PLANT

LOCATION

LEONARD C. YASEEN

Senior Partner, Fantus Factory Locating Service

PLANT

LOCATION

WITH AN INTRODUCTION BY

Joseph A. Russell

Head of the Department of Geography, University of Illinois

AMERICAN RESEARCH COUNCIL • NEW YORK

INTRODUCTION

American industry is on the move. For a variety of reasons, the managements of both large and small manufacturing establishments are reappraising existing locations of plants and seeking new sites which hold promise for more profitable operation. The resulting industrial migration has been from one major into another major region, but also between parts of the same region; it has included "decentralization" into small communities for some industries and "centralization" in major cities for others; it has been into traditional manufacturing belts and away from them.

Intense business competition has created a situation in which "hit or miss" selection of locations for industry must give way to thorough analysis of the comparative advantages afforded by many locations. The analytical process of selecting a location for an industry consists of matching the cost and other requirements of the industry with the abilities of several places to satisfy those requirements. Each industry has three basic needs—(1) to accumulate its required materials and services at a single place, (2) to manufacture the materials into products at that place, and (3) to distribute the products from that place to the intended markets. Each of these represents a large number of individual costs, and the relative importance of accumulation, processing, and distribution costs will be different at different places. The eventual site ideally should be the place where the total cost of the three is least, so long as the industry is socially and economically acceptable to the community. This successful merging of the interests of industry and community is one of the most critical problems facing our dynamic industrial scene. It requires the care and understanding of both the industry seeking a new location and the community seeking a new industry.

However, much of the promotional literature describing the attractions of communities seeking industry, and the occasional errors in management decision, demonstrate that this understanding is not always present. In part this is true because it is not generally appreciated that there is a *geography of industrial cost*. Just as there are mountains, hills, and valleys on the earth's surface there are also areas of relatively high or low industrial costs. Unlike the earth's surface features, however, the cost "mountains" and "valleys" are not the same to all viewers; a site located on a cost "mountain" for one industry may well be in a cost "valley" for another. In addition, an area that has high or low costs for a particular industry today may have its position reversed as new materials, improvements in transportation, new sources of industrial energy, new machines, or legislation affecting wages and taxes change particular cost characteristics of an existing plant or a proposed site. Such changes suddenly can depreciate the competitive value of any given location, and, because it takes some years to design and build a new plant and to put it into operation, and an even longer time to amortize the investment, it is necessary to project, insofar as possible, the geography of industrial costs as of the future.

The problem is further complicated by the increasingly wide choice of locations now open for industrialization. For example, automation permits plants with processes requiring large numbers of workers to be considered for sites which do not have access to dense populations; increased efficiency in the use of fuels, new methods of transporting them, and possibilities of industrial use of new kinds of fuels allow heavy consumers to appraise the possible advantages of locating at places which do not now offer cheap coal, oil, or gas.

Because smaller communities have thus become possible locations for industry, there has developed an intense community awareness of the economic advantages of securing new plants. Towns and villages compete with each other and with larger cities and metropolitan areas for favorable attention. This is desirable, but only if each such community has honestly studied its position in relation to the geography of cost for a wide variety of industrial operations and has recognized that it may be suited for a few but totally unsuited for many others. To attract an industry that will fail is worse than getting none at all.

Leonard C. Yaseen's book, PLANT LOCATION, represents ideas gained by many years of successfully matching industries and communities. It discusses in detail the factors which must be considered as plans are made to locate a plant; it recognizes the geography of cost and shows how the geographic variability in industrial costs can be determined. In this way it is an essential tool for the manufacturer who has plans for movement or expansion and for locational consultants employed to recommend new sites. But this book also should be of value to the leaders of communities that are hopeful of attracting industry because Mr. Yaseen points out the factors he has found to be of importance in locational decisions, and shows how those responsible for the decisions judge potential sites in terms of industrial cost.

To assist communities in doing this, Mr. Yaseen has devoted an entire chapter to the work that must be undertaken by the community if it is to enjoy the benefits and accept the responsibilities of increased industrialization.

Thoughtful use of this material will permit communities to wage a more aggressive and successful campaign to attract industry. The application of ideas expressed in this book will lead almost inevitably to the conclusion that a large number of industries are not good prospects for a particular community, but that a few industries can be assured that their costs will permit them to be competitive. Deficiencies in the community structure which limit industrialization will be brought to light; some of these may be correctable, and as they are corrected a wider range of industries may become feasible.

Because this book can be used with advantage by both industry and community it should provide a way of emphasizing the singleness of interest between them. It is vital to both that all of the factors bearing on the possibilities of mutually profitable operation be recognized and honestly analyzed. Mr. Yaseen's book makes this possible.

JOSEPH A. RUSSELL

Department of Geography
University of Illinois
Urbana, Illinois

CONTENTS

MAPS, CHARTS AND TABLES

PLANT

LOCATION

CHAPTER 1

Planning
for Plant Location

With over 300,000 manufacturing concerns and a gross national product approaching $400 billion, the United States can rightfully be termed the world's greatest industrial nation. Enormous progress has been made in utilization of raw materials, chemurgy, electronic engineering, jet propulsion, synthetic production and, in fact, in new processes and techniques of every description.

No such scientific advances, unfortunately, can be claimed in the determination of *where* new plants should be built. Too often, decisions are reached with scant regard for sound economic principles so highly prized in literally every other phase of industrial enterprise.

The importance of the application of scientific principles is apparent when it is realized that hundreds of billions have been expended for new plants and equipment in this generation.

Industry is expanding and relocating because of shifting markets, steadily

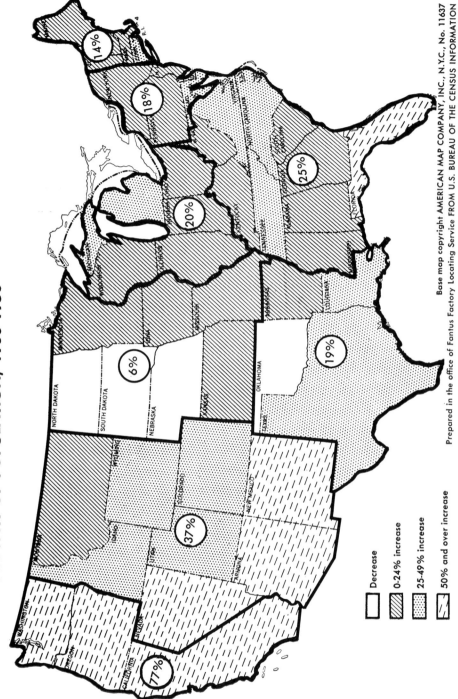

GROWTH OF POPULATION, 1930-1950

Decrease

0-24% increase

25-49% increase

50% and over increase

Base map copyright AMERICAN MAP COMPANY, INC., N.Y.C., No. 11637

Prepared in the office of Fantus Factory Locating Service FROM U.S. BUREAU OF THE CENSUS INFORMATION

mounting freight costs, the need for new labor reservoirs, the desire to operate in low-cost small communities, and the requirement for new, straight-line production facilities.

Massive shifts in our rapidly growing population have radically changed market potentialities in just a few decades. For example, California, with a population of around 12 million, has more than doubled its consumer purchasing power since 1929, and now ranks second in population in the nation. Practically one third of the country's population now lies west of the Mississippi River. Continued increase in number of people as well as geographical shifts of population are in prospect. By 1965 the country's population will reach 188 million.

Not only is the consumer flocking to hitherto unpopulated areas, but it costs a great deal more for the manufacturer to reach his customers today. Freight rates on class rated commodities moving in Official Classification Territory have increased as much as 120% since June, 1946.

In terms of geography, it isn't generally realized that *all cost factors are regionally variable,* including many raw materials, inbound and outbound freight, wage rates, fuel, power, gas, water, local and state taxes, workmen's compensation insurance rates, and even rental or other carrying charges.

It is an inescapable fact, therefore, that geographic location becomes as important to producers of goods as sound management, modern plant structure, and astute merchandising policies.

> *In many industries a differential of as much as 10% of total manufacturing and distribution costs can be effected simply by virtue of geography.*

Plants can no longer be located by intuition or on the basis of insufficient data; nor can the manufacturer automatically expand in his present location simply because it was chosen (often by accident) possibly fifty years before!

The paramount issue, therefore, that faces any manufacturer when considering plant expansion, is—Where? Ours is a big country with 4,270 communities of 2,500 population or more. There are 226,000 miles of railroads, 300,000 miles of regular truck freight lines, literally every type of climatic condition and degree of precipitation, 48 different sets of state labor laws and regulations, and a host of regional differences in temperament and working habits. The task of selecting the one best location for the new plant is formidable, and a sound decision requires the weighing of a great number of interdependent factors.

Hence, a definite plan based on clear-cut, sound business principles must be followed. The first and perhaps most important step for the executive considering plant location is to cast out personal predilections and honestly determine what makes his company "tick." Critical self-evaluation is essential if the inves-

PROJECTIONS OF THE POPULATION OF THE UNITED STATES
for 1960 and 1965, compared with figures for 1953

REGION, DIVISION AND STATE	1953 ESTIMATE	1960 PROJECTED	1965 PROJECTED
United States Total	158,306,000	176,103,000	188,593,000
Regions			
Northeast	40,726,000	44,124,000	46,436,000
North Central	46,262,000	50,586,000	53,554,000
South	49,483,000	54,776,000	58,436,000
West	21,834,000	26,617,000	30,167,000
Northeast			
New England	9,697,000	10,505,000	11,055,000
Middle Atlantic	31,030,000	33,619,000	35,381,000
North Central			
East North Central	31,879,000	35,385,000	37,804,000
West North Central	14,384,000	15,201,000	15,750,000
South			
South Atlantic	22,550,000	25,418,000	27,420,000
East South Central	11,592,000	12,493,000	13,105,000
West South Central	15,342,000	16,865,000	17,911,000
West			
Mountain	5,564,000	6,426,000	7,035,000
Pacific	16,270,000	20,191,000	23,132,000
New England			
Maine	914,000	964,000	996,000
New Hampshire	527,000	554,000	573,000
Vermont	377,000	393,000	404,000
Massachusetts	4,900,000	5,285,000	5,545,000
Rhode Island	817,000	876,000	916,000
Connecticut	2,162,000	2,433,000	2,621,000
Middle Atlantic			
New York	15,233,000	16,556,000	17,456,000
New Jersey	5,141,000	5,694,000	6,075,000
Pennsylvania	10,656,000	11,369,000	11,850,000
East North Central			
Ohio	8,369,000	9,291,000	9,925,000
Indiana	4,136,000	4,592,000	4,905,000
Illinois	9,003,000	9,826,000	10,388,000
Michigan	6,852,000	7,841,000	8,536,000
Wisconsin	3,518,000	3,835,000	4,050,000

(PROJECTIONS OF THE POPULATION OF THE UNITED STATES—continued)

REGION, DIVISION AND STATE	1953 ESTIMATE	1960 PROJECTED	1965 PROJECTED
West North Central			
Minnesota	3,053,000	3,279,000	3,431,000
Iowa	2,605,000	2,712,000	2,784,000
Missouri	4,096,000	4,361,000	4,538,000
North Dakota	621,000	633,000	642,000
South Dakota	657,000	680,000	696,000
Nebraska	1,347,000	1,401,000	1,437,000
Kansas	2,006,000	2,135,000	2,222,000
South Atlantic			
Delaware	358,000	417,000	457,000
Maryland	2,541,000	2,911,000	3,167,000
District of Columbia	841,000	935,000	999,000
Virginia	3,547,000	3,978,000	4,271,000
West Virginia	1,937,000	2,051,000	2,123,000
North Carolina	4,193,000	4,606,000	4,881,000
South Carolina	2,195,000	2,376,000	2,494,000
Georgia	3,585,000	3,864,000	4,045,000
Florida	3,353,000	4,280,000	4,983,000
East South Central			
Kentucky	2,965,000	3,153,000	3,279,000
Tennessee	3,329,000	3,658,000	3,885,000
Alabama	3,114,000	3,379,000	3,558,000
Mississippi	2,183,000	2,303,000	2,383,000
West South Central			
Arkansas	1,909,000	1,975,000	2,018,000
Louisiana	2,884,000	3,214,000	3,439,000
Oklahoma	2,251,000	2,320,000	2,366,000
Texas	8,298,000	9,356,000	10,088,000
Mountain			
Montana	614,000	649,000	671,000
Idaho	603,000	664,000	703,000
Wyoming	306,000	337,000	357,000
Colorado	1,413,000	1,575,000	1,681,000
New Mexico	758,000	878,000	962,000
Arizona	930,000	1,210,000	1,424,000
Utah	734,000	840,000	912,000
Nevada	206,000	273,000	325,000
Pacific			
Washington	2,478,000	2,883,000	3,171,000
Oregon	1,602,000	1,917,000	2,145,000
California	12,190,000	15,391,000	17,816,000

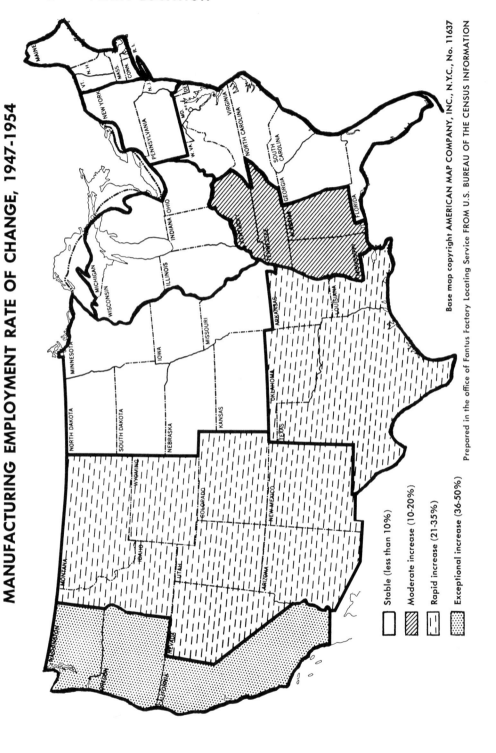

MANUFACTURING EMPLOYMENT RATE OF CHANGE, 1947-1954

Stable (less than 10%)

Moderate increase (10-20%)

Rapid increase (21-35%)

Exceptional increase (36-50%)

Base map copyright AMERICAN MAP COMPANY, INC., N.Y.C., No. 11637

Prepared in the office of Fantus Factory Locating Service FROM U.S. BUREAU OF THE CENSUS INFORMATION

tigator assigned to this task is to do a good job. "Know thyself" is as important today as it was in biblical times.

It is recommended that a complete historical outline be prepared, preferably by five-year spans, showing the chronological growth of the company, increase in number of employees, additions to floor space, and new products added. This will help visualize the eventual size of the proposed new unit, the possible future labor needs beyond the original plant size, plant size and orientation on the site, and other factors.

Primary reasons for considering relocation or branch plant expansion are obsolescence and crowding of present facilities due to company growth, shifts in markets, inability to properly service customers, inability to meet selling cost of competitors and still show a profit, and unduly high overhead and production costs. Careful analysis of all cost and competitive factors in present operations will pinpoint the tests which a new location must meet.

Honest introspection will probably reveal a whole series of blank areas to the investigator. Most companies don't know how much freight absorption is necessary to equalize competitors' favorable positions with respect to markets; nor are they usually cognizant of industry-wide terms of sale in their field.

Many manufacturers, in fact, are not aware of their actual distribution costs. Because production and *distribution* costs are seldom differentiated, many companies have constructed plants when they should have built warehouses.

In textiles, for example, transportation, selling, advertising, warehousing and credit combined, account for only around 9% of total manufacturing costs. In machinery and tools such "distribution" expenses average 25.8% of total manufacturing costs. High cost of shipping heavy products to users means that for this industry transportation plays an important part.

It will be advisable also for the investigator to determine how much of the company's excessive production and distribution costs is due to geography and how much is due to inefficient plant layout, unnecessary re-handling of materials and labor wastes due to congestion. It is axiomatic that re-handling adds nothing to a product except its cost! Storage of finished products and goods in process, wasted time at shipping platforms, lost time at elevators, are still other factors to be considered.

The company executive will, of course, want to examine his labor picture microscopically. Such factors as labor turnover, labor productivity, number of personnel to be transferred to a possible new plant site, length of training time required for direct and non-productive labor, and wage rates, are, of course, all important. Here, too, the investigator must probe deep if he is to be in a position to draw true geographic comparisons.

It is important in comparing wage rates, for example, to include the cost of all incentives, fringe benefits, shift differentials, and labor turnover which vary greatly by geographic area. In some areas, seven paid holidays, two-week vacations, bonus and pension plans, and medical and insurance benefits are standard practice. In other communities, fringe benefits are virtually non-existent. No practical comparison can be drawn unless *all* the facts are known.

Cost and reliability of power, gas, water, rail and truck motor carrier service, workmen's compensation insurance, and local and state taxation must be thoroughly charted. Too few corporations know whether their ad valorem taxes are being equitably assessed. Few have compared their neighbors' assessments, or have applied for writs of certiorari if unfairly assessed, or are familiar with the long term tax fluctuations of their area, or are aware of the present and future debt position of even their own community. A small minority know whether their tax dollar is bringing them presently a full measure of community service in the way of fire and police protection, schools, roads, sewage disposal and other facilities.

When all the facts are known, the investigator should be in a position to assign a relative value to all production and distribution cost components. Raw materials, labor, utility costs, transportation, taxes and plant overhead will then be seen in their true proportions.

In order to arrive at a correct valuation of the various factors involved, it is advisable for the investigator to chart present manufacturing costs. A suggested guide follows:

DIRECT & INDIRECT TRANSPORTATION COSTS

Inbound materials	$
Outbound products	$
Warehousing	$_____
TOTAL	$

LABOR

Direct productive	$
Non-productive	$_____
TOTAL	$

PLANT OVERHEAD

Rent or carrying costs, excluding taxes	$
Real estate taxes	$
Personal property and other locally assessed taxes	$
Fuel for heating purposes only	$_____
TOTAL	$

UTILITIES

Power	$
Gas	$
Water	$
Sewage disposal, etc.	$_____
TOTAL	$

STATE FACTORS

State taxes	$
Workmen's Compensation Insurance	$_____
TOTAL	$

MISCELLANEOUS

Other costs inherent or peculiar to your present locations(s)	$_____
TOTAL	$
GRAND TOTAL	$_____

Supplementary data for transportation costs should include a tonnage breakdown of finished products to principal markets, how shipped, i.e., rail (LCL or carload), truck (LTL or truckload), terms of sale, location of principal competitors, data on service to possible new markets, and development of new and alternative sources for vital raw materials.

In preparing labor data, it is advisable to consider labor productivity and attitude, present labor turnover, fringe benefits, shift differentials, training time for necessary skills, seasonal or cyclical fluctuations, union set-up, state labor laws, and housing for possible transferees. At this stage, the total annual loss of man-hours due to restrictive flow of work through the plant should be computed.

The operations carried on within the plant and the equipment utilized will determine the size and layout of the structure proposed and the site necessary in the new location. The dimensions of the prospective plant, floor loads, siding and loading facilities, the size of water, gas, power and sewage lines, and all-important off-street parking provisions will affect the topography and characteristics of the finally selected site.

Until the investigator has gathered and interpreted all the factors discussed, no opinion can be crystallized as to the general geographic area to be considered. But once this major and admittedly burdensome detail is out of the way, it is usually surprisingly easy to identify the specific area or areas that can best serve customers at lowest possible over-all cost. The selection and size of the community within the finally chosen area will depend to a great extent on labor skills or special services required.

CHAPTER 2

Our Complex
Transportation System

THE EFFECT OF TRANSPORTATION
ON INDUSTRIAL GROWTH

American historians generally have neglected the importance of transportation in the nation's development. Economists, on the other hand, agree that our most important economic accomplishments have depended directly on this factor.

In the colonies the dominant interest was commercial rather than industrial. The immature nation, its population clustered about the North Atlantic ports, conducted a lively trade exporting raw materials and importing manufactured goods. Inland commerce was confined to the navigable streams and a few poor roads.

The need for inland routes became apparent during the Revolution and was a national issue as early as the 5th Congress. While the federal government argued the matter, the rival port cities developed an extensive network of canals and turnpikes under State and private sponsorship. At the height of their development, the railroad appeared on the scene.

The early railroads were feeders to navigable streams. By 1840 short sections had been projected inland from most coastal cities, lake ports and river terminals. By 1850 New York State had been crossed, and by 1860 there were 30,000 miles of railroad in the United States.

Following the Civil War, the eastern seaports grew into industrial centers. Unlike the smaller inland cities, they had sufficient labor supply and financial resources to sustain the program. Perhaps of equal importance, the transportation facilities which they had developed enabled them to assemble production materials and distribute manufactured products in the growing markets west of the Appalachians.

Ironically, the railroads which had been constructed to tap the hinterland were to aid in the establishment of rival inland industrial communities. Attracted by new raw material sources, expanding markets and the vastly improved transportation system, industry began to migrate westward. The extractive industries led the movement. Processing and subsidiary industries followed, establishing plants to meet the eastward flow of materials. Expanding interior cities enticed local service industries, such as bakeries and printing establishments.

One pertinent observation can be made concerning the migration: *in virtually every instance the site selected was on or near an established transportation route.* The industrial communities which appeared along the strategic routes of the major trunk-line railroads were to develop into our major interior manufacturing cities.

THE INFLUENCE OF TOPOGRAPHY

Surface features have an important influence on the transportation routes which are developed in any particular area. Waterways are necessarily restricted to river valleys, lakes, bays and relatively level areas where canals can be easily constructed. Railroads and highways follow valleys and passes, seeking reduced grades and circumventing natural barriers.

Mountains, lakes and rivers obviously influence the pattern of traffic. Less obvious are the transportation problems of coastal areas. Because of their peninsular configuration such vast areas as southern New Jersey, the Delmarva Peninsula, and the Louisiana delta lie off the routes of through carriers. This affects their industrial potential.

PRINCIPAL RAILWAYS OF THE UNITED STATES

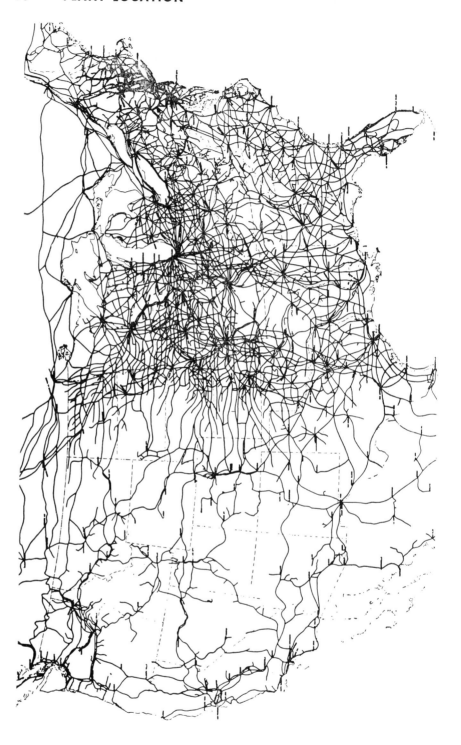

Similarly those sections of the country which are geographically removed from the major economic activity of the nation do not enjoy good transportation service. Industrial activity is limited in these areas which include northern New England, the upper peninsula of Michigan and certain Western states.

Despite the blanket of railroads in the country, large areas have been completely omitted from the system. The southeast, with good railroad coverage, furnishes an excellent example. One region in south central Kentucky 70 miles wide and 90 miles long (extending into northern Tennessee) has no railroad facilities whatsoever.

THE SYSTEM DESCRIBED

All manufacturing operations require inbound movement of raw materials and outbound movement of the finished product to the market. Accordingly, it is vital for the executive contemplating new plant location to understand the intricacies of the complex transportation system at his disposal.

Review of post-war industrial locations reveals some glaring errors concerning transportation geography. A common pitfall is the assumption that all sites adjacent to highway and railroad have adequate service. Only after operations have begun does the misinformed executive learn of his problems in obtaining shipments of raw materials and servicing his customers.

This section is devoted to a discussion of the principal transportation agencies of the United States as they exist today. Their distribution, the general character of their traffic, and their relative advantages and disadvantages are considered.

Railroads

The United States, with only about 6% of the world's population, has approximately 29% of the world's railroad mileage. In 1950, the combined length of our railways was 227,244 miles. Despite growth in population and industrial capacity during the past two decades, railroad mileage has actually been declining. In 1939, for example, only one mile of new rail line was added while 6,758 miles were abandoned.

The rail routes of the nation form a grid of east-west and north-south lines. Actual trackage distribution on the major routes is very uneven, however. As

PRINCIPAL RAIL ROUTES

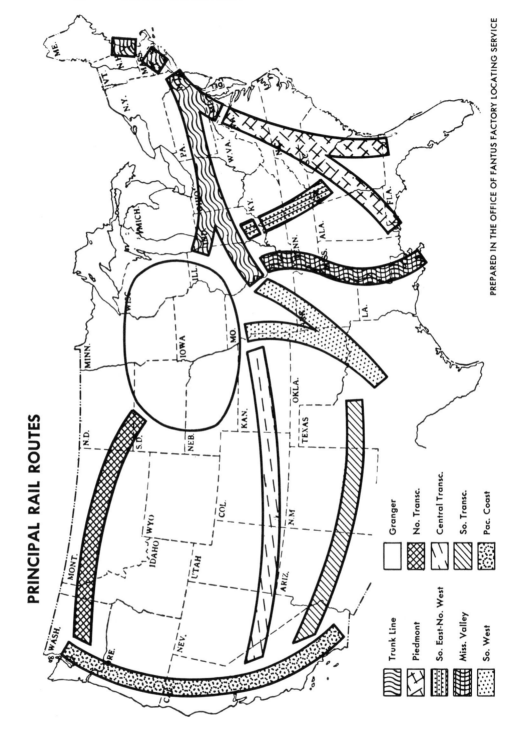

Trunk Line
Piedmont
So. East-No. West
Miss. Valley
So. West

Granger
No. Transc.
Central Transc.
So. Transc.
Pac. Coast

PREPARED IN THE OFFICE OF FANTUS FACTORY LOCATING SERVICE

illustrated in the map on page 14, density is greatest in the East and least in the West.

The present pattern reflects the concepts of the investment groups which constructed the original rail lines. In the East, railroads were built to connect urban centers. In the West, the emphasis was on tapping the mines and gathering the products of agriculture.

Vestiges of the original development are very much in evidence. Chicago is the hub of the American railroad system. Oddly enough, most railroads entering the city also terminate there. Divisions in the systems are common along major river crossings including the Mississippi, Missouri, Ohio, Hudson and Potomac Rivers. With long-haul interterritorial traffic increasing in importance, these transfer points are bothersome bottlenecks.

An executive planning plant location should know the groupings of the major railroad systems so he can be certain that major inbound and outbound movements will follow the natural flow rather than become subject to needless transfer. These groupings are as follows:

1. The *Trunk Line* route serves the northeast, connecting Chicago and St. Louis with the North Atlantic ports. These railroads generally terminate at the Mississippi, Ohio, Potomac and Hudson Rivers. Leading representative railroads include the New York Central, Pennsylvania, Baltimore & Ohio, Chesapeake & Ohio, and the Erie. Connecting lines such as the New York, New Haven & Hartford and the Boston & Albany serve New England.

2. The *Southeastern* route roughly parallels the Atlantic Coast, east of the Appalachian Mountains. These railroads serve Alabama and Florida ports, connecting with Trunk Line tracks at Richmond, Norfolk, or Washington, D. C. Representative lines include the Southern, Atlantic Coast Line, and the Seaboard Air Line. The Central of Georgia serves only the southern end of the route, and an important northern bridge line is the Richmond, Frederickstown & Potomac.

3. The *Southeast-Northwest* route extends from Atlanta to Chicago. Most carriers do not serve the entire distance but interchange at Ohio River crossing points. The Southern and the Louisville & Nashville serve that portion of the route south of the Ohio River. Major connections are with carriers serving Chicago. These include the Chicago & Eastern Illinois, the Chicago, Indianapolis & Louisville, and the Chesapeake & Ohio. The Birmingham-Chicago route of the Illinois Central competes for part of the traffic.

4. The *Mississippi Valley* route connects the central states with Louisiana and Alabama ports. The Illinois Central, serving the entire length of the route, and the Gulf, Mobile & Ohio operate on the east bank. The Missouri Pacific is on the west bank. Northern connections include the Wabash and the Chicago & Eastern Illinois.

5. The *Granger* railroads serve the states of Illinois, Iowa, Kansas, Missouri, Nebraska, Minnesota, South Dakota and North Dakota. Interchange is made with Southwestern or Mississippi Valley routes, forming a link between the Trunk Line and Transcontinental routes. Included in the group are the Chicago, Burlington & Quincy, and the Chicago & Northwestern. The Chicago, Rock Island & Pacific operates through the area in connection with its transcontinental route.

6. The *Southwestern* route connects the Texas Gulf ports with Chicago, St. Louis and Kansas City. Major lines in this service are the Chicago, Rock Island & Pacific, the St. Louis-San Francisco, and the Missouri-Kansas-Texas. The Atchison, Topeka & Santa Fe (a transcontinental route) and the Missouri Pacific (a Mississippi Valley route) claim part of this traffic.

7. The *Northern Transcontinental* route, like all other so-called transcontinental routes, does *not* operate from coast to coast. Rather, railroads in this group connect Chicago with the north Pacific Coast cities. Representative lines include the Chicago, Milwaukee, St. Paul & Pacific, the Great Northern, and the Northern Pacific. Chicago connections are made through subsidiaries, in some instances.

8. The *Central Transcontinental* route includes the Union Pacific with its eastern terminus at Omaha and branching lines from Salt Lake City to Los Angeles and the Puget Sound area. A popular central freight route utilizes these three railroads: the Chicago, Burlington & Quincy, the Denver & Rio Grande Western, and the Western Pacific.

9. The *Southern Trancontinental* route extends from Chicago to major California ports via Texas. The Atchison, Topeka & Santa Fe serves this route in its entirety, and the Southern Pacific operates most of the distance.

10. The *Pacific Coast* route roughly parallels the western coastline. It is served primarily by the Southern Pacific and extensions of the Great Northern.

Basically there are two major types of freight service rendered by the railroads, carload (CL) and less-than-carload (LCL). The distinction is based upon the weight tendered for shipment to one destination at one time.

Most carload shipments are loaded by the shippers on private sidings and unloaded by consignees on sidings or in the freight yards at destination. Because of standardizations in equipment, these shipments proceed to their destination without unloading en route. An ingenious method of "per diem" bookkeeping allows any of the 1,778,811 cars in service to be used on the tracks of all other railroads in the United States, Alaska, Canada, Mexico and Cuba.

LCL freight is generally trucked to the nearest freight station, where shipments are loaded into cars with other freight. These shipments are frequently unloaded and re-loaded at several transfer points before reaching their destinations for local delivery. Time-in-transit is necessarily slower than carload service. Rates are higher, reflecting the additional cost to the carrier of handling small lots.

The general dissatisfaction of the shipping public with the quality of LCL rail service has created the need for an assembler of freight called a "freight forwarder" or "carloading company". Two of the largest such organizations are owned by railroads themselves.

The function of the freight forwarder is to provide an expedited and complete door-to-door LCL service. The forwarder picks up LCL freight, assembles it with other like freight, and tenders a complete carload to the railroad for shipment. At destination, he arranges to distribute the shipments direct to the consignees.

As the forwarder charges the LCL rate for each small shipment and pays carload rates to the railroad, he has an opportunity for profit. He substitutes truck for rail service wherever it is to his advantage.

Between *key* points the railroads seek to retain LCL traffic by providing expedited merchandise cars. However, *most railroads do not encourage LCL movement at smaller stations.* They prefer to allow the the forwarders to assemble full carloads which can be transported at lower cost to the railroad.

Motor trucks

The highway system of the United States is more extensive than all other transportation routes combined, and is five times greater than the total railroad length in the country. Like railroads, the highways are concentrated in the East and are less numerous in the West.

There are three general types of motor freight operators: common, contract and private. *Common carriers,* comprising the majority of carriers for hire, serve the general public and are obligated to accept traffic at published rates. *Contract carriers* do not serve shippers in general, but operate under contract to specific companies. *Private carriers* operate vehicles in connection with their own manufacturing plant, store, farm, etc.

By no means are the routes of motor truck common carriers as clearly defined as the rail routes previously described. In fact, the Interstate Commerce Commission finds it necessary to classify carriers by the character of their services: (a) regular route, scheduled service; (b) regular route, non-scheduled service; (c) irregular route, radial service; (d) irregular route, non-radial service; or (e) local route, cartage service.

Administration Building, Sperry Gyroscope Company, Lake Success, Long Island. Plant Location Study—FANTUS FACTORY LOCATING SERVICE.

Motor carriers are also classified according to the *kind* of commodities handled, reflecting the type of equipment operated. There are 17 general classifications, but manufacturers are concerned with only four or five, such as general freight, heavy machinery, liquid petroleum, explosives and other dangerous articles, and carriers of motor vehicles.

While virtually every town and hamlet is reached by motor truck, the service is not uniformly distributed. Large centers of population are served by numerous motor carriers in intense competition for traffic to and from other large centers. However, a shipment from a remote community may require transfer en route to several independent trucking lines before reaching its destination.

The trucking lines tend to operate within restricted geographical regions, consistent with their inherent advantages over railroads for hauls up to 350 miles. Unlike the railroads, the long-haul trucking lines ignore sectional boundaries and follow the flow of interterritorial traffic.

The location of principal truck routes is keyed to the historical development of the motor trucking industry. During World War I, it was in its infancy, with operations confined to local business. Remnants of the industry's development from horse-drawn equipment still prevail in such terms as "drayage," "cartage," "team-truck," "teamster's union," etc.

As concrete highways developed and motor equipment was improved, these local cartage companies extended their services over greater areas. Competition developed with the railroads for short-haul traffic such as New York-Philadelphia, Chicago-Milwaukee.

Increased industrial tempo in the 1920's created the need for a premium motor express service between key manufacturing centers. Truck routes were lengthened accordingly, i.e., New York-Boston, Chicago-Detroit, Philadelphia-Pittsburgh. The shift of the textile industry from New England to the South developed a need for a long-haul rapid service to the New York market.

By 1935 truck competition between key centers had become so keen that the Interstate Commerce Commission was given the power of regulating the industry. Existing routes were frozen and franchises were granted only to those points to which operations had been extended prior to that year. All future development of routes required proof of economic necessity.

In the 1940's, the giant over-the-road trucking companies were developed. Most are consolidations, mergers or linking of existing routes with I.C.C. approval, similar to the activity in railroad development several decades before. New consolidated long-haul lines are still developing and one motor truck company now operates coast to coast. However, the bulk of motor traffic continues to move within geographical regions over routes established prior to 1935.

Motor carriers divide their services into truckload (TL) and less-than-truckload (LTL). However, the quantity necessary to meet the truckload minimum weight requirement is usually less than the rail carload minimum. This enables shippers to serve smaller markets at lower cost via motor truck.

In recent years, a flexible system of trailer interchange has been developed, enabling full truckload shipments to move from origin to destination without rehandling of the contents.

Unlike the railroads, the motor trucks recognize that when a shipper tenders large quantities of LTL freight to a single consignee, the carrier has lower handling costs per unit. Accordingly, in most territories LTL shipments of greater weights are afforded rate reductions.

LTL shipments are handled in much the same manner as less-than-carload movements via rail. A small pick-up truck brings the freight to a receiving dock where it awaits consolidation with other freight to the destination area. Interline transfers en route are common.

Because of the myriad of independent truck lines, routing of shipments is difficult where the same carrier does not serve both origin and destination. Where motor trucks are used extensively, the existence of direct motor truck service to major markets from prospective locations must be carefully checked.

Waterways

American school children continue to be taught that Holland has a complex system of canals. Few learn the fact that their own country has the world's greatest system of navigable channels and inland waterways.

On the Mississippi River controlling depths are 9 feet from Baton Rouge to Minneapolis. This is made possible by a series of 26 locks and dams. The Illinois Waterway, joining the Mississippi with Lake Michigan, is 327 miles long.

On the Ohio River, the world's most extensive system of locks and dams provides a dependable channel from Cairo to Pittsburgh, a distance of 981 miles. Important tributaries have been dredged to accommodate the Ohio River barges.

These improvements on the Mississippi-Ohio system have made possible the modern tow which may comprise 20 barges, carrying 20,000 tons of freight, equivalent to 400 carloads or *4 full trainloads.*

One of the most bitterly opposed developments in the transportation industry is the Federal Barge Lines (Inland Waterways Corporation) owned and operated by the Federal Government. This line competes with private barge companies on the Mississippi River as well as the railroads. Its heavy annual losses have been absorbed by public taxation in the interest of developing backward areas and new waterway techniques.

The Intracoastal Waterway when completed will allow commercial tows and other light-draft vessels to operate from New England to Brownsville, Texas, with most of the route protected from open sea.

Numerous routes extend from coastal shores to inland points. The Hudson River and New York State Barge Canal connect New York City with the Great Lakes. Birmingham, Ala. (470 miles inland) is connected to the Gulf of Mexico by an improved waterway via the Tombigbee, Warrior and Black Warrior rivers.

Included in the inland waterways system are the Great Lakes which form a 1500-mile route, the longest inland navigable waterway in the world. Open to traffic seven and one-half months each year and ice-blocked all winter, this route carries 85% of all iron ore produced in the United States as well as heavy bulk cargoes of coal, stone and grain.

COMMERCIALLY NAVIGABLE INLAND WATERWAYS
of the Eastern United States

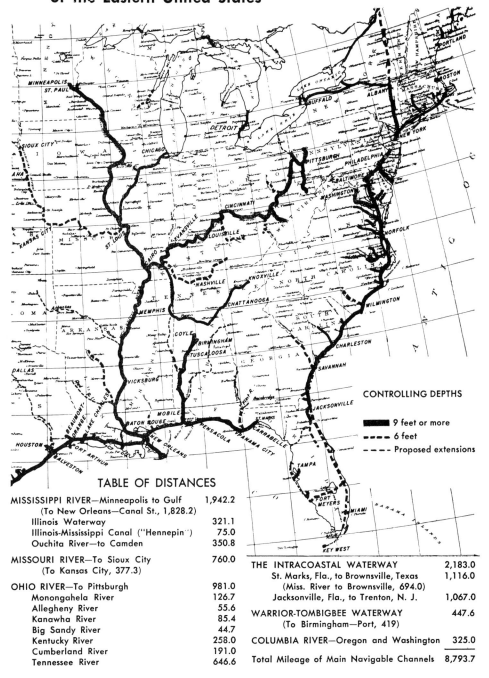

CONTROLLING DEPTHS

▬▬▬ 9 feet or more

▬ ▬ ▬ 6 feet

– – – Proposed extensions

TABLE OF DISTANCES

MISSISSIPPI RIVER—Minneapolis to Gulf	1,942.2
(To New Orleans—Canal St., 1,828.2)	
Illinois Waterway	321.1
Illinois-Mississippi Canal ("Hennepin")	75.0
Ouchita River—to Camden	350.8
MISSOURI RIVER—To Sioux City	760.0
(To Kansas City, 377.3)	
OHIO RIVER—To Pittsburgh	981.0
Monongahela River	126.7
Allegheny River	55.6
Kanawha River	85.4
Big Sandy River	44.7
Kentucky River	258.0
Cumberland River	191.0
Tennessee River	646.6

THE INTRACOASTAL WATERWAY	2,183.0
St. Marks, Fla., to Brownsville, Texas	1,116.0
(Miss. River to Brownsville, 694.0)	
Jacksonville, Fla., to Trenton, N. J.	1,067.0
WARRIOR-TOMBIGBEE WATERWAY	447.6
(To Birmingham—Port, 419)	
COLUMBIA RIVER—Oregon and Washington	325.0
Total Mileage of Main Navigable Channels	8,793.7

The inherent advantages of the river barge lie in its ability to handle bulk movements at low cost. Typical loadings are 300 to 500 tons, but some lines handle carload and even less-than-carload traffic.

Barge service is slow, with downstream movements somewhat faster than upstream movements. Despite the lack of speed, high-valued manufactured goods are being attracted to barge lines because of the substantial economies available.

Unlike other forms of freight transportation, the majority of movement on rivers and canals is by private carriers. On the Ohio River, 95% of the tonnage is handled by industrial barges. The number of private vessels on the New York State Barge Canal is increasing. Bulk cargoes are transported on the Great Lakes mainly by private or contract carriers. On return voyages, some private carriers become part-time common carriers seeking traffic to offset empty mileage costs.

While our discussion is confined to domestic carriers, it is interesting to note that ocean vessels can navigate directly to some major inland cities. Philadelphia is 100 miles inland on the Delaware River. The channel is being improved to admit ore-bearing ships to Morrisville, Pa., the site of the U. S. Steel Fairless Works.

Baltimore, 150 miles upstream and Washington, 150 miles inland, can both dock ocean vessels. Jacksonville, Wilmington, Savannah and Mobile are on river estuaries. New Orleans and Baton Rouge (250 miles inland) have deep draft facilities.

On the Pacific Coast, ocean vessels can serve ports of Portland, Oregon and Vancouver, Wash. via the Columbia River. Construction has started on a deep draft-channel to Sacramento, California, more than 100 miles from the Golden Gate.

The Intercoastal lines compete with the railroads for transcontinental domestic traffic, operating between the Atlantic and Pacific coastal cities via the Panama Canal. Their service, slower than all-rail, is offset by low rates. Those intercoastal lines which do not operate north of San Francisco transfer freight with common carriers serving Oregon and Washington ports.

Prior to World War II, considerable volume of coastwise shipping was found along the Atlantic Coast. Due to rising costs, few common carriers have restored the service in the post-war period.

The majority of tonnage moving coastwise in the Atlantic-Gulf seaboard route is handled by contract carriers or private industrial owners, operating tankers, special coal vessels, etc. This route competes with both the railroads and pipe lines.

A formidable competitor with the railroads for long-haul north-south traffic is the Seatrain Lines. In this unique operation, loaded rail cars are lifted into the hold of specially designed ocean-going ships. At destination ports, the cars are placed on rails of connecting railroads and hauled inland to final destinations. Routes have been established between New York and Gulf Coast points, and a new service to Savannah, Ga., has been installed.

On the Pacific Coast the most prominent ocean carriers are the "steam schooners" operated by lumbering interests. Common carriers operate between ports in all three Pacific Seaboard states in active competition with the railroads.

Airlines

There are two major classes of airlines in the United States, scheduled and non-scheduled. The scheduled lines follow three major transcontinental routes and three major north-south routes, and handle passengers, mail, air express and air cargo. They operate 36,982 miles of routes in the nation, with density greatest east of the Mississippi and north of the Ohio rivers.

Non-scheduled airlines handle air cargo in addition to passenger service. Air-freight forwarders assembling small shipments to be consolidated into plane-load lots for key destinations utilize the "non-skeds" primarily.

The importance of the airlines as cargo-handlers is negligible, as their total annual ton-miles do not exceed 1.0% of the U. S. volume. Yet, as handlers of high-grade commodities and expedited shipments, their service cannot be equalled by land transportation. Air service is provided to all major U. S. cities, with a feeder-system being improved to smaller communities.

Rockwell Manufacturing Company, Sulphur Springs, Texas. Plant Location Study—FANTUS FACTORY LOCATING SERVICE.

Express service

The Railway Express Agency, with 23,000 offices, is recognized as a nation-wide medium of expedited service. It is owned by the railroads, and the majority of shipments are forwarded in special cars usually included in passenger trains.

At most cities, pick-up and delivery service is provided by the Agency. The express service operates over 16,000 motor trucks, one of the largest fleets under commercial management.

In recent years the number of rail shipments handled by the Agency has been declining. This is due in part to the disparity between express and parcel post charges. Recent legislation has restricted the size of parcel post shipments which may divert larger shipments to the express service.

Since 1927 the Air Express division has been handling expedited shipments on regularly scheduled passenger and cargo flights. An attempt is made to co-ordinate rail express service with air express in order to provide air express service to communities off the air line routes.

The number of shipments, gross weight, and average weight per shipment have been increasing. In 1928 only 17,000 shipments were flown. In 1950, slightly over 4,230,000 shipments were handled with a gross weight of almost 100,000,000 lbs., averaging 23.5 lbs. per shipment.

Parcel post

Fourth class mailing matter is commonly known as domestic parcel post. An intricate transportation system has been developed by the Post Office Department which provides a convenient manner of transporting small shipments between virtually all points in the United States.

In the post-war period the common carriers, including the Railway Express Agency, were forced to raise rates and to impose minimum charges on small shipments. Shippers turned to the cheaper service provided by the postal service on small shipments not exceeding 70 pounds in weight.

Under pressure of private transportation interests and others seeking to promote efficiency in the postal service, in 1951 Congress limited the weight of shipments via parcel post to 40 pounds in Zones 1-2 and 20 pounds to all other zones.

Pipe lines

Trunk pipe lines, fed by gathering lines, move crude petroleum from the oil fields directly to refineries, or to trans-shipping points at junctions with railroads or waterways. Similar lines transport refined petroleum products to centers of distribution or reloading facilities. These trunk lines are generally 3″ to 24″ in diameter and the gathering lines range up to 20″ in diameter. Total length is 152,000 miles.

Most of the pipe lines are privately owned and unregulated. However, when the line handles products of other companies in addition to the products of its owners, it is classified as a common carrier subject to the Interstate Commerce Act.

Gasoline transportation by railroad costs about 10 times more than by pipe line for movements from Texas to the New York metropolitan area. Total refined oil pipe line length in operation is about 34,000 miles.

A total of 376,000 miles of transmission and distribution pipe lines carry natural gas from over 43,000 miles of field and gathering lines to users over the country. Diameter of pipe runs 16″ to 36″. The system competes with liquified petroleum (propane or butane) which moves via rail or truck in tankloads or cylinders, as well as other types of fuels which can be handled by these carriers. The natural gas lines have been regulated by the Federal Power Commission since 1938.

SELECTION OF TRANSPORTATION MEDIA

The domestic transportation system of the United States has been described in the foregoing sections. However, in actuality, there is no coordinated "system" as such. Each mode is directly or indirectly in competition with each of the others, and it is the shipper (or his customer) who selects the type of transportation to be used in each instance.

Whether or not the inherent advantages of each type of carrier will guide the selection of routes is dependent upon a group of factors. Under proper guidance, the shipper will consider the following:

(1) The relative cost of the service,
(2) the urgency of reaching the destination,
(3) special services which may be provided, and
(4) the physical facilities for handling shipments at origin and destination.

As freight charges are part of the delivered-to-customer cost, the relative cost of the service in most instances will determine the type of carrier which will be selected. Expedited services such as air express, air cargo, and railway express are relatively expensive, and the urgency of the shipment must be balanced against the price of the service.

The vast majority of high or medium grade traffic is routed via rail or truck, with the choice determined by relative rates, convenience, length of haul, etc. Low grade cargo which cannot stand high transportation costs will move in water service when within reach of these carriers by rail, or by both water and rail.

Certain carriers provide specialized equipment to meet shippers' needs. If such services are utilized, their existence in the new area must be carefully checked. Anyone who has ever waited for a freight train to clear a grade crossing is familiar with the special rail cars used for bulk commodities, liquids, machinery, refrigerated products, etc. Less commonly known are the following: heaters to prevent freezing, box cars with ends that open, covered hopper cars and a large variety of other equipment designed for specific commodities. In the post-war period, motor trucks have become increasingly specialized.

The routing of small shipments depends upon weight and dimensions as well as relative rates and minimum charges. Choice of carrier involves consideration of rail less-than-carload, carloading company, truck, railway express, air express, parcel post and air parcel post.

* * *

From a locational viewpoint, it is necessary to first determine which of these many types of services are used by the company and then ascertain that specific sites have all these services available. Do not be satisfied with general statements from local promotional officials who are usually untrained in traffic matters. Check with reliable representatives of the carriers themselves.

CHAPTER 3

Competitive Advantages in Raw Materials Sources and Markets

The domestic transportation system described in the previous chapter allows manufacturing processes to be established at the source of raw materials, at the market, or almost any intermediate point.

In plant location study, distance is measured in terms of freight costs. Just as the relative costs of assembling raw materials and distributing finished products will vary from industry to industry, so will the locational "pull" of raw materials and markets differ in each problem.

The few economists who have treated plant location theory have given great stress to this relationship of "transfer costs" of raw materials and finished products. They treat raw materials in three classes:

> 1. Pure materials which are included in the manufactured article without loss of weight.

2. Weight-losing materials, only a part of whose weight is represented in the weight of the finished article.
3. Ubiquities, or materials found virtually everywhere.

Oversimplifying the problem by assuming uniform rates per mile, these writers have concluded the following:

1. Where a single pure material is used, location can be at the source of the material, at the market, or at any point in between.
2. If a weight-losing material is used, it is cheaper to carry on the manufacture at the source than to transport it to market as the finished product is lighter.
3. If a ubiquity is used, location should be at the market since the material is universally available.

All other things being equal, an industry will tend to locate at that point where it will have the lowest aggregate transportation cost. Hence, while the economic theories are highly academic, they do suggest the factors which must be considered.

Historically the proximity of primary raw materials has vitally influenced the location of American industry. Early shoe manufacturing was concentrated near the supply of leather in Massachusetts and the tanning industry itself was located nearby because of the presence of tanning materials, such as the bark of oak or hemlock or tannin. Today, however, only one out of five manufacturers in the United States directly processes basic raw materials—most industrial firms purchase partially processed materials. In other industries, technical improvements, and substitute or synthetic materials reduce the former locational pulls of raw material sources.

Raw material oriented plants are continually diminishing in number as the locational attractions of labor and markets increase. Furthermore, our vast nationwide transportation network, the decentralization process of all industry, and competitive sales equalization practices have made it more and more possible for manufacturers to widen the gap between their own producing plants and the actual raw material source. This flexibility and freedom of movement has been particularly noticeable in the last few decades.

Obviously those industries utilizing raw materials of an extractive nature incurring tremendous weight loss in manufacturing will still tend to be located as close to the working-face of the mine as possible. Typical industries are those involved in the smelting or concentrating of ores. This locational pull is particularly strong if the ore is of low grade.

In other industries where the raw material is bulky or unwieldy in proportion to its value or where the raw material is perishable, the locational pull of the source remains dominant. Sawmills, paper mills, cotton gins, beet sugar refineries, food packing and freezing plants, and dairy products manufacturers locate as close to the growing or producing areas as possible.

When substantial weight loss is not involved in the manufacturing process, the relative rate levels on raw materials and finished goods will tend to govern the location of the plant. Freight rates generally increase as value is added in manufacture. Therefore, raw materials normally enjoy lower levels than manufactured goods.

However, where the finished product is of relatively low value or offers other favorable transportation characteristics, it may take a rate that is not greatly above that applying on the raw materials used in its production. In such situations the attraction of the market may become minimized. Some further processing of steel is conducted at Pittsburgh rather than at metal-working centers for this reason. Similarly, rates on raw cotton are almost equal to those applying on some finished cotton goods and mills can be located near the growing fields without penalty.

Generally, intermediate locations between material sources and markets are expensive. Every freight rate is composed of two terminal costs plus a line-haul cost. As hauls increase in length, the terminal charges assume less and less importance, being absorbed in the line-haul revenue. When average hauls are shortened by an intermediate location, both the inbound and outbound rates must continue to support terminal charges. Accordingly, the aggregate freight cost at an intermediate location may be higher than would result from location at either the material source or at the market.

The disadvantage of intermediate locations has been overcome in some industries through the extension of in-transit privileges. Under this arrangement the through-rate from origin to final destination is applied. Interruption of the movement is allowed at the intermediate location for a nominal charge. These privileges have been extended to the milling of grain, compressing of cotton, mixing, simple fabrication, packing, cleaning and storage processes.

Freight rates are not determined by means of mathematical formulas. The number of variables is too great, therefore, to offer a generalized answer to the material—market controversy. Rather, there can be offered a procedure for comparing the net "pull" toward the market and toward materials. The answer appears in freight differentials. The procedure is illustrated in the comparisons of locations A and B.

COMMODITY	TOTAL ANNUAL WEIGHT IN LBS.	CARLOAD RATE (IN CENTS PER 100 LBS.)		TOTAL FREIGHT COSTS	
		"A"	"B"	"A"	"B"
Raw Material					
#1	16,000,000	225	170	$360,000	$272,000
#2	9,000,000	350	100	315,000	90,000
#3	4,000,000	60	30	24,000	12,000
#4	2,000,000	240	180	48,000	36,000
Finished Products	25,000,000	300	500	750,000	1,250,000
				$1,497,000	$1,660,000

DIFFERENTIAL IN FAVOR OF "A" — $163,000.

Further study might show other points to have a lower total assembly and distribution cost than "A". It must be concluded from this calculation that point "B" is too close to the raw material source and too far removed from the market despite the "rule" that weight-losing processes should be located at the source of materials.

The goal is clearly to determine that point which yields the minimum sum. However, countless combinations can be made and two or more points can obtain the same net advantage. Oil is profitably refined both near the oil fields and near the consuming markets. Steel is manufactured successfully near ore fields, near coal fields, and at assembly points (like Gary, Indiana) where neither raw material is locally produced.

THE EFFECT OF GENERAL RATE INCREASES

Our mass production technique is based partly upon the hypothesis that a worker specializing on a small part of the finished job becomes expert in this task and greatly expands his output. The extent to which specialization may be conducted is limited by the size of market which can be reached for the differential between the mass-produced unit price and the cost of manufacturing the article locally on a smaller scale.

The application of general increases in freight rates since 1946 has affected the extent of the market which can be served from any given location. These percentage increases have not only inflated the rates but have increased the *differential* between competitive producing points. Below the first-class Exception rates from Chicago to New York and from St. Louis to New York are compared. Note the 100% increase in the differential.

These increasing rates and differentials limit the size of specialized plants and accelerate the trend toward regional production.

FIRST-CLASS EXCEPTION RATE (IN CENTS PER 100 LBS.)
TO: NEW YORK, N. Y.

GENERAL INCREASES SINCE JUNE 30, 1946	FROM CHICAGO	FROM ST. LOUIS	DIFFERENTIAL IN FAVOR OF CHICAGO
Base Rate	167	184	17¢
X-162 (25%)	209	230	21¢
X-166 (30%)	272	299	27¢
X-168 (10%)	299	329	30¢
X-175 (15%)	344	378	34¢

One example will serve to illustrate how these general increases tend to destroy the advantages of the specialized producer. Assume originally that local manufacturer "A" can sell a product f.o.b. his plant for $10, whereas specialized manufacturer "B" in a distant city can make the same product for $7.

When "A" has a local delivery cost of $1.00 per unit and "B" has a freight cost of $3.00, specialized producer "B" dominates the local market with a delivered price of $10.

Applying a general 75% increase in freight rates, the cost of delivery for "A" becomes $1.75 and for "B" the cost is increased to $5.25. Now the local, small-scale producer "A" can outbid his large competitor with a delivered price of $11.75 compared to "B's" cost of $12.25.

CHARTING OF RAW MATERIALS

Intelligent choice of raw material sources can only be made from examination of factual information. The charted data should include the following detail for each major material from all possible origins:

(a) location of source
(b) availability
(c) price
(d) terms of sale
(e) freight rates to site

MINERALS AND PRINCIPAL PRODUCING STATES

RANK IN VALUE	MINERAL	PRINCIPAL PRODUCING STATES	
		IN ORDER OF QUANTITY	IN ORDER OF VALUE
	Abrasive stone:		
69	Grindstones & pulpstones	Ohio, W. V., Wash.	Rank same as for quantity
82	Millstones	Not available	N. C., Va.
74	Pebbles (grinding)	Minn., Wisc., Tex., N. C.	Rank same as for quantity
77	Tube-mill liners (natural)	Minn., N. C., Wisc.	Minn., Wisc., N. C.
86	Andalusite	Nev.	Rank same as for quantity
50	Antimony ore and concentrates	Ida., Nev., Ore., Wash.	"
67	Aplite	Va.	"
41	Asbestos	Vt., Ariz., Ga., Cal.	"
31	Asphalt (native)	Tex., Ky., Ala., Okla.	Tex., Ky., Utah, Ala.
30	Barite (crude)	Ark., Mo., Nev., Ga.	Ark., Mo., Ga., Nev.
27	Bauxite	Ark., Ga., Ala.	Rank same as for quantity
72	Beryllium concentrates	N. H., Colo., S. D., N. M.	"
24	Boron minerals	Cal.	"
22	Bromine	Tex., Mich., Cal., W. Va.	Tex., Mich., W. Va., Cal.
66	Brucite	Nev.	Rank same as for quantity
39	Calcium-magnesium chloride	Mich., W. Va., Cal., Ohio	Mich., Cal., W. Va., Ohio
64	Carbon dioxide (natural)	Cal., Utah, N. M., Ore.	Cal., Ore., Wash., Utah
3	Cement	Pa., Cal., Tex., N. Y.	Rank same as for quantity
81	Chromite	Cal.	"
13	Clays	Ohio, Pa., Cal., Ill.	Ga., Pa., Ohio, Mo.
2	Coal:		
	Bituminous	W. Va., Pa., Ky., Ill.	Rank same as for quantity
	Lignite	N. D., Tex., Mont., S. D.	N. D., Mont., S. D., Tex.
	Pennsylvania anthracite	Pa.	Rank same as for quantity
70	Cobalt	Pa.	"
8	Copper	Ariz., Utah, Mont., N. M.	"
29	Diatomite	Cal., Ore., Nev., Wash.	"
85	Dumortierite	Nev.	"
75	Emery	N. Y.	"
83	Epsomite	Wash.	"
44	Feldspar (crude)	N. C., Colo., Va., S. D.	N. C., Colo., N. H., Va.
25	Fluorspar	Ill., Ky., Colo., N. M.	Rank same as for quantity
57	Garnet (abrasive)	N. Y., Ida.	
61	Gem stones	Not available	Ore., Cal., Wash., Tex.
15	Gold	S. D., Cal., Utah, Nev.	Rank same as for quantity
60	Graphite:		
	Amorphous	R. I.	Rank same as for quantity
	Crystalline	Tex., Ala.	"
21	Gypsum (crude)	Mich., N. Y., Ia., Tex.	"
55	Helium	Tex.	"
49	Iodine	Cal.	"
4	Iron ore (usable)	Minn., Mich., Ala., Utah	Minn., Mich., Ala., N. Y.
63	Kyanite	Va., S. C., Ga.	Rank same as for quantity
11	Lead	Mo., Ida., Utah, Ariz.	"
14	Lime (open-market)	Ohio, Pa., Mo., Ala.	Ohio, Pa., Mo., W. Va.
65	Lithium minerals	S. D., Cal.	Cal., S. D.
46	Magnesite (crude)	Wash., Nev., Tex., Cal.	Rank same as for quantity
45	Magnesium chloride (for magnesium metal)	Tex.	"
34	Magnesium compounds from sea water and brines (except for metal)	Cal., Mich., N. J., Tex.	Mich., Cal., N. J., Tex.

(MINERALS AND PRINCIPAL PRODUCING STATES—continued)

RANK IN VALUE	MINERAL	PRINCIPAL PRODUCING STATES IN ORDER OF QUANTITY	IN ORDER OF VALUE
33	Manganese ore	Mont., Ark., Cal., Va.	Mont., Ark., Ariz., Tenn.
37	Manganiferous ore	Minn., N. M., Ark., Mont.	Minn., N. M., Mont., Ark.
48	Manganiferous residuum	N. J.	Rank same as for quantity
	Marl:		
71	Calcareous	Va., Ind., Wisc., W. Va.	Va., Ind., Nev., W. Va.
68	Greensand	N. J.	Rank same as for quantity
53	Mercury	Cal., Nev., Ore.	"
52	Mica	N. C., Colo., Pa., S. D.	"
	Scrap	N. C., Colo., Pa., S. D.	
	Sheet	N. C., N. H., Ga., S. D.	N. C., N. H., S. D., Ga.
20	Molybdenum concentrates	Utah, Colo., N. M., Ariz.	Colo., Utah, N. M., Ariz.
6	Natural gas	Tex., La., Cal., Okla.	Tex., Cal., W. Va., La.
5	Natural-gas liquids:		
	Natural gasoline and cycle products	Tex., Cal., La., Okla.	Rank same as for quantity
	LP-gases	Tex., Cal., Okla., La.	"
76	Olivine	N. C., Wash.	"
51	Peat	N. J., Ohio, Minn., Fla.	Ohio, N. J., Mich., Me.
56	Perlite (crude)	Nev., N. M., Colo., Ore.	Nev., Ore., N. M., Colo.
1	Petroleum (crude)	Tex., Cal., La., Okla.	Rank same as for quantity
17	Phosphate rock	Fla., Tenn., Ida., Mont.	Fla., Tenn., Mont., Ida.
79	Platinum-group metals (crude)	Cal.	Rank same as for quantity
18	Potassium salts	N. M., Cal., Utah, Mich.	"
43	Pumice and pumicite	N. M., Cal., Ore., Ida.	"
38	Pyrites	Tenn., Va., Mont., Cal.	Tenn., Va., Cal., Mont.
59	Quartz from pegmatites and quartzite	Wash., N. C., Conn., Wisc.	Wash., N. C., Conn., Ariz.
16	Salt (common)	Mich., N. Y., Ohio, La.	Mich., N. Y., La., Kan.
9	Sand and gravel	Cal., Mich., N. Y., Ill.	Cal., N. Y., Ill., Pa.
32	Sand and sandstone (ground)	Ill., N. J., W. Va., Ohio	Ill., W. Va., N. J., Ohio
80	Sharpening stones	Ark., Ind., Ohio, N. H.	Rank same as for quantity
19	Silver	Ida., Utah, Mont., Ariz.	"
23	Slate	Pa., Vt., N. Y., Md.	Pa., Vt., N. Y., Va.
36	Sodium carbonate (natural)	Cal.	Rank same as for quantity
40	Sodium sulfate (natural)	Cal., Tex., Wyo.	"
7	Stone	Pa., Ohio, Ill., Mich.	Pa., Ohio, Ill., N. Y.
12	Sulfur (refined)	Tex., La.	Rank same as for quantity
73	Sulfur ore for direct agricultural use	Wyo., Cal., Nev., Colo.	"
26	Talc, pyrophyllite, and ground soapstone	N. Y., N. C., Cal., Vt.	N. Y., Cal., N. C., Vt.
78	Tin concentrates	Colo.	Rank same as for quantity
	Titanium concentrates:		
28	Ilmenite	N. Y., Fla., N. C., Va.	N. Y., Fla., Va., N. C.
58	Rutile	Fla., Va.	Rank same as for quantity
87	Topaz (industrial)	S. C.	"
54	Tripoli	Mo., Ill., Pa.	"
35	Tungsten concentrates	Cal., N. C., Nev., Colo.	Cal., Nev., N. C., Colo.
42	Vanadium concentrates	Colo., Utah, Ida., Ariz.	Rank same as for quantity
47	Vermiculite	Mont., S. C., N. C., Colo.	"
84	Wollastonite	N. Y.	"
10	Zinc	Ida., Ariz., Mont., N. J.	Ida., Ariz., N. J., Mont.
62	Zirconium concentrates	Fla.	Rank same as for quantity

The chart on the preceding two pages gives source data on eighty-seven minerals produced in the United States for industrial purposes. The first column notes their rank in value. Principal producing states are mentioned opposite each mineral named, the third column listing high quantity producers, the fourth noting producers according to value. This chart is offered as a guide to possible basic raw material sources.

Under normal conditions, those raw material sources are preferred which are:

(1) closest to the site, and

(2) can guarantee continued productivity.

Given equal quality and equal extraction costs, these closer sources enjoy lower delivered costs to the site than apply from distant producers.

More commonly, extraction costs are not equal but vary from source to source, with the f.o.b. mine price reflecting these differences. The choice involves a simple problem in arithmetic and may favor more distant sources:

SOURCE	PRICE PER NET TON F.O.B. MINE	FREIGHT PER NET TON	TOTAL DELIVERED COSTS
A	$5.10	$0.80	$5.90
B	4.55	1.25	5.80
C	4.40	1.55	5.95

In modern industrial terminology, "raw materials" include commodities which are purchased in the partially processed state or as completed components.

For example, the machinery manufacturer considers his raw material to be iron and steel shapes rather than the ore, fuel and flux used in the production. A radio manufacturer may purchase his "raw materials" as completed cabinets, transformers, tubes, tuning units, etc.

Hence, in the locational sense, raw materials include all purchased materials and supplies necessary to manufacture a given product.

It may become advisable in some studies (particularly those involving divisions of national corporations) to divide raw materials into "static" and "dynamic" supplies:

Static supplies represent captive producers or others with long-term commitments which cannot be readily shifted.

Dynamic sources include those which are entirely dependent upon location of the plant and can be adjusted easily.

In the selection of raw material sources there is a tendency to overemphasize the competitive position of the local producer. Actually the more distant source may be able to effectively compete due to a favorable rate relationship.

Most raw materials have been accorded low rate levels under various "commodity rate" structures. These rates, which are designed to reflect the delicate balance between competitive sources, place less emphasis upon distance than upon the ability to reach the market.

Commodity rates are dynamic and new rates can be readily established to meet shipper and carrier needs at new manufacturing locations. Each carrier is eager to develop new traffic or receive a "fair share" of the movement.

The more distant raw material producer, anxious to enter the market in competition with other sources, usually finds a sympathetic reception to reasonable proposals.

Basing point pricing was eliminated in some industries following a postwar Supreme Court decision. However, the practice of equalization, freight allowance, and zone pricing has not been disturbed. On raw materials involving such adjustments, the competitive relationship between producers must be examined to determine whether the program will be continued, curtailed, or expanded at the new location.

CHARTING THE MARKET

Whether the product of the plant will go directly to the general public for consumption or to other manufacturers as materials for further processing, every plant location study envisions a market to be served from the site.

Proximity to markets is always desirable. In many instances, however, a compromise may be necessary in order to accomplish other economies.

At the outset the market should be carefully analyzed. Preferably a large map should be prepared indicating the extent of the market to be served by the new plant, the location of competitors, and local distribution facilities available.

Accurate comparisons can only be made if present outbound freight costs are known. Cost data should be prepared showing (a) the shipping weight to each destination and (b) the percentage of this weight handled by various types of carriers. Where LTL distribution is used, knowledge of the weight normally shipped at one time will be necessary in determining the applicable rates.

Unless a very small market area is being considered, it will be advisable to reduce the number of individual rate calculations from the present plant and proposed locations. This can best be accomplished by grouping destinations into retail trading areas. The following map shows this for Ohio. Rates checked to the central city will usually be representative for the entire group.

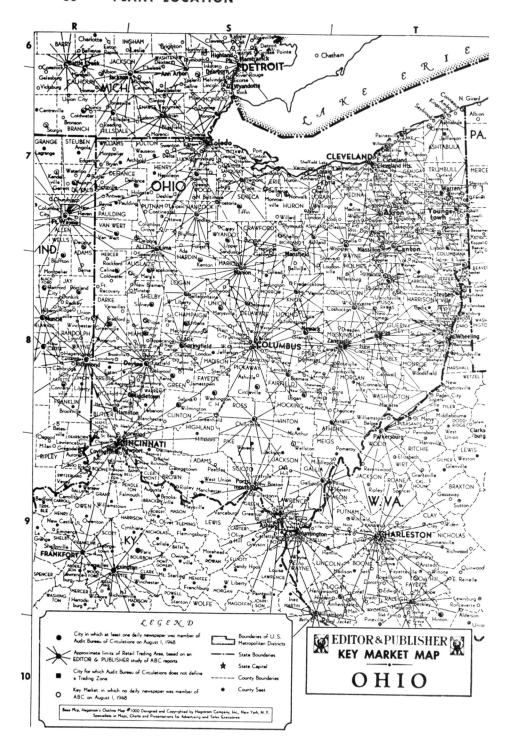

EDITOR & PUBLISHER
KEY MARKET MAP

OHIO

THE CENTER OF THE MARKET

The center of markets is a statistical device helpful in approximating that point which will provide the lowest cost for distribution of outbound products. Caution must be used in its application for, like other techniques employing averages, it can only be used as a guide.

The following procedure is used in calculating the center of markets:

1. First a large-scale map of the market area to be serviced by the new plant is obtained, and an overlay is made on graph paper. (It is imperative that the number of squares per unit of measurement be equal in each direction.)
2. Customer locations (identified by code) are plotted on the graph paper according to their geographic position determined from the base map.
3. Horizontal and vertical axis lines are constructed with their origin as close to the lower left-hand corner as possible. The location of these lines with respect to the plotted points is immaterial, provided the entire market area is included within them. The graph now represents Quadrant I of a Cartesian co-ordinate.
4. A uniform scale is laid out along the horizontal or "X" axis and the vertical or "Y" axis.
5. The number of distance units along the "X" axis and along the "Y" axis of each destination are found and then entered in a table.

An arithmetic mean (or average) is determined along the "X" axis by adding together all of the distance units and then dividing by the number of points plotted. The arithmetic mean along the "Y" axis is determined in a similar manner.

That point located at the intersection of the mean number of units along the "X" axis and the mean number of units along the "Y" axis is the geographic center of markets. It is a *simple* geographic center in that each of the destinations has been weighted equally with no regard to the actual magnitude of tonnage to the individual point.

CENTER OF MARKET,
NEW YORK, 1951

● Simple Center

● Weighted Center

FROM AN ACTUAL STUDY BY FANTUS FACTORY LOCATING SERVICE

The *weighted* center of markets can be determined as follows: (a) multiply the number of distance units along each axis for each entry by the volume of tonnage moved to that destination during a representative period, (b) determine the weighted arithmetic mean along each axis by dividing the sum of individual multiplications by the total tonnage moving to all points considered. That point located at the intersection of the weighted arithmetic mean along each axis is the weighted center of markets.

The accompanying example has been taken directly from a report of the Fantus Factory Locating Service. The territory to be served by the proposed plant included all of upper New York State and border areas in Pennsylvania and Vermont. The simple center of markets is near Auburn, New York (T-2) and the weighted center is south of Rochester (T-32).

As stated at the outset, this type of presentation is highly theoretical, but the final result when adjusted by applicable rates will normally fall close to these centers. In this example, actual distribution charges are lowest from a point midway between the weighted center and Buffalo (T-6), which city represents about 50% of the total volume. Lowest *average* rates prevail from the simple geographic center.

OBTAINING A FREIGHT ADVANTAGE TO THE MARKET

Under normal circumstances, new plant facilities should be established at that point where a definite freight advantage can insure control of a substantial market and where a good competitive position can be maintained in important adjoining market areas.

Study should first be made of competitive rate levels to define the "natural" markets of competitors. Those areas which are presently served at *greatest penalty* from all competitive producing points will generally prove to be most fruitful, provided they possess a sufficiently large market.

After a study has determined that such an area can support an economical operation, rates should be checked using hypothetical locations within the selected area. A shift of a few miles in one direction or another can secure a freight advantage over competitors to important destinations. In this manner, the "natural" market areas of competitors can be *re-defined* to the benefit of the new plant location.

As an example, consider a manufacturer of electrical appliances who is considering central Ohio as a location for his new plant. The majority of his distribution is in Ohio and neighboring states, but he has an important carload movement to a distributor in Los Angeles. His major competitor is located in Cleveland, Ohio.

If he selects Marysville as his location, he and his Cleveland competitor will have a rate of $5.56 per 100 lbs. to Los Angeles. Due to rate blanketing, his location 100 miles nearer the West Coast will have no effect on his competitive position. However, if he shifts only 7 miles further northwest of Marysville to Peoria, Ohio, Group C rates will replace Group B, and his rate will be $4.83. On every carload to Los Angeles, he will enjoy a differential of $60 or more over his competitor.

Equalization of competitive advantages

A typical problem in plant location study is the determination of the competitive position of various points in serving a single market.

Assume it is desired to serve Mobile, Alabama at a lower cost than prevails for a Charleston, South Carolina competitor. Yet, because it is necessary to give good service to other southeastern markets, the new plant can be no farther west than the Georgia-Alabama line.

Use of airline distances will yield an erroneous conclusion. Rather, the applicable rate from Charleston to Mobile should be determined. All points having the *same* rate should then be plotted on the map. An arc will be circumscribed with its focal point at Mobile. It will extend westward from Charleston through these plotted points, terminating on the Gulf some distance west of Mobile.

Those origins lying within the plotted arc will have lower rates to the Mobile market than apply from Charleston. Those outside the arc will have higher rates.

Rate-making geography

The thousands of entirely distinct sub-structures and delicate interterritorial relationships involved in rate-making are beyond the scope of this study. However, the executive considering new plant locations should be familiar with general aspects of rate-making geography. Because the truck lines have copied the railroad system, our attention will be directed to the railroad terminology.

The country is basically divided into three major classification territories. For our purposes, the exact definition of their boundaries is unnecessary.

Basically, *Official Classification Territory* consists of the northeastern portion of the United States lying north of the Ohio and Potomac Rivers and east of the Mississippi River. Omitted from the territory are the northern peninsula of Michigan, the states of Wisconsin and Minnesota, as well as the northwestern portion of the state of Illinois.

Southern Classification Territory consists of that portion of the country lying south of the Ohio and Potomac Rivers and east of the Mississippi.

Western Classification is the balance of the United States west of the Mississippi River and including those states east of the Mississippi River and including those states east of the Mississippi which are not part of Official Classification Territory.

Each section of the country has its own traffic and rate-making problems. To deal with them the railroads have organized themselves into freight traffic associations. Under recent legislation these rate-making bodies were exempted from anti-trust regulation.

The names of most of the associations will indicate the geographic area which they cover. The boundaries of these areas are shown on the accompanying map of rate-making territories.

Principles of rail rates

Every article produced in the country is classified into one of a limited number of "class ratings". These ratings are percentages of the first class rate (100%) and can be multiples above it.

First class rates are prescribed on a distance basis between virtually all origins and destinations in the nation. In order to simplify their publication, points are arbitrarily grouped into rate-basing areas. The rates are filed with the Interstate Commerce Commission and appear in publications called "Tariffs".

Class rates are named in cents per 100 lbs. If the first class rate from "A" to "B" is 147 cents, and the article being shipped has been assigned a Column 70 classification rating, the rate applied to the shipment will be 70% of the first class rate, or 103 cents.

Because of commercial and operating conditions within rate-making territories, the carriers may wish to alter the classification ratings. Accordingly, "Exceptions" to the classification are published. These Exception ratings appear as percentages of the first class rate. When an article is listed in the Exceptions, the rating named *supersedes* the classification rating unless otherwise specified.

Exception ratings in turn can be superseded by the publication of a Commodity rate. This is a rate (as opposed to a "rating" which is a percentage) usually restricted to apply between specific points on a given article. The rate is normally lower than would result from application of the Exception rating between the same points.

The list which appears below compares the basic mileage rates prescribed in the Eastern Class Rate Investigation and maximum rate levels named on various commodities as a result of hearings before the Interstate Commerce Commission. While all are related to mileage, each commodity has been handled separately, reflecting the competitive situation between producers and the revenue needs of the carriers.

The Transcontinental Rate Bureau deals with rates between points on the West Coast and regions east of the Rocky Mountains. This bureau publishes carload and LCL commodity rates on virtually all important articles of commerce moving to and from West Coast markets. These rates reflect the competition of intercoastal waterways operating via the Panama Canal.

The great bulk of tonnage in the U. S. moves on either Exception ratings or Commodity rates.

Comparison of Basic Exception Scales and Maximum Rates Presented on Various Commodities
(Subject to Increases X-123, 162, 166, 168, 175)

	DK. 15879 6th CL. EXC. (27½%)	DK. 17260 ACID SULPHURIC	DK. 16496 CASTINGS	DK. 18112 CEMENT	DK. 17.00-6 IRON & STEEL	229-1CC-4 LIME
5	8	5.0	—	5.0	6.0	—
25	10	7.0	—	8.0	8.5	—
50	12	9.5	—	9.5	11.0	10.0
100	15	13.0	15.0	12.0	16.0	11.5
150	18	15.5	17.5	13.5	19.0	13.0
200	20	—	20.0	15.0	21.5	14.0
250	23	—	22.5	17.0	24.0	15.5
300	24	—	25.0	18.5	26.5	16.5
350	26	—	—	19.5	29.0	17.5
400	27	—	—	21.0	31.0	18.0
450	29	—	—	22.0	33.0	19.0
500	31	—	—	23.5	35.0	20.0
550	32	—	—	24.5	37.0	20.5
600	34	—	—	26.0	38.0	21.5
650	36	—	—	27.0	40.0	22.5
700	37	—	—	28.5	41.0	23.0
750	39	—	—	29.5	43.0	24.0
800	40	—	—	31.0	44.0	25.0

The effect of the new uniform
freight classification

On May 30, 1952 a major adjustment was made in the rail rate-making technique. Upon the insistence of the Interstate Commerce Commission the railroads issued a Uniform Freight Classification to apply nationwide. It replaced the Consolidated Freight Classification which had named varying ratings by classification territory. Simultaneously a new rate structure was placed into effect on all class-rated traffic.

The railroads have attempted to compromise ratings which varied from territory to territory on virtually all the items appearing in the Consolidated Freight Classification. Excerpts for an identical entry are shown below for comparison:

ITEM 26100 LEAD, PIG OR SLAB, LOOSE OR IN PACKAGES

	LESS-CARLOAD RATINGS	CARLOAD MINIMUM (LBS.)	CARLOAD RATINGS
Excerpt from Consolidated Freight Classification No. 20	4-50-4	36,000	6-7-5
Excerpt from Uniform Freight Classification No. 1	55	40,000	35

In the Consolidated Freight Classification separate ratings are shown for LCL and CL shipments in the three major classification territories. The first symbol, reading from left to right, is for Official, the second for Southern, and the third for Western Classification. The symbol 4 shown for LCL shipments governed by Official Classification represents 4th class. Prior to this recent adjustment, class 4 in Official Territory was 50% of 1st class. The 50 shown in the second entry represents 50% of 1st class in Southern Classification Territory. In Western Classification, the symbol 4 represents 4th class, which was 55% of 1st class in that territory.

In the carload entry, the symbol 6 represents 6th class in Official Classification Territory ($27\frac{1}{2}$ of 1st class), the symbol 7 represents 7th class in Southern Classification Territory (35% of 1st class), and the symbol 5 represents 5th class in Western Classification Territory ($37\frac{1}{2}\%$ of 1st class).

The Uniform Freight Classification effectively eliminates the former boundaries of the classification territories for rate-making purposes *on class-rated traffic only*. Note that the compromise symbol for LCL in the Uniform Freight Classification is 55, or 55% of 1st class. In this case, as in many others, the highest percentage relationship to 1st class was selected as the compromise. Similarly, a compromise was reached of 35% of 1st class for carload movements in all territories, *but the carload minimum was raised from 36,000 to 40,000 lbs. to meet the revenue needs of western railroads.*

The effect of the Uniform Freight Classification on plant location cannot be predicted. Each commodity is affected differently, some experiencing drastic increases, others receiving moderate decreases. Much of the individual effect depends upon the location of markets.

Western and Southern interests have been in favor of a uniform scale of class rates, insisting that the higher level of rates which prevailed in those areas (mile for mile) tended to restrict industry to Official Classification Territory. A review of many individual cases reveals that the new scale may actually postpone movement of plants into these regions. While rates within Official Territory generally increased, the rates to Western and Southern markets from the East decreased. This is the other side of the double-edged sword which was to attract industry by offering lower rates within and from the West and South.

The chart which appears below illustrates the relationship between the new class rates and the exception rates which conform to the original mileage scales within the various territories. All rates should be inflated by 15% which is actually applicable as a surcharge on freight bills under Ex Parte 175 as amended.

Comparison of Uniform Classification Rates and Exception Rates Applying Within Various Territories
(SUBJECT TO X-175 INCREASES)

1st CLASS (100%) RATES

MILES	UNIFORM CLASS RATES ALL TERRITORIES	EXCEPTION RATES OFFICIAL TERRITORY	EXCEPTION RATES SOUTHERN TERRITORY	EXCEPTION RATES SOUTHWESTERN RAILROADS	EXCEPTION RATES WESTERN RR ZONE 1
25	76	72	76	79	69
50	91	85	94	102	85
75	103	100	113	122	101
100	114	111	131	140	118
200	149	143	185	193	164
300	179	172	221	231	195
400	206	195	257	267	227
500	231	219	286	305	256
750	295	277	356	397	334
1000	345	326	411	467	392
1250	395	373	465	539	456
1500	445	424	520	613	516

Motor carrier rates

Most of the motor carrier rate technique is similar to that of the railroads. Rates are published point-to-point and involve a classification, exceptions to the classification, commodity rates, truckload rates and less-than-truckload rates.

The National Motor Freight Classification is very similar to the rail classification, and names less-than-truckload and volume rates for East, South and West Territories. In some areas, such as New England, the carriers have attempted to write truck classifications based on density of the commodities. Other truck lines utilize the railroad classification. Adjustments are being made to meet the competitive rail rates published effective May 30, 1952.

Motor truck class rates, for the most part, are based on rail rates. In recent years, their level has been slightly below rail due to the application of general increases on rail rates. The commodity rate structure is competitive, but it is more closely related to distances than is true of rail commodity rates.

Several important differences exist between motor truck rate structure and rail rates. Rates on small LTL shipments approximate railroad LCL rates, but larger LTL shipments have been accorded important rate reductions. In general, truckload rates approximate carload rates.

Unlike the railroads, the truck lines are able to pick and choose the traffic which they will handle and the level of rates which will apply. The carriers publish minimum rate restrictions or "rate stops", which device enables them to insure their revenues for off-line hauls or where excessive transfer is involved.

An example of this restriction is that of a carrier whose tariffs prohibit the assessment of any rate lower than 2nd class to specific destinations, regardless of the classification rating of the commodity tendered for shipment.

Express rates

The Railway Express Agency divides commodities into three general classes: first class, second class, and commodities having special rates. General merchandise falls into the first class category. Goods and liquids are in second class, and such things as printed matter, fresh fruit and vegetables are accorded special rates. Second class rates are 75% of first class rates. Ratings and rules are contained in the Official Express Classification.

Express rates are fixed according to geographical block system. For this purpose, the country is divided into areas of one square degree of latitude and longitude. The blocks are 69 miles long and from 45 to 65 miles wide. Each block is divided into 16 squares identified by letters of the alphabet from A to Q, omitting J.

Where large numbers of express shipments are made, it is advisable to check the relationship of proposed sites to the dividing line of express blocks. Movement of a few miles can sometimes result in important economies to major markets served by express shipments.

Parcel post zone system

Parcel Post rate-making divides the whole country into blocks that are approximately one-fourth the size of the major express blocks. Each square degree is divided into four parts. Rate zones are measured from center to center of these blocks, and a graduated scale of rates is applied.

There are 9 zones as follows:

Local	
First Zone	Up to 50 miles
Second Zone	50 to 150 miles
Third Zone	150 to 300 miles
Fourth Zone	300 to 600 miles
Fifth Zone	600 to 1000 miles
Sixth Zone	1000 to 1400 miles
Seventh Zone	1400 to 1800 miles
Eighth Zone	Over 1800 miles

Near critical block lines, postal zones should be carefully checked before a site is selected.

Other rate techniques

Water carriers usually publish port-to-port commodity rates. Some of the coastwise carriers, Great Lakes carriers, and barge operators participate in through rail-water or rail-water-rail rates on class and commodity traffic, however.

The freight forwarders publish tariffs which refer to rail tariffs in most instances. In effect, they are a collection of minimum rate restrictions between given points, with rates above or below rail less-than-carload rates depending on the cost of providing the service.

More and more airline freight traffic is moving on commodity rates, but no real pattern of rate-making has emerged as yet.

Construction stage of new Flint River plant of Merck & Co., Inc., vicinity of Albany, Georgia. CONTRACTOR: *A. C. Sanford, Inc.* Plant Location Study—FANTUS FACTORY LOCATING SERVICE.

CHAPTER 4

Labor Availability

Selection of the broad, general geographic area for the plant is an obvious but necessary preliminary step in the selection of the specific community. This determination is based upon the costs of raw material assembly, market accessibility and the economic background which affects such factors as labor cost, utility availability and cost, etc. However, once the general area has been determined, the selection of the particular community within that area will depend largely on labor in all its ramifications.

It is not too far fetched to state that labor for some companies is the *greatest single influence* motivating plant relocation. Similarly, branch plant selection is, to a large extent, determined by local labor cost, labor availability and labor stability and productivity.

Despite its importance, nevertheless, few reliable standards have been developed for measuring labor resources of a given area. So many intangibles are involved that most manufacturing concerns, after purely superficial examination, act by "hunch."

Each individual firm has its own criteria and, within each management, individuals also possess strong personal opinions. The resultant conflict is not altogether disastrous for there is usually a sub-stratum of agreement and, ultimately, if the management is wise, facts will be taken as the ultimate guide. Here is a typical example of the kind of disagreement with which companies are often beset:

Two executives of a manufacturing concern may disagree between themselves as to the effect of size of community on the supply and productivity of a labor force. Vice President Smith insists that only in a large city can they secure an adequate pool of workers, accustomed to factory employment, familiar with machine operations, and replaceable in the event of turnover.

President Jones, on the other hand, argues that the smaller the city, within reasonable limits of course, the better. Workers, when trained, are less likely to seek other jobs. With fewer big city distractions, less time and effort in travelling to and from work, the employee is likely to work more happily and productively.

We have here a kind of disagreement which is hard to resolve, for the simple reason that a fairly sound case can be made for both points of view. Unless additional FACTS are brought to bear on the size and type of labor market required, action based exclusively on one or the other contention can lead to disappointment and—what is more important—to serious financial loss.

First of all, the term "labor market" should be defined. The United States Employment Service furnishes the following definition:

> The labor market is a "place" within which the factors influencing the employment process operate. It is the "place" where employers recruit workers and in which workers seek employment. It is the general field in which labor demand and supply, wage differentials, variations in hours and shifts of work, employer hiring practices, and a multitude of other working conditions shape employer-worker job relationships.
>
> A labor market area may be defined as the geographic area consisting of a central city (or cities) and the surrounding territory in which there is a concentration of urban economic activity, or urban labor demand, and in which workers can change jobs without changing their residences.

The labor market, thus, is considered as a geographic entity—a place. That conception, however, is true only in the consideration of relatively static unskilled labor. Actually, skilled labor is seldom static, and moves freely from one area to another, dependent upon demand.

Labor shortages must be considered as part of a long-term trend. The number of older persons is increasing, whereas the number of younger people is declining. Each decade proportionately fewer reach the minimum entrance age.

Approximately 67,000,000 persons are now in the nation's work force. Of this number, *1 out of every 3 workers is over age* by accepted industrial standards. The fact is that while over-all national population increased 14.5% between 1940 and 1950, the group between 25 and 29 years increased only 8.7%; but the group 75 years and over increased 40.2%. There were 4.1% *fewer* males in 1950 between the ages of 20 to 24 years.

Growing dependence on female labor, as a result, is apparent when we note that some 19,000,000 women are in the work force.

Industrial firms that have operated successfully for years in certain localities have gradually been forced to the realization that their personnel departments must hire marginal and heretofore unacceptable labor because of intense competition. The lowering of entrance qualifications, such as educational background, manual dexterity and emotional stability, results in the employment of substandard labor with attendant turnover, unrest and lowered plant efficiency.

The manufacturer setting out to determine a new plant location must first of all ascertain whether sufficient stable labor is available for his needs, bearing in mind the general character of the area involved, its growth and the probable future requirements of rival industries.

Let us assume that you are now that manufacturer seeking a stable unskilled labor reservoir. Before time is wasted in expensive and time-consuming field investigation, it is advisable to eliminate as many localized areas as possible for due and sufficient cause. The general rules that follow are the result of actual experience gained in locating over 1300 industrial plants.

1. Caution is advised in evaluating the labor potential of resort and vacation areas. Many workers, temporarily available off-season, will leave full-time employment for the allure of high-paying seasonal work. This is true to a lesser degree in areas where canning, packing and agricultural production prevail.

2. It is not necessarily true that a large city will have more of a permanent labor surplus than a small town. The number of people in a community is only important in relation to the *number of people gainfully at work* in the community.

3. In semi-urban and rural areas, population and work force figures should be applied county-wide. The county seat, for example, may have a population of only 4,000, yet the county itself may easily have tenfold that population. In many areas the county seat is the natural shopping orbit, school, social and recreational center. Area residents naturally gravitate towards it. Do not make the common mistake of precluding examination of a town because its size does not initially indicate sufficient manpower for your needs. In this connection, the density of the population, public highway transportation, commuting patterns and shopping habits all have significance.

4. The most desirable community is the diversified community where industry, commerce and services are well balanced. Care should be exercised in considering a community where employment in manufacturing is more than 50% of aggregate employment in manufacturing, trade and service.

5. A self-contained, independent labor supply is vital to long-term success. Anticipating the recruitment of a large percentage of the necessary work force beyond a twenty-mile radius may be hazardous. Constant sniping and utilization of workers by incoming plants in such contiguous areas can eventually deplete the labor resources of the central area.

6. In considering the over-all work force, investigate and eliminate those persons who are listed as residents, but are confined to mental or other hospitals, prisons, or similar institutions. (In an extreme case, a recent survey in a New York State county revealed 11,000 persons so confined out of a total reported population of 70,000.)

7. In suburban communities adjacent to large metropolitan areas, thoroughly investigate the commuting population. Do not consider the commuting population as potential recruits for an industrial work force. In most cases it is difficult, in fact well nigh impossible, to persuade the white collar worker to accept industrial employment.

8. For those concerns utilizing female labor, it is important to ascertain the average *family* income in the area under investigation. Generally the need for *supplementary* income draws females into the labor market. Estimates of female labor supply must be based on the correlation between primary and secondary (or supplementary) income.

9. A partial index to the female labor market is the availability of domestic help. Whenever the demand for female labor exceeds the supply, domestics are virtually unavailable.

10. In general, areas tending to attract migratory labor of the "flotsam and jetsam" type (large ports, for example), should be avoided by certain types of manufacturing operations.

The recommendations outlined above are only a few suggestions that can be amplified by the manufacturer in the light of his own special requirements, forming the basis of his preliminary "at home" investigation.

Field investigation of remaining communities is, of course, the next logical step. A standard procedure should be to interview the local office of the State Employment Service (formerly U.S.E.S.). There are now over 1700 such offices scattered throughout the United States.

With due deference to the State Employment offices, most of which are ably managed and perform a creditable community service, reasonable care must be exercised in assessing the data supplied. Inexperience, lack of comparative knowledge of other areas, personal opinion, and community pressure may sway the Employment Service Manager.

A *personal* inspection of applicants' cards is recommended wherever possible. The age, former position, primary and secondary skills, previous wages, and residence are listed for each applicant.

The total number of Employment Office registrations may be quite deceiving. The ratio of female and male applicants is easily apparent, but it is important to ascertain the number of *qualified* applicants after weeding out the over-age, those eligible for military service, drifters, and applicants who are only interested in domestic, professional, commercial and work other than industrial employment.

The season of the year again plays a great part in analyzing current unemployment. The necessity for analyzing the *permanent labor surplus* cannot be over-emphasized. The bricklayer, mason and carpenter may be drawing unem-

POPULATION AND LABOR FORCE
by Age and Sex, United States, 1950

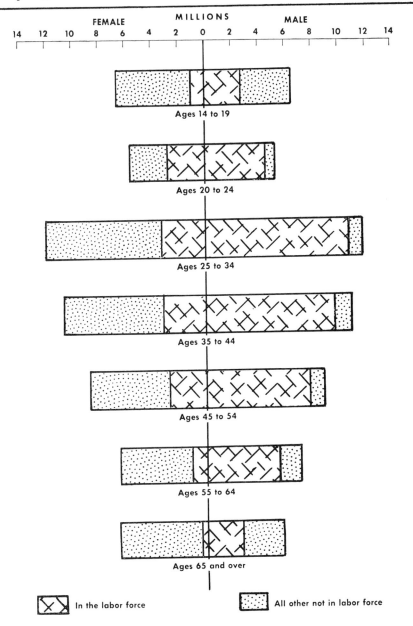

MILLIONS

FEMALE   MALE

14 12 10 8 6 4 2 0 2 4 6 8 10 12 14

Ages 14 to 19

Ages 20 to 24

Ages 25 to 34

Ages 35 to 44

Ages 45 to 54

Ages 55 to 64

Ages 65 and over

In the labor force   All other not in labor force

Prepared in the office of Fantus Factory Locating Service FROM U.S. BUREAU OF THE CENSUS INFORMATION

SHIFT IN OCCUPATIONAL GROUPS OF WOMEN
in Manufacturing, Trade and Service Industries*
1940-1950

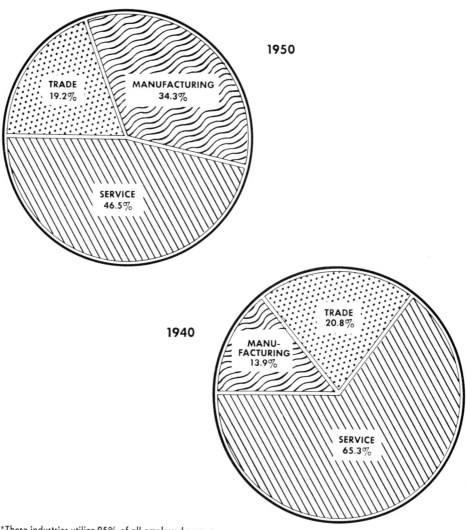

1950

TRADE
19.2%

MANUFACTURING
34.3%

SERVICE
46.5%

1940

MANU-
FACTURING
13.9%

TRADE
20.8%

SERVICE
65.3%

*These industries utilize 95% of all employed women.

Prepared in the office of Fantus Factory Locating Service FROM U.S. BUREAU OF THE CENSUS INFORMATION

ployment compensation in the winter but, used to high seasonal wages in his trade, will not usually accept steady industrial employment. Conversely, it must be realized that the average labor force increases as much as 6% in the summer when schools are closed and when agricultural workers enter the market.

Too, when seeking an unskilled labor reservoir, skilled industrial labor registrants, specializing in high-paying skills other than those required, should be deducted from the indicated total.

Finally, in assessing the validity of Employment Service figures, compare the net number of availables against monthly *job openings* for a period of one year. Very often the caliber of available help can be determined by the number of *unfilled* jobs.

If, on the basis of the foregoing suggested investigation, the community appears superficially qualified, a most important procedure is recommended, namely, personal conferences with the principal manufacturing concerns of the area.

If there is any single factor which should receive the greatest amount of attention, it is probably the experience of other manufacturers and employers. Here the investigator can find the true reflection of the spirit and nature of the community.

Civic agencies, Chambers of Commerce, Industrial Development groups on a State or utility basis, all can make claims about a given location. And they all do! However, the proof of the pudding lies in the testimony of the people who are faced with the day-to-day problems of the manufacturer. What have his experiences been while operating in the city? Does the company's Personnel Department have difficulty in attracting all the labor it needs and can it be selective in its hiring? Are local safety inspections conscientious attempts to look after the well-being of the employees or are they disguised efforts at graft? How willing is the local labor force to give an honest day's work? Are local committees of the union constantly bickering over petty grievances?

Following is an example of a conference by an investigator taken from an actual field study.

"The largest single plant in the _____ area is that of _____. 2300, 80% female, are currently employed in the manufacture and assembly of radio and television sets.

"The minimum rate paid in the plant is 87¢. Increases in rate are on an automatic basis. Top rate is paid to toolmakers, first class, with a minimum rate of $1.50 and a maximum rate of $1.83. A set-up man is paid between $1.20 and $1.53 an hour. No improvement factors or cost of living increases are provided for, although all rates were increased by 4¢ an hour on July 31, 1951.

New plant of Charles Bruning Co., Inc., Teterboro, New Jersey. BUILDER: *Joseph L. Muscarelle, Ltd., under direction of Alexander Summer Co.* Plant Location Study—FANTUS FACTORY LOCATING SERVICE.

"The company has good relations with the IBEW-AFL. Indeed, Mr. _____ believes them to be better than the relation with labor at any other of the company's many plants, and certainly better than for the rest of the country. The only strike during their ten years of operation here occurred in August of 1951 and lasted 36 hours. The issue was a matter of wages and of insurance with _____ offering a company hospitalization plan and the union holding out for the Blue Cross Plan. A compromise on wages was effected and the Blue Cross Plan instituted. It is interesting to observe that, on the morning following termination of the strike, all workers reported for work, and full production was achieved by 10 a.m.

"The company offers and pays full cost of a group life insurance program (average of $4000 per employee) and health and accident insurance. Since 1944, a pension program has been in effect with company and employee each paying 50% of the cost.

"An unusual feature is the seventh paid holiday, Armistice Day. No shift premium is paid for the second shift although 10% is paid for the night shift. Employees are paid time and a half for Saturday work and double time for Sunday work.

"The seniority provisions of the union contract seem to be entirely satisfactory to the company management. The contract in this, and other company plants, is negotiated in its entirety on a local basis.

"Mr. _____ was enthusiastic about the city administration and said, 'Taxes are equitably assessed.' He registered no complaint as to utility services."

Meetings with present manufacturers can easily be arranged when it is explained that it is in their own interest, as well as in that of the prospective newcomer, to disclose the facts.

If local manufacturers are dissatisfied, they will hesitate to unburden themselves when local interests are present for fear of later unfavorable repercussions. Thus, despite the possible sincere interest of the Chamber of Commerce or other civic agencies, it is imperative that no community witness be present to restrain a free flow of information. From past experience, most intelligent Chamber of Commerce secretaries will respect this viewpoint.

Other procedures are available to ascertain labor availability—casual conversations in the street, at the filling station, in the restaurants, are typical. Examination of newspaper want-ads over a period of time will reveal the urgency of labor needs (as well as wage rates and the skills most in demand).

At this stage, most communities can be placed in an unqualified favorable or unfavorable category, insofar as labor needs are concerned. But if no positive

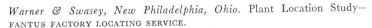

Warner & Swasey, New Philadelphia, Ohio. Plant Location Study—
FANTUS FACTORY LOCATING SERVICE.

COMPARATIVE COMMUNITY STATISTICS

	ADAIR	BOYLE	CHRISTIAN	CLARK	CRITTENDEN	FAYETTE	FRANKLIN
(1) Population 1950	16,900	18,600	43,600	18,800	11,100	90,900	28,400
(2) % white population	94	83	69	86	98	79	91
(3) % employed agriculture	77.0	33.3	41.1	42.0	49.9	12.8	21.8
(4) Total employed manufacturing	274	718	1,433	262	24	2,859	6,128
(5) Total employed mining operations	5	29	254	28	660	132	37
(6) % males in labor force	85.8	77.1	74.2	79.7	82.1	72.0	75.0
(7) Deviation from norm (male)	—	2.9	5.8	.3	—	8.0	5.0
(8) % of all females in labor force	9.0	22.3	20.5	22.6	10.4	28.7	30.8
(9) Deviation from norm (female)	17.0	3.7	5.5	3.4	15.6	—	—
(10) Density per sq. mile	47.2	94.3	49.8	69.5	33.2	281.8	110.5

reaction has been obtained, if the community "looks good" but no decision can be reached, two courses of action can be taken:

(1) Mathematical formula of potential labor force, and

(2) Labor registration.

UTILIZATION OF "DEVIATION FROM NORM" FORMULA

The *available* supply of labor comes from workers who are unemployed. The *potential* supply of labor comes from those persons 14 years of age and over who are not within the labor force (and from agricultural workers who are so employed because of a lack of other employment opportunity*). To determine the amount of potential labor from non-agricultural sources, the percentage of males in the work force (Line 6 in the chart opposite) is compared with the normal relationship in the nation, or 80.0% for white and non-white males. Where the figure in Line 6 exceeds the national norm, no deviation is shown, and where it is below the national norm, the deviation is shown as a decimal. This difference is the percentage of the total local labor pool that can be assumed to be the *potential* supply of males who accept jobs if they become available but are not reported as *available* by the various Unemployment Compensation Commissions. Female labor is charted in the same manner except that deviation figures are based on 26.0% instead of 80.0% as above.

The location investigator is cautioned never to rely upon this test alone or without corroboration from other sources. Peculiarities in the economic background of an area, unless recognized and accounted for, may distort the deviation figure in one direction or another.

The chart opposite is taken from an actual survey conducted by the Fantus

---

* The desire of farm labor to enter the industrial work force is illustrated in a study completed by Prof. Geo. T. Starnes of the University of Virginia, published in 1951. Of 101 employees of the U.S. Rubber Company plant at Scottsville, Va., 13 were previously employed in farming or dairy work. It is also interesting to note that in this survey it was found that 20% of present employees were formerly occupied in such seasonal trades as construction, lumbering, day labor, etc. Some 18% were attracted from mercantile work, and included such occupations as service station attendant, waitress, and store clerk. Naturally, industrial wages were higher than in any of the occupations listed, and almost one third of employees interviewed in this study admitted that they had changed jobs for "more money."

Factory Locating Service. In interpreting these figures, it is apparent that in Adair County, males (Line 6) are fully employed (national average 80%), whereas females (Line 9) should be available for employment (national employment average 26%). Franklin and Fayette Counties, conversely, reveal that males are not fully employed, but that the number of females currently employed is well above the national average.

LABOR REGISTRATION

In marginal cases where field investigation and statistical analysis fail to produce conclusive measurement of available labor resources, some companies resort to a labor registration. Such a registration offers greatest chance for success in smaller communities, rather than in already highly industrialized metropolitan centers.

Through blanket area-wide publicity, the purpose of the labor registration is actually to solicit applicants for the proposed new plant. Newspapers, direct mail, circulars in retail outlets, sound-truck and radio publicity are the usual mediums. Obviously, such a program should be used sparingly and only when there is a reasonable certainty that positive action will be taken to construct the plant in the community should the registration prove favorable.

Essential data will not be received unless it is asked for. If females are necessary for night shift work, if a certain wage rate is contemplated, if the work is seasonal, the attitude of applicants will not be determined unless the question is asked and phrased for positive results.

When analyzing applications, it is important to check residence for feasibility of commuting distance, age, educational background, unusual physical characteristics and present employment. If the applicant is currently working in an industrial plant, it is wise from a community relations standpoint to rule him out. Unless unusual conditions exist locally, no good can come from establishing a plant in a new community and recruiting labor from fellow manufacturers.

In an ideal labor situation, the number of qualified applicants should exceed the actual number to be employed in the ratio of at least three-to-one.

Following is a partial questionnaire recapitulation of an actual labor registration conducted by the Fantus Factory Locating Service:

Total Applicants (Female)	1,373	
Age 18-35	841	
Percent of Total Returns		61.3%

Over 35	532
Percent of Total Returns	38.7%
Age 18-35, Presently Employed	472
Percent of Total in Age Group	56.1%
Over 35, Presently Employed	274
Percent of Total in Age Group	51.5%
Age 18-35, Willing to Work Shifts	530
Percent of Total in Age Groups	63.0%
Over 35, Willing to Work Shifts	374
Percent of Total in Age Group	70.3%
Age 18-35, Married	477
Percent of Total in Age Groups	56.7%
Over 35, Married	387
Percent of Total in Age Group	72.7%
Age 18-35, Not Employed and Willing to Work Shifts	224
Percent of Total in Age Group	26.6%

	AGE DISTRIBUTION						
RESIDENCE	18-25	26-30	31-35	36-40	41-45	46-OVER	TOTAL
Local	310	162	140	131	95	173	1,011
Suburban	56	25	26	25	13	31	176
County	63	28	31	31	21	12	186
TOTAL	429	215	197	187	129	216	1,373

In evaluating the foregoing registration, it is evident that despite the impressive total of 1,373 female applicants, only 224 are qualified for consideration, i.e., do not object to shift work, are not presently employed, and are in the preferred age bracket. An aptitude test for the specific type of industrial process involved might eliminate at least half of these remaining applicants.

STRAIGHT-TIME AVERAGE HOURLY EARNINGS[1] FOR MEN
in selected occupations in ferrous foundries in 20 areas — 1953

AREA	CHIPPERS AND GRINDERS	CORE-MAKERS, HAND	LABORERS, MATERIAL HANDLING	MOLDERS, FLOOR	MOLDERS, HAND, BENCH	MOLDERS, MACHINE	PATTERN-MAKERS, WOOD	SHAKE-OUT MEN
Birmingham	$1.13	$1.43	$0.92	$1.43	(2)	$1.52	(2)	$1.16
Boston	1.48	1.97	(2)	1.96	$1.96	2.03	$2.04	1.53
Buffalo	2.06	2.14	1.66	2.13	1.92	2.41	2.24	1.90
Chicago	1.87	2.18	1.56	2.10	2.07	2.21	2.46	1.72
Cincinnati	1.59	2.19	1.47	2.22	1.98	2.42	(2)	1.57
Cleveland	1.95	2.20	1.53	2.13	2.08	2.18	2.60	1.89
Denver	1.49	1.81	(2)	1.81	(2)	1.79	(2)	1.49
Detroit	2.09	2.32	1.72	2.26	2.21	2.26	(2)	1.92
Hartford	1.76	1.84	1.34	2.28	1.98	2.26	2.22	1.51
Houston	1.45	1.88	(2)	1.95	(2)	2.02	(2)	1.45
Los Angeles	1.64	2.04	1.46	2.16	2.02	2.42	2.66	1.54
Milwaukee	1.99	2.26	1.52	2.26	1.97	2.41	2.07	1.69
Minneapolis-St. Paul	1.69	1.94	1.56	1.95	1.93	2.05	(2)	1.76
Newark-Jersey City	1.56	2.01	1.50	2.17	2.23	2.40	(2)	1.67
New York	1.54	2.00	(2)	2.02	2.00	1.96	(2)	1.52
Philadelphia	2.12	2.43	1.53	2.13	2.11	2.27	(2)	1.56
Pittsburgh	1.86	2.19	1.47	2.02	1.99	2.05	2.32	1.63
Portland, Oregon	1.86	2.17	1.72	2.16	2.16	2.15	2.70	1.72
St. Louis	2.17	2.28	1.44	2.11	2.00	2.13	2.36	1.58
San Francisco	1.90	2.24	1.75	2.25	(2)	2.21	2.79	1.85

[1] Excludes premium pay for overtime and nightwork.
[2] Insufficient data to justify presentation of an average.

CHAPTER 5

Labor:
Costs and Stability

Wide variations exist in wage rates between geographic areas, between large cities and small communities, and often between neighboring communities. Wage scales for unskilled labor and many skilled occupations are traditionally lowest throughout the southeastern area of the United States. Highest wages appear most often on the Pacific Coast.

Of course a manufacturer must recognize that wage differentials are affected by such factors as the skill and industries represented and the degree of male, female, white and non-whites employed. But despite the claims of certain economists that income is leveling off, important regional differentials persist. In fact, the geographic spread in actual *dollars and cents* is as great today as in any previous period. Illustrations of such variations appear in the table on the facing page showing wages by cities for specified occupations.

Differences in states are illustrated by figures on average weekly hours and average hourly earnings of production workers for 1952 and 1955:

	AVERAGE WEEKLY HOURS		AVERAGE HOURLY EARNINGS	
	1952	1955	1952	1955
Oregon	38.9	40.1	$1.97	$2.29
California	41.3	40.5	1.79	2.11
Illinois	41.4	41.4	1.67	1.98
Pennsylvania	40.0	40.0	1.61	1.90
New York	39.0	39.5	1.65	1.89
Massachusetts	39.1	40.6	1.53	1.71
Tennessee	40.0	41.2	1.29	1.48
North Carolina	38.3	40.0	1.17	1.28
Mississippi	41.0	43.4	1.05	1.19

Some economists have advanced the theory that when rural areas become industrialized, wage rate differentials cease to exist. However, North Carolina's low average rate of $1.28 hourly is maintained despite the fact that over 240,000 are now employed in the manufacture of textile-mill products alone in that state.

Wage differentials between cities are just as pronounced. Following are rates in effect in 1952 and 1955:

	AVERAGE WEEKLY HOURS		AVERAGE HOURLY EARNINGS	
	1952	1955	1952	1955
Detroit, Mich.	39.9	41.2	$1.98	$2.29
San Francisco, Cal.	41.2	39.8	1.87	2.20
Portland, Ore.	39.7	38.7	1.83	2.11
Rochester, N. Y.	41.2	40.6	1.70	2.00
Newark, N. J.	40.7	40.4	1.68	1.96
Boston, Mass.	39.0	40.3	1.55	1.78
Atlanta, Ga.	40.1	40.2	1.33	1.64
Providence, R. I.	39.1	40.8	1.42	1.55
Chattanooga, Tenn.	40.5	40.7	1.33	1.52
Charlotte, N. C.	39.0	42.0	1.24	1.35
Little Rock, Ark.	43.5	40.7	1.10	1.27

There is a marked disparity in wage structure between communities within the same state and often between neighboring cities. In Pennsylvania, for example, average hourly earnings in 1955 ranged from a low of $1.45 in Wilkes-Barre and Hazelton to a high of $2.24 in Pittsburgh. A 6% differential exists between York and Lancaster, Pa. with only 30 minutes of easy driving time separating them.

The effect of such disparities on cost of production in 17 different cities is seen in the following table showing relative pay levels for plant workers in indirect manufacturing jobs (1953-4), compared with New York City as 100:

LABOR MARKET	TOTAL FOR MAINTENANCE, CUSTODIAL, AND MATERIAL MOVEMENT	MAINTE-NANCE	CUSTO-DIAL	MATERIAL MOVEMENT
Memphis	77	85	82	72
New Orleans	78	87	87	70
Atlanta	79	88	85	71
Dallas	85	90	88	81
Denver	94	92	100	92
Boston	95	92	101	93
Philadelphia	97	96	102	94
New York City	100	100	100	100
Minneapolis-St. Paul	102	99	110	99
St. Louis	102	101	105	100
Chicago	105	102	111	103
Portland	105	101	111	104
Milwaukee	108	103	112	108
Newark-Jersey City	108	101	109	111
Los Angeles	109	102	115	109
Detroit	114	107	126	111
San Francisco-Oakland	115	107	125	114

The earnings spread tends to diminish somewhat in skilled occupations, but significant differentials are maintained in all industries. In a survey conducted by the U. S. Bureau of Labor Statistics in the winter of 1954-1955, it was found that in machinery manufacturing establishments class A welders earned $1.77 in Dallas, $1.94 in Boston, $2.19 in Pittsburgh, and $2.37 in Newark-Jersey City.

In spite of unionization, vast differences exist in wage rates for identical work performed. In the construction field, a bricklayer is paid $3.625 an hour in Dallas, Texas and $3.50 in Oklahoma City. His counterpart in Tampa, Florida will receive $2.95 an hour.

Wage rates in large metropolitan areas are generally higher than in smaller communities.

In studies made by the U. S. Dept. of Labor in October, 1951, wage rates for union local-transit employees ranged from $1.637 in cities with a population of 1,000,000 or over, down to an average of $1.357 in cities of 40,000 to 100,000 population.

Hourly wage levels, according to the Department of Labor, on July 1, 1951, for printing-trades workers in commercial and newspaper establishments in the various city-size groups were as follows:

CITIES WITH POPULATIONS OF —	AVERAGE HOURLY SCALE	
	BOOK AND JOB	NEWSPAPERS
1,000,000 and over	$2.302	$2.757
500,000 to 1,000,000	2.155	2.659
250,000 to 500,000	2.119	2.641
100,000 to 250,000	2.032	2.456
40,000 to 100,000	1.963	2.219

It is obvious, therefore, that *if labor cost is an important proportion of total delivered-to-customer cost of a given product, the community finally chosen will exert tremendous influence on the competitive position of the new plant.*

The question often rises, "Don't low wage rates mean lower productivity?" The whole subject of output per man hour has received much attention, but so far few valid conclusions have been reached. In a special round table conference on worker productivity called by the National Industrial Conference Board, Dr. Fabricant of the National Bureau of Economic Research said, "If we look over the industrial area . . . this fact sticks out clearly: Employment and output were highly correlated with one another. When output was high, employment also was high. When output was low, employment was low."

The second speaker at this round table discussion devoted to "Measuring Labor's Productivity" was Mr. A. W. Rucker, consultant. Mr. Rucker said, ". . . in slack times, marginal workers are laid off first, and the more efficient workers retained, thus raising the average level of productivity of those who remain on the job. In boom times, the additions of marginal workers tend to lower the average level of efficiency for the same but reverse reasons."

The diverse viewpoints expressed by these competent economists is indicative of the difficulty that exists in measuring labor productivity. In many contacts throughout industry, specialists in the Fantus organization have been presented with all shades of opinion. One of our investigators in New England was told recently: "We manufacture textile machinery and due to the recession in the textile field, have laid off 900 men in the last ten months. We have weeded out the inexperienced workers as much as possible, but our remaining employees are now 'stretching' their jobs; as a result our productivity has gone down enormously."

From a practical standpoint, the difference in comparative efficiency (or

WEEKLY OFFICE PAY IN 25 CITIES

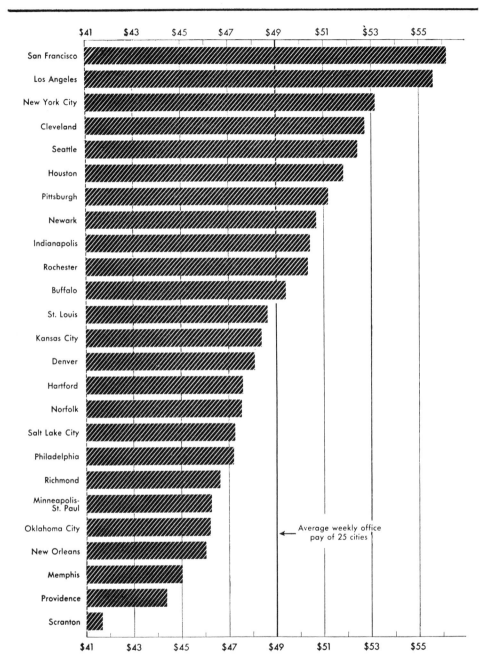

Prepared in the office of Fantus Factory Locating Service FROM U.S. BUREAU OF LABOR STATISTICS INFORMATION

labor output) between lathe operators on the West Coast and in New England, or between a large city and a small town,* is not so much a difference in individual characteristics but the result of external pressures and influences beyond their respective control.

Climatic and other environmental conditions, efficiency of equipment, management techniques, wage incentives, employee-management relations, business conditions, and numerous other factors have a direct bearing on ultimate worker output. Furthermore, comparative studies of efficiency are valid only in *identical* industries which have *identical* production methods.

Utilizing figures taken from the most recent U. S. Census of Manufactures (1947), we find for example that in the manufacture of "Textile Mill Products" each dollar of payroll expended produced $2.02 of value added in the State of Massachusetts, $2.08 in Rhode Island, and $2.20 in Pennsylvania. Each dollar of payroll expended in typical southern states produced the following: $2.24 of value in North Carolina, $2.24 in Mississippi, and $2.34 in South Carolina.

The above comparison is not meant to be conclusive, but is merely one index to refute the oft-heard allegation that labor inefficiency and low wage rates are synonymous.

LIVING COSTS

A most important influence on wage rates is the *expenditure standard* of a community. One of the keys to worker satisfaction is the relationship between his pay and the money he spends to feed, clothe and house his family.

There is rarely a material difference in the cost of identical quality food products. During 1951 five pounds of sugar cost 54.4¢ in Louisville, 54.0¢ in Minneapolis, 54.3¢ in Wichita, 52.9¢ in Detroit.

There is a tremendous differential, however, in *buying habits* (are residents accustomed to buying low, medium or high-quality merchandise). There are huge differences in the *tempo* of spending.

Illustrating this point is an incident related by a department store executive

---

* The claim is still being made that only "city" people are production minded. Who are "city" people? T. Lynn Smith in his *Population Analysis* (McGraw-Hill, 1948) says, "The twentieth-century city is still a kind of colony which must be repopulated each year by the rural parts of the nation. The bulk of the people who live in cities are either migrants from the country or children of migrants. Few families, very few indeed, have been urban residents for as many as three generations."

in a medium-sized city in Pennsylvania. He said, "Our company has department store interests here as well as in Wilmington, Del. and Trenton, N. J. Recently we ran an advertisement promoting the _____ ladies' slip, which is made in three price ranges, $2.00, $2.50 and $3.00. At Wilmington the $3.00 slip was by far the best seller. At Trenton, the two top-priced goods shared the bulk of sales. Here, in Pennsylvania, 90% of our slips sold were at the $2.00 level."

In criticizing the move by Lever Bros. administrative offices from Cambridge, Mass. to New York City, the writer commented as follows (*Saturday Evening Post*, February 11, 1950):

> While the cost of living, measured by the market-basket yardstick, is but little higher here (New York), and sometimes is even lower than in Chicago and Detroit, Mr. Yaseen holds that this measure is deceptive. "A can of tomatoes may cost no more in a New York supermarket than in Cedar Rapids," he agrees. "Topeka doesn't undersell New York on a pair of nylons. But while a woman who is willing to shop can buy her staples here for little or no more, this ignores subtle factors known to all who have lived in New York. Its tempo of expenditure is vastly higher. There is an immense choice in how you spend here, an unceasing incitement to spend. It takes more character to be thrifty. In smaller places there is a saner regard for the potential worth of a dollar. Pleasures and luxuries are simpler, less expensive, probably less frequent. In New York the wage earner demands more money principally because the family spends more.
>
> "New Yorkers relax in their apartments only as a last choice; they go out for relaxation and pay high for it. Contentment is an individual thing. There are discontented people everywhere, but where so high a proportion as here? The same dynamic qualities that attract the creator and the doer also attract the restless and the unstable, and aggravate their unrest. This overcharged city excites and disturbs. This is an intangible, hard to prove statistically, though we are prepared to prove that New Yorkers go to bed later, sleep fewer hours and less soundly. We don't have to prove that regularity and ample hours of sleep are an efficiency factor."

Buying habits can be illustrated by a comparison of food purchases. In 1950, the average family in New York State spent $930 in food stores whereas the average family in the State of Tennessee spent $525.

CITY WORKER'S FAMILY BUDGET

ESTIMATED ANNUAL COSTS AND RELATIVE INTERCITY DIFFERENCES IN CITY WORKER'S FAMILY BUDGET FOR FOUR PERSONS, 34 LARGE CITIES. LATEST CENSUS FIGURES.

CITY	TOTAL BUDGET	HOUSING[1]	FOOD[2]	OTHER GOODS	OTHER COSTS[3]	PERSONAL TAXES[4]
Atlanta, Ga.	$4,315	$934	$1,381	$1,529	$161	$310
Baltimore, Md.	4,217	875	1,354	1,532	161	295
Birmingham, Ala.	4,252	805	1,371	1,590	191	295
Boston, Mass.	4,217	801	1,356	1,596	161	303
Buffalo, N. Y.	4,127	775	1,324	1,575	177	276
Chicago, Ill.	4,185	825	1,353	1,567	161	279
Cincinnati, Ohio	4,208	901	1,316	1,547	161	283
Cleveland, Ohio	4,103	715	1,330	1,633	161	264
Denver, Colo.	4,199	857	1,331	1,560	161	290
Detroit, Mich.	4,195	758	1,360	1,635	161	281
Houston, Texas	4,304	964	1,362	1,513	161	304
Indianapolis, Ind.	4,044	689	1,326	1,575	161	293
Jacksonville, Fla.	4,202	866	1,359	1,534	161	282
Kansas City, Mo.	3,960	683	1,305	1,570	161	241
Los Angeles, Calif.	4,311	854	1,335	1,629	191	302
Manchester, N. H.	4,090	765	1,327	1,562	161	275
Memphis, Tenn.	4,190	865	1,348	1,535	161	281
Milwaukee, Wisc.	4,387	964	1,296	1,618	161	348
Minneapolis, Minn.	4,161	797	1,298	1,592	161	313
Mobile, Ala.	3,969	611	1,401	1,524	191	242
New Orleans, La.	3,812	581	1,363	1,497	161	210
New York, N. Y.	4,083	724	1,367	1,549	177	267
Norfolk, Va.	4,146	815	1,335	1,536	161	299
Philadelphia, Pa.	4,078	784	1,370	1,453	161	310
Pittsburgh, Pa.	4,203	758	1,363	1,629	161	292
Portland, Maine	4,021	716	1,321	1,571	161	252
Portland, Oregon	4,153	764	1,311	1,606	161	311
Richmond, Va.	4,338	997	1,328	1,515	161	337
St. Louis, Mo.	4,112	751	1,350	1,580	161	270
San Francisco, Calif.	4,263	798	1,353	1,628	191	293
Savannah, Ga.	4,067	746	1,409	1,489	161	262
Scranton, Pa.	4,002	707	1,314	1,535	161	285
Seattle, Wash.	4,280	804	1,373	1,646	161	296
Washington, D. C.	4,454	1,034	1,352	1,579	161	328

[1] Estimated average rent, including cost of heat and utilities, of 5-room dwelling units meeting standards specified for budget.

[2] Includes allowance for 189 meals away from home, and alcoholic beverages, snacks, etc.

[3] Includes allowances for life insurance, $85; occupational expenses, $22; Federal old-age and survivors' insurance, $54; and, as required by State law in Alabama, California, and New York, employee contributions to unemployment or disability insurance.

[4] Includes Federal and State or local income taxes at 1951 calendar year rates and per capita taxes as required by State or local law.

Supporting the intangible variation of expenditure standards and "buying tempo" are the measurable differences in heating costs, for winter apparel in colder climes, rentals, community utility and service costs, taxes on the local level, etc.

Let us compare the relationship of earnings and living costs more specifically. Rochester, N. Y., industrial employees in June, 1955, received $2.00 hourly. Employees in Nashville, Tenn., received $1.50 hourly. The chart following reveals some of the basic living-cost differentials, allowing the Nashville worker to live as comfortably with lower earnings as the Rochester employee does with higher wages.

	ROCHESTER, N. Y.	NASHVILLE, TENN.
Median monthly rent (1950 census)	$41.00	$27.00
500 KW residential electric bill	$11.10	$6.90
Number of degree days (Determines heating costs. See Chapter 8)	6755	3620

Many Chambers of Commerce and civic agencies advertise high retail expenditures per capita in their area as an index of desirability. These figures will, in all probability, be quite accurate. It is their interpretation that becomes important since high levels of expenditure standards often mean a correspondingly high level of earnings.

LABOR STABILITY

Thorough precautions to assure low production costs are of no avail unless the proposed new plant can operate with continuity and with tranquil labor-management relations. More than one company has been forced out of business because of unreasonable or prohibitive labor demands fostered, in extreme cases, by community-wide antagonisms.

As unions become increasingly stronger, relatively fewer worker stoppages are due to the fundamental question of union organization. Wage increase demands and jurisdictional disputes continue to be important points of conflict, but in recent years, the majority of stoppages are caused by fringe benefit demands such as pension and insurance plans.

The most serious wave of strikes in the United States up to this date occurred in 1946. Four million six hundred thousand workers were involved and

WORK STOPPAGES BY STATE, 1954

STATE	STOPPAGES BEGINNING IN 1954			MAN-DAYS IDLE DURING 1954 (ALL STOPPAGES)	
	NUMBER	WORKERS INVOLVED			
		NUMBER	PERCENT OF TOTAL	NUMBER	PERCENT OF TOTAL
United States	[1] 3,468	1,530,000	100.0	22,600,000	100.0
Alabama	84	23,400	1.5	355,000	1.6
Arizona	12	7,020	.5	107,000	.5
Arkansas	29	6,450	.4	163,000	.7
California	206	88,100	5.7	1,070,000	4.7
Colorado	30	7,440	.5	98,300	.4
Connecticut	62	19,800	1.3	448,000	2.0
Delaware	15	1,350	.1	16,100	.1
District of Columbia	15	2,440	.2	30,500	.1
Florida	62	8,020	.5	65,200	.3
Georgia	36	13,100	.9	367,000	1.6
Idaho	11	1,190	.1	9,240	([2])
Illinois	206	56,300	3.7	737,000	3.3
Indiana	107	51,600	3.4	536,000	2.4
Iowa	47	19,700	1.3	235,000	1.0
Kansas	26	5,670	.4	205,000	.9
Kentucky	103	31,600	2.1	160,000	.7
Louisiana	40	16,900	1.1	394,000	1.7
Maine	22	2,360	.2	40,800	.2
Maryland	42	14,600	1.0	135,000	.6
Massachusetts	113	23,400	1.5	300,000	1.3
Michigan	204	171,000	11.2	1,060,000	4.7
Minnesota	56	20,300	1.3	314,000	1.4
Mississippi	14	1,610	.1	11,200	([2])
Missouri	87	38,300	2.5	862,000	3.8
Montana	10	11,500	.7	430,000	1.9
Nebraska	15	5,270	.3	60,400	.3
Nevada	10	2,750	.2	20,100	.1
New Hampshire	16	2,900	.2	28,700	.1
New Jersey	198	95,900	6.3	791,000	3.5
New Mexico	15	3,510	.2	47,400	.2
New York	539	182,000	11.9	2,010,000	8.9
North Carolina	31	5,540	.4	82,900	.4
North Dakota	11	1,680	.1	4,540	([2])
Ohio	266	134,000	8.8	1,830,000	8.1
Oklahoma	34	9,560	.6	220,000	1.0
Oregon	38	39,000	2.5	1,810,000	8.0
Pennsylvania	387	174,000	11.3	3,030,000	13.4
Rhode Island	28	4,880	.3	60,900	.3
South Carolina	14	2,350	.2	15,900	.1
South Dakota	4	400	([2])	670	([2])
Tennessee	90	50,900	3.3	415,000	1.8
Texas	103	42,600	2.8	655,000	2.9
Utah	14	12,000	.8	143,000	.6
Vermont	10	2,410	.2	65,200	.3
Virginia	43	7,840	.5	97,500	.4
Washington	70	63,600	4.2	2,120,000	9.4
West Virginia	107	29,300	1.9	266,000	1.2
Wisconsin	59	16,600	1.1	641,000	2.8
Wyoming	7	240	([2])	380	([2])

[1] The sum of the figures in this column exceeds 3,468 because stoppages extending across State lines have been counted in each State affected, but workers involved and man-days idle were divided among them.

[2] Less than 0.05 percent.

928,000,000 man-hours were irretrievably lost in that one year alone. Even in these days of astronomical figures, it is difficult to comprehend the staggering losses sustained by industry and labor alike.

In that year of violent disputes, coming as an aftermath of World War II, many communities and whole regions were nevertheless untroubled by work stoppages. There can be no guarantee, of course, that in such areas management-employee relations will continue enlightened. Economic realities are often and suddenly thrown overboard by volatile human emotions, deep prejudices, and lack of patience.

Nevertheless, the question of labor stability must be approached from a positive standpoint. There *are* certain strong indices of community attitude that should influence its selection. Perhaps the most crucial question that can be asked about a community is "What is its *past* history?"

While the past record of a city offers no *guarantee* of what is going to happen in the future, there is reasonable certainty that given continued sound management, a community which has had industrial peace should prosper better than its neighbor with a lengthy history of labor strife.

Intensive research, therefore, is recommended in this phase of the plant location survey. It may be difficult to develop this data, but the extra time spent will more than be repaid.

We have discussed the necessity for interviewing present manufacturers in an area. If approached carefully, this procedure should prove a prolific source of confidential information.

Consult the publications of the Bureau of Labor Statistics which annually list strikes in a number of selected cities. Plan to allot at least several days to examining selected issues of the leading local newspaper for information bearing on labor disputes. Many newspapers, in fact, have a strike "morgue" which will simplify the search.

An investigation of the most aggressive labor organization and conferences with local union heads will often provide an inkling of their long-term attitudes. An examination of the terms of prevailing union contracts in the area will indicate the nature of union thinking on many controversial considerations. The presence or absence of unemployed councils and radical groups will also influence the final decision.

When the community itself has no comparable type or size industry, it is wise to examine neighboring areas within reasonable proximity as to their record of employee-management relations. Remember too, that if the wage rate intended in the proposed new plant is substantially *lower* than prevailing levels, labor difficulties will eventually occur.

FACTORS AFFECTING FUTURE
LABOR STABILITY

The articulate expression of concerted mob or crowd action takes the form of strikes, sit-downs or slow-downs. The number of disturbances and their duration are, of course, obvious and measurable barometers of management-employee relations in the community.

There are other indicators of community harmony, however, almost as significant in determining future tranquility as work stoppages. These may be classified under the heading of individual, *inarticulate* unrest which manifests itself in excessive absenteeism, tardiness, labor turnover, and disrespect for work rules and regulations. Any evidences of this nature are danger signs that no manufacturer can ignore, even though the community background of actual work stoppages seems to be relatively clear.

In the plant with a healthy labor-management "climate" it is entirely normal and expected that employees will occasionally be absent or late for work —an absentee rate of 3% is typical. When employers in the community report, however, that such rates are double or triple the average for work comparable to that of the proposed new plant, a potentially volatile labor situation may exist.

Labor turnover is perhaps the most important element of inarticulate unrest, particularly in industries where training time and costs for developing worker skill are sizeable. Turnover may be attributed to a number of basic economic factors including dissatisfaction with working conditions, ease of changing jobs in a "tight" labor market, as well as seasonal and cyclical fluctuations.

Full knowledge of all influences affecting specific industries is necessary before sound conclusions can be drawn. A monthly net turnover rate in the average manufacturing concern of over 5% can definitely be construed as a cause for alarm, but in such industries as logging or shipbuilding, separation rates of 11% to 12% are not uncommon.

CHAPTER **6**

Power—Fuel—Water

Historically, the location of power resources has been an outstanding factor in the choice of manufacturing sites. Prior to the invention of the steam engine, water power was the chief source of mechanical energy, and power sites along streams were the most favored manufacturing locations.

The relative importance of various sources of energy has undergone marked change, especially since the turn of the century. The discovery and production of oil and gas and the construction of the dams to generate water power have affected availability of energy from these sources. Technical developments, changes in the method and cost of transportation and transmission have altered delivered prices.

Traditional sources of electrical energy will not be readily replaced by atomic energy. But the ease of providing power in compact form without costly distribution lines can revolutionize plant location economics in many areas.

PRINCIPAL SOURCES OF ENERGY SUPPLY
Mineral Fuels and Water Power—United States, 1900-1954

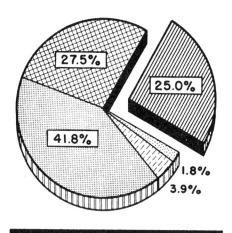

1954
TOTAL - 37,415 Trillion B.t.u

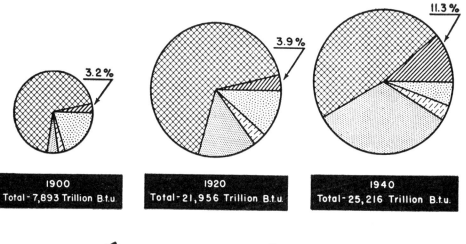

| 1900 | 1920 | 1940 |
| Total - 7,893 Trillion B.t.u. | Total - 21,956 Trillion B.t.u. | Total - 25,216 Trillion B.t.u. |

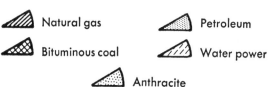

Natural gas   Petroleum

Bituminous coal   Water power

Anthracite

In New England, the birthplace of American manufacturing, original orientation to water power is still evident, for much of the older industry in the region is dispersed in small towns and cities bordering on streams. This dispersion contrasts sharply with the industrial concentration found in those cities which developed after the advent of steam power.

To the early industrialist, the most attractive sites were located on the fall line of navigable streams, that point where the river left the Piedmont uplands and entered the coastal plain. Here water power would be available to turn the wheels, and the smaller ocean-going vessels of the day could navigate to wharves just below the plant. This combination of factors attributed to the growth of such fall line cities as Trenton, Philadelphia, Wilmington, Baltimore, Washington and Richmond. Southern fall line cities similarly were attractive to industry, including Raleigh, Columbia, Augusta, Macon and Columbus.

The development of hydroelectric power plants and the means for transmitting electric power over considerable distances made general manufacturing less dependent on proximity to power resources. Important exceptions are the electro-metallurgical and electro-chemical groups. In these industries, power is the dominant locational factor. Typical products are aluminum, magnesium, liquified gas, lime, calcium carbide and artificial abrasives such as fused alumina and silicon carbide.

Niagara Falls was the first major hydroelectric installation in the United States. Clustered nearby today are manufacturing operations requiring large blocks of power, primarily for electro-chemical processes. The enormous hydroelectric potentialities of the states of Washington and Oregon have attracted industries in the electro-metallurgical group—particularly non-ferrous reduction plants. At Calvert City, Kentucky, new units of both the electro-chemical and electro-metallurgical industries are being established in the shadow of the gigantic Kentucky Dam.

The cost of power as a percentage of total delivered-to-customer costs in most industries is not significant. Hence, the average industrialist will not relocate his plant or establish a branch unit solely because of a power differential. Nevertheless, power costs do constitute a sizable, constantly recurring expense for many industries and should be carefully compared along with adequacy, reliability and type of service available in the area under consideration.

Most companies considering plant location are prepared to purchase rather than manufacture their own power. The size of the average utility, the diversified load, and particularly the increased efficiency of generating plants, have maintained the cost of purchased power at comparatively low levels. If the plant is in operation 24 hours a day or a sizable amount of exhaust steam can be used for processing or heating, it may be advisable to generate rather than pur-

PRIMARY ENERGY SOURCES OF ELECTRIC UTILITY PRODUCTION
by Geographic Divisions—1953

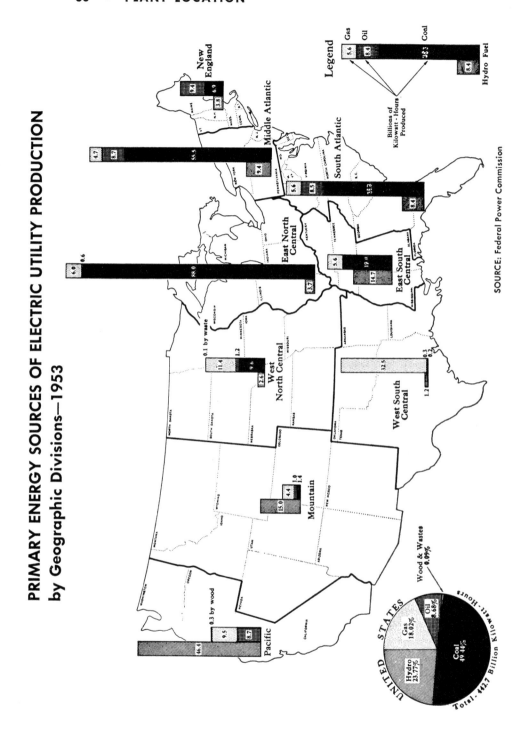

SOURCE: Federal Power Commission

chase power. Even so, careful consideration must be given to the capital outlay, cost of failures and repair, and cost of standby service, all of which must be assessed against the total kilowatt-hour annual bill.

Some of the factors to be considered when examining the power situation in a given area may be found in the following suggested check list:*

    a. Type of service
        1. Hydro-electric
        2. Steam
        3. Other
    b. Reliability of service; history of stoppages
    c. Adequacy of supply: seasonal restrictions
    d. Kind
        1. Phase
        2. Cycle
        3. Voltage
    e. Rates
    f. Availability of off-peak contracts
    g. Fuel adjustment
    h. Lighting allowances
    i. Discounts and penalties

The type of generation will have an effect on power bills. Hydroelectric power is usually associated with cheap rates, although the original installation cost of the generating plant is considerably more than for steam plants with similar capacity.

At most hydroelectric sites, stream flow fluctuates widely. Unless steam-developed power is available to carry part of the load during deficient flow periods, industry may be subject to interruptions in service. Interconnection of transmission lines with systems utilizing steam generation can insure continuous supply. These tie-in arrangements should be carefully investigated in hydro-electric districts. The remoteness of the hydroelectric installation from consuming areas and difficult terrain conditions may increase the frequency of service interruptions due to transmission line failures.

The publicly-owned Tennessee Valley Authority has been remarkably successful in providing reliable hydroelectric service at low rates. The project was originally considered "primarily for the benefit of the people in the area as a whole, particularly domestic and rural sources." Sale of power to industries spe-

---

* Standards of Industrial Analysis. Copyright 1950. Fantus Factory Locating Service.

EXISTING AND UNDEVELOPED HYDROELECTRIC POWER
Federal Power Commission—January 1, 1951

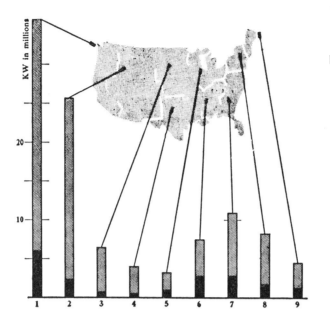

BY GEOGRAPHIC DIVISIONS

1 Pacific
2 Mountain
3 West North Central
4 West South Central
5 East North Central
6 East South Central
7 South Atlantic
8 Middle Atlantic
9 New England

Undeveloped power
Existing power

BY MAJOR DRAINAGE BASINS

1 North Pacific
2 South Pacific
3 Great Basin
4 Colorado River
5 Missouri River
6 Lower Mississippi River
7 Western Gulf
8 Hudson Bay
9 Upper Mississippi River
10 Eastern Gulf
11 Ohio River
12 Great Lakes-St. Lawrence
13 South Atlantic
14 North Atlantic

Undeveloped power
Existing power

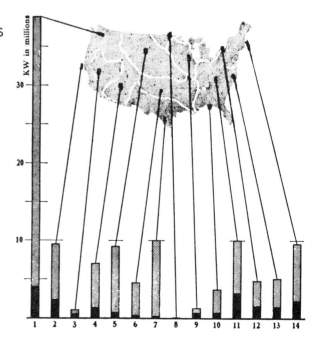

cifically was made a secondary issue. Offering lower rates than most other regions, it was inevitable that the T. V. A. would attract industries with large power demands. Expanded use of power in the region has required the Government to build huge steam plants to double its generating capacity.

Steam generating plants account for approximately 71% of the total primary energy sources in the country. While rates are usually higher than those prevailing in areas served by hydroelectric plants, major strides have been made toward increased efficiency. In 1902, about 5.5 pounds of coal were required to produce one kilowatt-hour of output. Large modern plants now operate on less than one pound of coal per kilowatt-hour. The load factor of the steam plants is raised in some regions by auxiliary hydroelectric generators which furnish the base load in periods of maximum stream flow and peak power the balance of the time.

In New England, oil is the major fuel, accounting for about two thirds of total thermal energy. Coal is the major fuel for steam generating plants in the South Atlantic and Middle Atlantic regions. Gas-fired boilers are used principally in the West-Southcentral region. In the East-Southcentral and the Pacific Mountain regions, the major portion of the kilowatt-hour output is derived from waterpower.

It is important to ascertain the *reserve* power of a community before definite steps are taken to establish a manufacturing plant. Despite an installed capacity of electric utility generating plants in 1952 of 74-million kilowatts and an estimated production of 400-billion kilowatt-hours, some areas of the United States had insufficient power to cope with mushrooming industrial expansion. Even certain portions of the huge T. V. A. could not immediately provide additional power to potential new customers. As a stop-gap measure, T. V. A. purchased power from private-owned utility companies on its periphery.

Because of seasonal operations in some agricultural areas, power availability may be strained during harvest months when packing and canning plants are in full operation. Similar seasonal peaks exist in coastal areas during fish canning periods and at resort communities. In some portions of the South, power is in short supply in mid-winter months when household electrical heating units are in operation.

The phase, cycle and voltage of the supply must be carefully checked. Motor wiring in plants in long established areas of the country may not conform to the power furnished in decentralized areas. Accordingly, the manufacturer faces either an expensive conversion process or a sizable transformer loss. In rural areas, the distribution lines are normally of insufficient capacity to serve large manufacturing plants. While power companies are willing to make reasonable improvements to accommodate industrial plants, responsible utility execu-

250 KWH MONTHLY RESIDENTIAL BILLS—1955
Cities of 50,000 population and more

Federal Power Commission

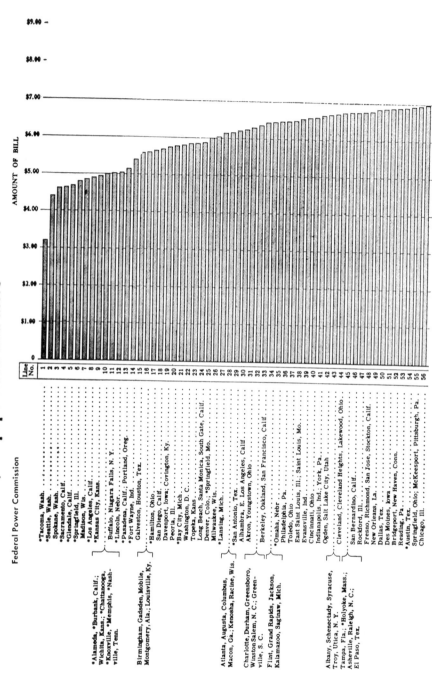

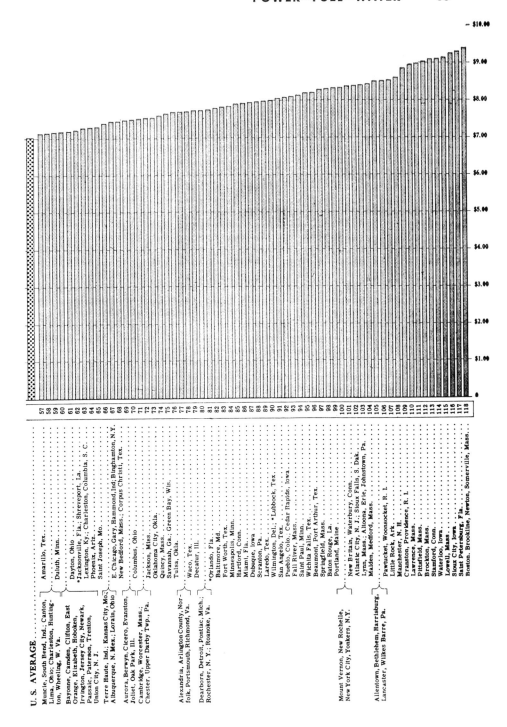

tives must be consulted to determine the extent of cooperation which will be extended.

Geographically there is a wide variation in industrial utility rates. Following is a chart prepared from data by the Federal Power Commission depicting typical net electric bills in January 1955 for industries in selected cities using 60,000 kilowatt-hours and 200,000 kilowatt-hours monthly. The cost of power with gas-fired generating systems, such as Houston, Texas, compares favorably with T. V. A. rates:

CITIES OF 50,000 POPULATION AND MORE	INDUSTRIAL BILLING DEMAND (KILOWATTS) AND MONTHLY CONSUMPTION (KILOWATT-HOURS)	
	300 KILOWATTS 60,000 KWH	1000 KILOWATTS 200,000 KWH
Cedar Rapids, Iowa	$1,394	$4,116
Hartford, Conn.	1,317	4,069
New Rochelle, N. Y.	1,440	4,025
Toledo, Ohio	1,290	3,894
Nashua, N. H.	1,154	3,680
Worcester, Mass.	1,093	3,580
Philadelphia, Pa.	1,140	3,571
Woonsocket, R. I.	1,244	3,523
Erie, Pa.	1,255	3,402
Bayonne, N. J.	1,126	3,329
Jacksonville, Fla.	1,059	3,270
Lexington, Ky.	1,074	3,226
Peoria, Ill.	1,328	3,225
Jackson, Miss.	1,110	3,187
Columbia, S. C.	1,048	2,824
New Orleans, La.	955	2,679
Syracuse, N. Y.	906	2,573
Birmingham, Ala.	820	2,550
Houston, Texas	891	2,502
Charlotte, N. C.	820	2,480
Memphis, Tenn.	748	2,082
Seattle, Wash.	572	1,798
Los Angeles, Calif.	529	1,649

Most steam-generating plants have rate schedules which contain fuel adjustment clauses. They provide for fluctuations in cost as well as B. t. u.* content. A typical adjustment clause for a coal-fired plant is the following:

---

* British thermal unit—the amount of heat required to raise the temperature of one pound of water 1 degree Fahrenheit.

> When the cost of coal to the Company, as determined under the standard classification of accounts approved by the Commission, exceeds $4.00 or is less than $3.50 per ton of 2,000 pounds, then for each whole 10¢ variation in the cost of coal above $4.00 or below $3.50 per ton, the cost of energy delivered hereunder shall be increased or decreased at the rate of sixty-three ten-thousandths (.0063) cents per kwhr. When the B. t. u. content per pound of coal is in excess of 14,500 or below 13,500 B. t. u. per pound, the cost of coal will be adjusted to a basis of 14,000 B. t. u. per pound.

A typical example of a fuel adjustment clause for oil burning steam plants is as follows:

> After the Authority's steam generating plant goes into production, the purchaser's monthly bill computed under the above rate schedule shall be increased by $.00010 (.10 mills) per kilowatt hour for each whole five (5) cents increase over $2.15 per barrel cost to the Authority (including freight and handling) of bunker "C" (150,000 B. T. U. per gallon) fuel oil burned at the Authority's steam electric generating plant at Pinopolis during the calendar month for which the purchaser's electric power and energy consumption is billed.

Similar adjustment clauses are published for those plants utilizing gas as their source of energy. The B. t. u. content for each of the fuels will vary from company to company.

For maximum flexibility, it is preferable to have a choice of several alternate industrial rate schedules to meet varying demands. Power companies attempt to apply the tariff which will provide the lowest possible cost to the customer. In this connection, the phrasing of demand measurement clauses is particularly important. Each power schedule contains such a clause, some being more beneficial than others to manufacturing operations which have widely fluctuating demands. Sample clauses are shown below.

> (a) The billing demand in kw shall be taken each month as the highest single 30-minute integrated peak in kw as registered during the month by a demand meter or indicator, or, at the company's option, as the highest registration of a thermal type demand meter or indicator, but the monthly billing demand so established shall in no event be less than 60% of

the contract capacity of the customer, nor less than 1,000 kw.

The reactive demand in kvars shall be taken each month as the highest single 30-minute integrated peak in kvars as registered during the month by a demand meter or indicator, or, at the company's option, as the highest registration of a thermal type demand meter or indicator.

(b) The Billing Demand shall be the maximum kw registered during the current month by a demand meter suitable for measuring the demands used during a 15-minute interval, but shall not be less than 60% of the Contract Demand and in no event less than 50 kw.

(c) Class 1: For Consumers contracting to take their entire power requirements from the Power Company, the demand for billing purposes each month shall be the maximum integrated thirty-minute demand in the previous three months, including the month for which the bill is rendered, but not less than 50 per cent of the contract demand, nor less than 30 kilowatts.

Class 2: For Consumers who do not contract to take their entire power requirements from the Power Company, the demand for billing purposes each month shall be the maximum integrated thirty-minute demand during said month, but not less than 75 per cent of the highest integrated thirty-minute demand in the previous twelve months, including the month for which the bill is rendered, nor less than 75 per cent of the contract demand, nor less than 30 kilowatts.

Residential power rates obviously affect the cost of living and, thus, indirectly industrial wage rates. Wide variations exist. Monthly payment for 100 kilowatt hours runs from a low of $1.70 in Tacoma, Washington, to a high of $7.50 in Beloit, Kansas. The 250 kilowatt user pays a high of $9.51 in Somerville, Massachusetts, against Tacoma's low rate of $3.20. The following chart, compiled from statistics of the Federal Power Commission, shows variations in average rates by states.

STATE AVERAGE BILLS 250 KWH RESIDENTIAL SERVICE

1954 UNITED STATES AVERAGE BILL—$7.10

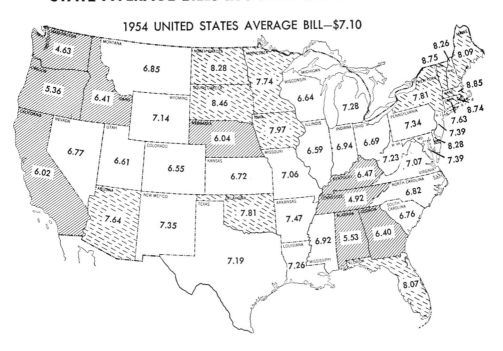

1941 UNITED STATES AVERAGE BILL—$7.21

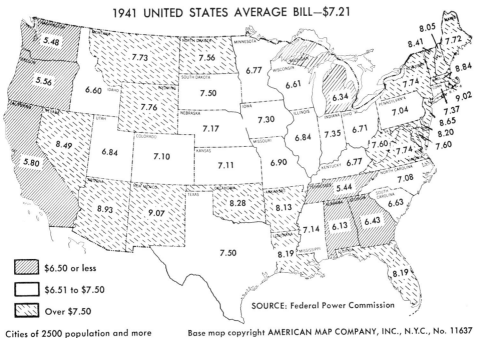

$6.50 or less

$6.51 to $7.50

Over $7.50

Cities of 2500 population and more

SOURCE: Federal Power Commission

Base map copyright AMERICAN MAP COMPANY, INC., N.Y.C., No. 11637

FUEL

The widest common denominator as applied to all American industry is the utilization of fuel resources, primarily coal, petroleum and gas. This chapter treats them chiefly as sources of thermal energy, readily substituted one for another and highly competitive.

Fuel as a locational factor varies in importance from industry to industry. In those processes utilizing fuel as a basic raw material, the plant may be entirely oriented to low cost supply of the commodity. Substitution of other fuels may be difficult or impossible. Typical examples are the manufacture of coke and coking by-products from bituminous coal and carbon black from natural gas.

Considered along with assembly cost of raw materials and freight rates to markets, fuel has influenced the location of an important segment of heavy industry. For example, the production of one ton of pig iron requires the assembly of 1.73 tons of iron ore, 0.41 tons of limestone and 0.93 tons of coke. Derived

No-Mend Hosiery Company, Gainesville, Florida. Plant Location Study— FANTUS FACTORY LOCATING SERVICE.

from certain grades of bituminous coal, coke is used in the smelting process as both a reducing agent and as a fuel. Orientation to coke sources has accounted for the development of iron and steel making in Pittsburgh and the Mahoning Valley. However, even in this basic industry, changes in pricing policy and shifting markets are reducing the influence of fuel supply on the location of blast furnaces.

Another example of the secondary effect of fuel costs on location are glass plants which are usually oriented both to markets and nearby gas fields. Temperatures as high as 2867° F. are required in the process. In the manufacture of glass containers, fuel represents as much as 33% of the total production cost. However, modern glass plants are being established closer to markets, indicating a subordination of the locational attraction of cheap natural gas supplies.

Most industries find the locational significance of fuels to be negligible. Within given economic regions slight differentials in fuel costs are usually far outweighted by other variable factors.

The delivered cost of coal, despite F. O. B. mine pricing, is virtually equal over a large area due to depressed freight rate levels and broad groupings of destinations for rate-making purposes. Natural gas transmission costs via pipeline vary only slightly mile for mile within geographic regions. Fuel oil prices are normally equalized F. O. B. refinery in marketing zones so that the differential lies only in transportation costs from the nearest refinery or pumping station to competitive sites.

The expansion of American industry since 1900 has been accompanied by a sharp rise in consumption of energy. However, all fuels did not experience equal increase in demand and a striking shift in relative importance occurred.

In 1899, according to the Bureau of Mines, 89% of all energy output was in the form of coal. By 1954 coal (anthracite included) dropped to 29.3%. Natural gas amounted to less than 4% in 1899 but with phenomenal gains in the past few years now accounts for one-fourth of the nation's energy output. Petroleum represents 41.8% of the 1954 total.

Several factors contributed to this change in relative importance of fuels:

1. Higher operating costs at coal mines and freight rate increases have reduced the competitive advantage of coal.
2. Public and private extension of the pipeline network provided cheap transportation of petroleum and natural gas into major fuel-consuming areas.
3. Increased efficiency of fuel conversion, particularly coal, reduced the required tonnage per unit of output.

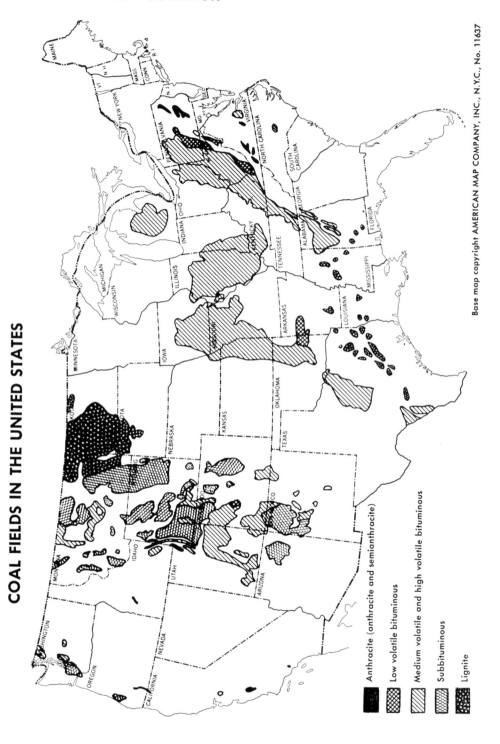

COAL FIELDS IN THE UNITED STATES

Anthracite (anthracite and semianthracite)

Low volatile bituminous

Medium volatile and high volatile bituminous

Subbituminous

Lignite

Base map copyright AMERICAN MAP COMPANY, INC., N.Y.C., No. 11637

The increased demand for fuels in the next twenty-five years is expected to create some acute supply problems as domestic energy sources become depleted. In a recent report of the President's Materials Policy Commission (PMPC), the following increased requirements are predicted for 1975 based on normal growth:

	1950	1975	INCREASE
Coal (in millions of short tons)	522	815	56%
Petroleum (in millions of barrels)	2,375	5,000	110%
Natural Gas (in billions of cubic feet)	6,300	15,000	150%

The investigator should be familiar with both the quantity and quality of present and future availability of fuel supplies at given locations.

Coal

The importance of coal in our economy must not be underestimated. The dollar value of coal mined in an average year exceeds that of all metals combined. Coal generates most of our power and its carbonization produces ammonia, tars and light oils, which in turn are utilized as the base of such varying commodities as medicines, explosives, insecticides, plastics, perfumes, dyes and hundreds of other products.

West Virginia, Pennsylvania, Kentucky and Illinois, respectively the principal producers of bituminous coal, accounted for 292 million of the country's 1954 production of 392 million tons. Total value was $1,889,000,000.

The total U. S. tonnage compares with a wartime peak of 630.6 million net tons, and a 1929 level of 535 million net tons. Excepting four years between 1931 and 1938, production in 1954 was the lowest since 1909.

Pennsylvania contributes the bulk of anthracite mined in the United States. Total output in 1954 was 26 million net tons, valued at around $285,000,000. This represents a marked decline from peak production in 1920 of over 80 million tons. The chief market for anthracite is now domestic heating as industrial consumption has declined.

Vast differences exist in the quality of coal mined in various areas. Coals found in the central part of the country, for example, are usually of inferior quality to coal found in the Appalachian highlands—having less fixed carbon and more volatile matter and moisture. Coal in southern Illinois has a much higher carbon content than coal mined just a few hundred miles north.

Here is an analysis of heat values found in bituminous coal mined in several areas. Note the wide variations that exist between states and even within the same state. Of the samples shown, calorific value ranges from a low of 10,450 to a high of 14,870 B. t. u.

STATE AND COUNTY	BED	MOIS-TURE	VOLA-TILE MATTER	FIXED CARBON	ASH	SUL-PHUR	CALORIFIC VALUE OF SAMPLE, AS REC'L B.T.U. PER POUND
ALABAMA							
Bibb	Yeshic	4.4	31.7	47.7	16.2	1.3	11,620
Jefferson:							
Warrior Field	Black Creek	2.9	31.8	61.5	3.8	.7	14,410
ILLINOIS							
Fulton	Springfield (#5)	15.2	34.3	38.5	12.0	3.1	10,450
Gallatin	Harrisburg (#5)	4.5	36.6	50.7	8.2	2.8	13,030
KENTUCKY							
Daviess	#9 (western Ky.)	11.2	34.5	41.5	12.8	4.1	10,830
Harlan	Harlan	2.5	37.1	55.8	4.6	.8	14,000
VIRGINIA							
Buchanan	Jewell	2.6	20.8	73.2	3.4	.5	14,870

Prices of bituminous coal

Prices of bituminous coal for industrial use vary by source and type of coal. Run-of-mine coal prices are currently (October, 1955) quoted from $3.60 to $7.25. Prices of run-of-mine coal from important regions include:

Southern West Virginia	smokeless	$7.25;
Northern West Virginia		3.85 - $4.50;
Western Kentucky	Seam #6	4.80;
Indiana		4.00 - $4.85;
Central Pennsylvania		5.25 - $6.40;
Southern Illinois		5.85;
Western Kentucky	Seam #9	3.60.

Screenings may be bought at around 50¢ per ton below the run-of-mine price.

The manufacturer is, of course, interested in the cost of coal *delivered* at his plant. Consequently, freight rates as well as prices at the mine must enter into his calculations. In many instances freight rate per ton will equal or even exceed the F. O. B. price.

In the future coal may again regain its importance as the nation's major source of energy. Unlike the shrinking sources of other fuels, proven reserves of coal exceed 250 billion short tons. The declining trend in the percentage of total energy requirements supplied by coal will probably continue until other domestic fuel sources run out. However, output will be increased 60% to meet increasing demands for coking coal for smelting of iron ore and increased use of coal in electric power generation.

Technological improvements in mining and processing methods may improve the competitive position of coal in the future and important research projects are under way in coal hydrogenation, coal gasification, pipeline distribution of pulverized coal, and coal-fired gas turbines.

There has been some indication that the natural gas industry may turn to coal to fill its pipelines when reserves of that commodity become depleted.

Natural gas

Within a short period of time it is expected that natural gas will be piped into every important metropolitan area of the United States. The discovery of huge natural gas reserves in the Gulf Coast and Southwest areas, the improvements made in seamless and welded steel pipe to withstand the high pressure necessary for its transport, and the need of industry for an ideal fuel easily convertible to steam or electric power, created a boom. Net production increased each year from 2.4 trillion cubic feet in 1935 to 9.6 trillion cubic feet in 1954. An average of 1.5 million new natural gas customers a year have been added for the past eight years.

In the year 1954 alone, 3,977 new gas wells were drilled in the United States. Construction of natural gas transmission and distribution facilities will exceed $1 billion for 1955. At the end of 1954 there were 419,670 miles of natural gas pipelines.

Unquestionably there is a potential market for all the natural gas that can be produced in the United States as long as the price is lower than other fuels. However, the cost of natural gas is increasing. The producing states, reluctant

NATURAL GAS FIELDS AND PIPE LINES

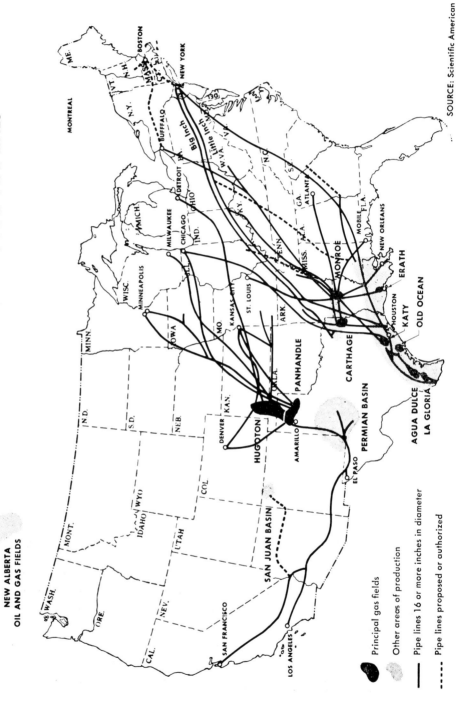

SOURCE: Scientific American

to see a prime natural reserve drained off from transmission to other areas, are applying higher and higher severance taxes. Costs of pipeline construction and maintenance are also increasing, as are the prices at producing points. Despite the economical transportation characteristics of pipelines, natural gas may cost eight to ten times as much in New York or Chicago as it does in the Texas fields.

Proven reserves in 1954 were 211 trillion cubic feet. As currently as 1950 the ratio of new discoveries to net production was approximately 2 to 1. During 1954 additions to reserves hardly exceeded production. If this trend continues, a slowdown in production can be anticipated.

It is interesting to consider the rate at which the reserves in the Gulf Coast area of Louisiana and Texas are dropping as these states represent the principal source for the large interstate pipelines. Life expectancy in Louisiana dropped from 36.8 years in 1946 to 31.15 years in 1950, a decline of 5.71 years in the four year period. In Texas, life expectancy was decreased from 41.13 years in 1946 to 30.29 years in 1950, a drop of 10.84 years in the four year period. For the entire country, extensions and discoveries virtually balanced to leave reserves at the end of 1954 unchanged from the previous year.

The industrialist contemplating use of natural gas should be guided by history. In the 1880's local communities in Indiana began to drill gas wells, offering the supply free of charge to prospective industries. This enticed the glass industry, woodworking plants, some smaller iron and steel manufacturers, and the brick and tile producers. The reserves were exhausted by 1900. Some plants became stranded and were forced to shift to other fuels and sustained large economic loss. Similar short-lived "booms" have occurred in Southwestern states. Accordingly, industry must be prepared for that inevitable time after 1975 when total national production of gas may be depleted.

Carter Underwear Company, Senatabia, Mississippi. Plant Location Study—FANTUS FACTORY LOCATING SERVICE.

When considering natural gas as a source of fuel for the proposed plant, the following suggestions may be of value:

1. The presence of a trunk line is no indication of *availability*.
2. Despite the fact that the community is presently served by natural gas, it may not have sufficiently large allocations to supply a new industry.
3. Users must be exceptionally large to allow economical tapping of a main line in the absence of local distribution facilities.
4. Only points near the gas fields can guarantee a "firm supply"—in other areas service is on an interruptible basis.
5. If a firm supply is offered, carefully check the rates quoted as interruptible rate schedules may be lower.
6. Where interruptible supplies are to be utilized, the cost of standby or storage facilities must be considered part of the fuel cost.
7. The source of the supply must be carefully checked. There is danger in depending on a single field unless tie-in arrangements are assured.
8. The *pumping capacity* of the site can be as important as the size of the line.
9. In comparing costs, the average B. t. u. content must be ascertained.

Petroleum

Petroleum has progressed from the "kerosene and axle grease" stage until today its indispensable use in the industrial field is extensive. During World War II, over 60% of all products shipped to our armed forces was in the form of oil or its derivatives.

Petroleum resources are in insufficient supply to meet anticipated demands in the next twenty-five years. The United States, once one of the world's largest exporters of oil, has shifted to one of the largest importers. Domestic production has increased greatly, but to keep pace with future demands new discoveries and developments must exceed 1.4 times annual production. Anticipated con-

New plant of Helena Rubenstein at East Hills, Long Island. DESIGN AND CONSTRUCTION: *Brown & Matthews, Inc.* Plant Location Study—FANTUS FACTORY LOCATING SERVICE.

sumption in the next twenty-five years will be more than double the present demand. Most of the increase is expected in motor fuel, and in kerosene and distillates. There may be insufficient domestic supply to meet the anticipated doubling of residual oil requirements for industry, transportation, power generation and heating.

The Federal Government, concerned with possible loss of Middle East supplies, is encouraging research in recovery of oil from domestic sources now considered uneconomical to operate. It is also promoting industrial shifts to other fuels.

Regional differences in oil prices are relatively small due to the efficient pipeline system (160,000 miles) and economical tanker transportation.

The competitive aspect

The decision on utilization of fuel supply is normally determined by arithmetic. The following example, taken directly from a survey of the Fantus Factory Locating Service, illustrates the necessary computations. Note that the source of coal with the lowest delivered cost to the site may not necessarily produce the lowest cost per thermal unit due to differences in characteristics.

With the exception of natural gas, freight costs must be included in the study and may involve several alternate types of transportation. To these calculations should be added the additional cost of handling and storage of coal and oil. The gas price, due to interruptible supply, must be inflated to cover the cost of standby facilities.

EXAMPLE OF FUEL COST COMPUTATION

	SOURCE A	SOURCE B
Coal		
Price per 2000 pounds f.o.b. mine	$ 3.50	$ 3.75
Freight per net ton	3.71	4.09
Delivered cost to site per ton	$ 7.21	$ 7.84
B.t.u.'s per pound	11,620	13,030
Delivered cost per 1,000,000 B.t.u.	$ .31024	$ .30084
Oil		
Price per barrel (42 gallons) f.o.b. delivery		$ 2.45
Tank truck rate per gallon to site		.009
Delivered cost to site per barrel		$ 2.828
B.t.u.'s per gallon		150,000
Delivered cost per 1,000,000 B.t.u.		$ .44889
Gas		
Price per MCF (1000 cu. ft.) delivered to site		$ .245
B.t.u.'s per cu. ft.		1,050
Cost per 1,000,000 B.t.u.		$ .23334

WATER

The domination of water over all forms of life is evident throughout history. Water is precious and the continuing serious waste of this resource could impoverish succeeding generations.

As the population of the nation expands, the demand for water increases. The average United States city requires about 113 gallons per day per capita. Four acres of land are required to support each person in our economy and, of necessity, over 22,000,000 acres of land in the nation must be irrigated.

New industrial techniques, including the harnessing of atomic power and the production of synthetic fuels, require more and more water. In many industries the problem of securing usable water at reasonable rates is a pressing one. In fact, water supply is prerequisite in site selection in steel, paper pulp, paper board, wool scouring, food and chemical processes. Typical water requirements for various industries are shown below:

Produce a ton of bromine	5,000,000 gallons
Produce a ton of synthetic rubber	600,000 "
Produce a ton of aluminum	320,000 "
Produce a ton of viscose rayon	200,000 "
Make a ton of steel	65,000 "
Test an airplane engine	50,000 "
Generate one KWH	6,000 "
Produce a ton of coke from coal	3,600 "
Refine a barrel of petroleum	770 "
Brew a barrel of beer	470 "

In the majority of manufacturing operations public water supplies will prove satisfactory directly from the tap or with minor treatment. The quality of the supply will depend upon the source from which it is derived. Shown below is a comparative study of public water supplies in one region of a southeastern state. The table illustrates the wide variations in characteristics to be found within a limited area.

COMPARATIVE TYPICAL ANALYSIS OF PUBLIC WATER SUPPLIES
PIEDMONT PROVINCE, SOUTHEASTERN STATE

	SOURCE		
	SURFACE	SPRINGS	WELLS
Total Solids (180°C)	58.8	83.0	484.4
Volatile residue	12.0	28.5	188.4
Mineral residue	46.8	54.5	296.0
Dissolved silica (SiO_2)	11.6	24.2	30.6
Iron and Aluminum oxides (Fe_2O_3 and Al_2O_3)	1.6	2.2	2.4
Calcium (Ca)	3.6	7.3	55.9
Magnesium (Mg)	4.3	1.4	16.8
Chlorides (Cl)	4.8	3.12	125.8
Nitrates (NO_3)	.06	.12	3.6
Sulfates (SO_4)	4.8	14.9	24.7
Bicarbonates (HCO_3)	35.0	45.0	107.4
Soap Hardness	11.1	78.6	145.8
Calculated Hardness	28.0	74.4	208.6
Iron (Fe) colorimetric	None	—	Trace
Free carbon dioxide (CO_2)	2.6	—	174.3
Normal carbonates (CO_3)	None	None	None
Sodium (Na), calculated	6.4	15.0	39.3
pH	6.8	6.8	6.4

Industrial rates normally range between 4 and 20¢ per 1000 gallons. Where rates are quoted in terms of cubic feet measurement, they must be converted to gallons for comparative study. One cubic foot equals 7.480512 gallons.

Whenever a water shortage develops, it is industry which first feels the effect. If there is not enough water to go around the order of priority is: domestic and sanitary use first, agriculture (if any) second, and industrial use *last*. Industries which utilize water in their manufacturing process will not wish to depend upon public supply systems. Hence, the investigator should be familiar with water sources as they occur in nature.

Basically water is available from three sources:

> Surface (water from lakes, streams, etc.)
> Ground (springs, wells, etc.)
> Rain water

Impounded supplies (lakes and reservoirs) are usually clear, soft and high in oxygen as impurities tend to settle out during storage. Of the various possible sources, supplies taken from impounded waters show the most consistency in composition. During summer months, however, microscopic organisms and vegetation may add taste and color harmful to certain manufacturing processes. Decomposing organic matter easily combines with the free oxygen to form carbon dioxide which is injurious to pipe lines and industrial equipment.

Rivers and streams vary greatly in their analyses, even during relatively short periods of time. The character of the drainage area will dictate relative hardness, turbidity and other characteristics. Surface waters are subject to contamination from animal wastes, sewage, seepage from coal mines. The existence of anti-pollution regulations and their enforcement are important.

The prudent investigator will determine maximum and minimum flow, seasonal variations, tidal influence, temperature, etc. Several analyses should be studied from samples taken at various times of the year. On larger streams, lengthy flow records may be available for numerous gauging stations, but data on smaller tributaries may be completely lacking.

Experienced engineers can estimate flow data by examining topographic conditions, rainfall in the drainage area, etc. Similar study will reveal the most advantageous location for the erection of private dams to impound the supply.

The dispersal of industry into semi-rural areas beyond city water mains has revived keen interest in the study of ground water supplies. The geology of an area will dictate the quality, quantity and location of underground sources. If wells are contemplated, a basic understanding of ground water principles is necessary.

Precipitation is the principal source of ground water supply. Rain and melted snow percolate down through soil particles and through cracks, joints and bedding planes of rocks. At the zone of saturation, all cracks and pores become filled with water. The upper limit of this zone is commonly called the "water table". Depending upon geographic location, the water table may lie a few inches under the land surface or hundreds of feet below it, and will be constantly fluctuating.

The underlying water bearing formations are called aquifers. The quantity of water which they contain will depend upon the characteristics of the rock, which are known as porosity, specific yield and permeability. The most important property of the underlying aquifer to the industrialist is its permeability, or ability to transmit water. Clays, for example, transmit water very slowly. Clean, medium grained sands give up water very rapidly. In rocks, the size and number of openings will determine the yield. The *tilt* of the bedding planes also affects the yield as the number of planes intersected by a well is greater in areas of moderate tilt than where the planes are steeper.

Removal of water from a well causes a decrease in pressure and the water table in the vicinity will have a shape similar to an inverted cone, known as the "cone of depression". If two or more wells are drilled in close proximity, these cones may overlap, interfering with each other and lowering the yield of both wells. This limits the number of wells which may be sunk on a given site.

In some densely populated areas this mutual interference of wells has been of grave concern to industry. Some coastal cities report a drastic lowering of the water table to the point where all supplies have been contaminated by sea water drawn into the low pressure areas.

The necessity of finding a water supply that does not require extensive conditioning is important. High pressure and low pressure steam are important throughout industry in general, particularly in chemicals and food industries, paper and textile finishing. Large amounts of cooling water are required in the manufacture of iron and steel, in metal processes, and in modern plants using air conditioning and other refrigeration devices.

Even rain water is contaminated, and most raw water requires some conditioning before it is fit for industrial or domestic use. As rain falls it absorbs the gases of the atmosphere. When this water comes in contact with soils and rocks, it dissolves considerable mineral matter due to the solvent activity of the atmospheric gases in solution. As water passes over the ground or percolates through it, it will therefore undergo many changes in its chemical composition.

Set out below are the minerals usually found in water and their effect upon industrial processes and equipment:

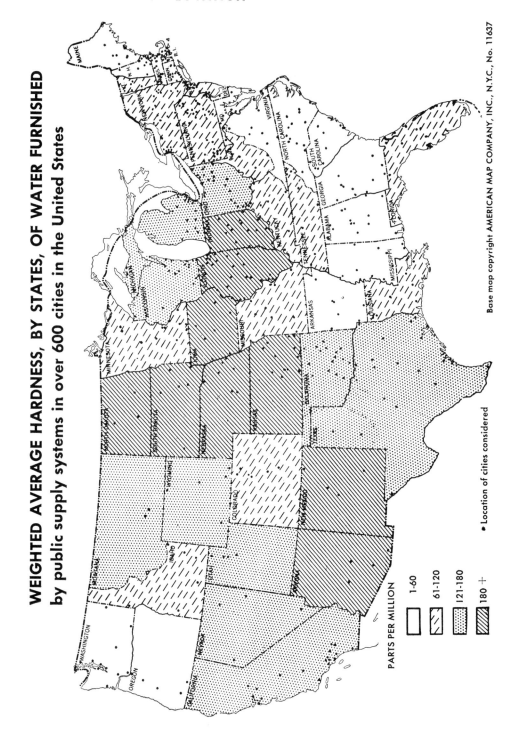

WEIGHTED AVERAGE HARDNESS, BY STATES, OF WATER FURNISHED
by public supply systems in over 600 cities in the United States

PARTS PER MILLION

1-60

61-120

121-180

180 +

• Location of cities considered

Base map copyright AMERICAN MAP COMPANY, INC., N.Y.C., No. 11637

MINERAL	EFFECT ON INDUSTRIAL EQUIPMENT AND PRODUCTS
Bicarbonate (HCO_3)	Taste
Calcium (Ca)	Forms an insoluble curd in pipes and boiler tubes. Soap consuming.
Chloride (Cl)	Taste. Increases corrosiveness.
Fluoride (F)	Amounts larger than 1.5 parts per million will mottle enamelware.
Iron (Fe)	About 0.3 parts per million will stain cloth, porcelain fixtures and other materials.
Magnesium (Mg)	Forms an insoluble curd in piles and boiler tubes. Soap consuming.
Manganese (Mn)	About 0.3 parts per million will stain cloth, porcelain fixtures and other materials.
Nitrate (NO_3)	Large amounts indicate pollution.
Potassium (K)	Large amounts will cause foaming in boilers.
Silica (SiO_2)	Results in boiler scale and destructive hard deposits on equipment.
Sulfate (SO_4)	Can form permanent hardness and scale.

Hard water can eventually create havoc in steam boilers, hot water pipes, pumps and circulating systems, diesel engines and other water-jacketed equipment, bleach tanks and many industrial processes. The corrosion and scale resulting from its use means increased costs for replacements and disruptions in operations. A helpful chart on relative hardness is shown below:

HARDNESS	CLASSIFICATION
Less than 15 p.p.m	Very soft water
15 to 50 p.p.m.	Soft water
50 to 100 p.p.m.	Medium hard water
100 to 200 p.p.m.	Hard water
Over 200 p.p.m.	Very hard water

The results of water analysis are usually expressed in parts per million (p. p. m.). An exception is the indication of the pH factor. This is a measure of hydrogen-ion concentration of water and is an expression of its acidity or alkalinity. Neutral water has a pH of 7.0. Values below 7.0 and approaching Zero denote increasing acidity while values above 7.0 to 14 indicate increasing alkalinity.

Manufacturers who propose to utilize water for cooling purposes will do well to examine carefully *climatic* data for the region under consideration. The temperature of surface water follows change in area temperature. However, ground water temperature generally is about the same as the *mean annual air temperature.*

Under normal conditions, as revealed in a study of over 3,000 records of ground water temperatures by the U. S. Geological Survey, water obtained from wells drilled to a depth of 30 to 60 feet will generally exceed mean annual air temperature by about 2° to 3°. An increase in 1° in temperature for each 64 feet of additional depth is the average condition.

As a practical illustration, a manufacturer seeking a plant location to serve the Southwest, and requiring large amounts of cooling water at a maximum temperature of 60°, could not locate his plant in the state of Texas without erection of cooling towers. Below Galveston well water ranges from 72°-75°; average lowest temperature (63°) is found in the northwestern corner of the state. In order to assure a safe supply, he would have to go north through the adjoining state of Oklahoma to Kansas where ground water temperatures from south to north range from 60° down to a low of 52°.

A quick check list* for the executive interested in community water data follows:

    1. Water from city mains
        a. Description of system
        b. Pressure
        c. Capacity
            1. Pumping
            2. Softening
        d. Purification treatment
        e. Consumption
        f. If hard, is it suitable for boiler use?
        g. Rates (industrial)
        h. Chemical analysis
        i. Temperature
    2. Water from rivers
        a. Describe source of supply, distance from city and volume of flow
        b. Is special treatment necessary?
        c. Approximate cost

*Standards of Industrial Analysis. Copyright 1950. Fantus Factory Locating Service.

WASTE DISPOSAL

In many industries, the problem of obtaining a suitable supply of water is aggravated by the necessity of disposing of resulting effluent at the same site. There are increasingly few areas of the country where industrial wastes can be disposed of without treatment. Manufacturers who located along the Ohio River, for example, have created a situation that has backfired in the form of the Ohio River Pollution Control program. In the Cincinnati area alone, organic wastes with a population equivalent of 1,784,700 people are discharged. These wastes are 64% industrial.

Due to this type of situation and the dumping of dangerous wastes by some unheeding industries, serious consideration must be given to the rate of flow of streams that can absorb effluent, the conditions above stream, the degree of treatment required under existing regulations and the possibility of future legislation in the area.

Most states have enacted some type of water pollution control law. Effluent, especially that of new plants, must therefore be treated before disposal. Woolen and worsted mills, chemical industries, dye plants and others are subject to unusually stringent controls. Robert E. Oberholtzer, in *Textile World,* (October 1949) said "Waste-treatment (at James Lees & Sons Co. carpet mill at Glasgow, Va.) removed 97% of the grease, 96% of the suspended solids, and 60% of the biochemical oxygen demand (B. O. D.) from mill dyeing and wool scouring waste before effluent is allowed to return to the Maury (North) River . . ."

Many industries having nothing more than normal sanitary sewage disposal requirements will find local community sewage disposal systems satisfactory. Over 9,000 communities in the United States now have sewer systems serving more than 90,000,000 people—99.1% of all cities of 25,000-50,000 population, and 100% of cities over 50,000 population have sewer systems.

CHAPTER 7

Taxes—Labor Laws

The impact of state and local taxation is tempered by huge federal tax impositions. Few industries have relocated their plants solely because of unfavorable state taxes—it is rather the *cumulative* effect of this and other high costs that prompt a manufacturer to consider relocation.

In a survey conducted by Burkhead and Steels and printed in the *Journal of Business of the University of Chicago,* July, 1950, it was found that taxes in approximately half of the manufacturing corporations studied in the state of Pennsylvania amounted to 1% or more of the total net income—and in one out of every seven corporations state taxes amounted to 2% or more of the total income. In the latter category especially, companies with other undue cost factors, workmen's compensation insurance rates, high local taxes or burdensome labor costs, might be prompted to consider relocation.

The Tax Foundation of New York stated in their booklet *Facts and Figures* as early as 1951, ". . . the states' expanded activities left them short of revenue requirements and they turned more and more to the federal government for aid. At the beginning of the decade the states were receiving about $645 million in such aid. By 1949, this federal aid had increased nearly two-fold.

"Thus state and local taxpayers were doubly burdened. To meet the states' demands for more aid, federal taxes were increased. Helped by this federal aid, the states' programs were enlarged still more, necessitating demands for still larger state levies to support them."

Perhaps most important in any discussion of state taxes is the net debt now being incurred by many states, which eventually cannot help but be detrimental to its industry and other business interests. At the close of fiscal 1951, the total state debt rose to an unprecedented high of $7,824,000,000.

Since the net debt of a state is at least a partial indication of future revenue needs, the finances of a state should be investigated prior to plant location. The table on the next page shows the trend in state debt.

Because of huge budgetary increases, the various states have sought new forms of taxation and have increased existing sales, property, alcoholic beverage, and other taxes. As of October 1955, 16 states assessed no corporation income tax and 32 other states plus the District of Columbia (see page 111) imposed a tax ranging from 1% to 8%. Because of differences in application of the income tax and the wide variation in regulations, it is difficult, if not completely misleading, to compare simple tax rates. Some states employ a formula for the apportionment of income, some do not. Some states permit deduction of Federal income tax, some do not, etc.

Property taxes, one of the oldest forms of taxation and still a principal source of revenue, are levied by every community.

Variation appears in actual rates, in the ratio of assessment to actual value, in distinctions between real, personal, tangible and intangible property, in the existence of special taxes on corporate securities or on specified types of business; and in the exemptions allowed. These variations indicate the necessity of ascertaining liability to requirements of property taxing procedures.

The general property tax rate is the total of all school, county, township and state levies assessed against the property. Since most property valuations for assessment purposes are made *on a local level,* municipal or county practices are very important when estimating the total property tax to which a new plant might be subject.

With full realization that tax rates are not a measure of the type of service rendered by a municipality, data on the following cities from a chart prepared by the National Municipal League (*National Municipal Review,* January, 1955) reveals sizable variations not only in tax rates but in local assessment

NET LONG-TERM DEBT OF STATE GOVERNMENTS

TOTAL AND PER CAPITA End of Fiscal Years 1942, 1946, and 1953

STATE	NET LONG-TERM DEBT (THOUSANDS)			PER CAPITA (a)		
	1942	1946	1953	1942	1946	1953
Total	$2,563,493	$1,727,107	$6,296,320	$19.26	$12.41	$39.99
Alabama	66,700(b)	45,409(b)	56,267(b)	22.68	15.60	18.07
Arizona	3,483	2,505	2,263	6.65	4.07	2.43
Arkansas	148,419	129,762	111,196	75.07	72.21	58.25
California	144,749	88,497	344,417	18.71	9.26	28.25
Colorado	23,686	18,924	13,214	21.28	15.73	9.35
Connecticut	30,213	9,921	80,200	16.86	5.21	37.10
Delaware	5,717	4,535	110,309	20.49	15.17	308.13
Florida	4,465	4,017	65,204	2.08	1.65	19.45
Georgia	26,163	66	66,026	8.16	.02	18.42
Idaho	2,548(b)	234	1,088	5.33	.46	1.80
Illinois	142,573	103,356	347,696	17.70	12.67	38.62
Indiana	7,214	4,471	18,604	2.06	1.21	4.50
Iowa	2,941	1,219	30,649	1.21	.49	11.77
Kansas	14,544	8,713	3,417	8.26	4.83	1.70
Kentucky	6,221	2,929	9,751	2.22	1.06	3.29
Louisiana	178,005(b)	148,233	199,277	69.92	57.99	69.10
Maine	26,811	16,813	63,726	31.96	20.21	69.72
Maryland	50,104(b)	30,135	176,898	25.08	13.61	69.62
Massachusetts	76,631(b)	54,216	409,382	17.54	12.06	83.55
Michigan	15,493	19,356	345,612	2.79	3.30	50.44
Minnesota	78,925	53,557	106,163	29.65	19.59	34.77
Mississippi	78,441	44,105	75,713	35.49	21.37	34.68
Missouri	84,710(b)	53,146	14,557	22.12	14.19	3.55
Montana	12,004	9,004	34,888	23.17	17.52	56.82
Nebraska	1,384	850	3,001	1.12	.68	2.23
Nevada	587	—	840	4.28	—	4.08
New Hampshire	16,389	10,721	27,037	34.07	21.70	51.30
New Jersey	58,889	37,667	402,555	13.70	8.39	78.30
New Mexico	26,707	20,647	25,681	53.20	36.80	33.88
New York	517,595	384,784	469,878	39.81	28.72	30.85
North Carolina	108,329	33,570	202,503	30.35	9.06	48.30
North Dakota	4,027	6	8,551	6.91	.01	13.77
Ohio	6,432(b)	3,352(b)	474,331	.92	.45	56.68
Oklahoma	53,280	17,000	115,941	24.05	8.02	51.51
Oregon	14,359	5,009	98,726	12.97	3.74	61.63
Pennsylvania	168,964	89,307	930,635	17.41	9.05	87.33
Rhode Island	23,946	20,517	49,396	32.01	26.65	60.46
South Carolina	84,130	67,521	128,772	41.92	34.88	58.67
South Dakota	22,898	18,236	3,431	38.88	31.01	5.22
Tennessee	83,968	70,029	104,760	28.57	22.78	31.47
Texas	17,786(b)	11,108(b)	89,817(b)	2.65	1.54	10.82
Utah	2,590	293	1,095	4.50	.46	1.49
Vermont	6,204	2,236	4,350	18.09	6.54	11.54
Virginia	19,258	6,032	27,496	6.34	1.88	7.75
Washington	11,925	6,161	188,347	6.27	2.69	76.01
West Virginia	74,115	62,236	242,874	40.48	34.08	125.39
Wisconsin	5,403	3,731	5,419	1.77	1.18	1.54
Wyoming	3,568(b)	2,901(b)	4,367(b)	14.22	11.42	14.27

(a) Based on estimated population residing in the United States, excluding armed forces overseas, as of July 1 of each calendar year.

(b) Fiscal year ending in preceding calendar year.

Source: Department of Commerce.

practices that change the effective rate paid. Variations in exemption of home-steads also affect taxes paid on residential property.

CITY	1950 POPULATION	TOTAL ACTUAL TAX RATE AS LEVIED PER $1000 ASSESSED VALUATION	REPORTED RATIO OF ASSESSED VALUE TO CURRENT MARKET VALUE (PER CENT)	ADJUSTED TAX RATE ON 100% BASIS OF ASSESSMENT
Atlanta, Ga.	331,314	$47.75	28	$13.37
Newark, N. J.	438,776	85.50	56	47.88
Buffalo, N. Y.	580,132	46.64	60	27.98
Milwaukee, Wis.	637,392	49.85	52	25.92
San Francisco, Calif.	775,357	68.50	50	34.25
Los Angeles, Calif.	1,970,358	67.40	50	33.70
Houston, Tex.	596,163	53.00	77	40.81
Baltimore, Md.	949,708	28.77	65	18.70
Cleveland, Ohio	914,808	31.30	50	15.65
Seattle, Wash.	467,591	52.51	24	12.60
Pittsburgh, Pa.	676,806	44.09	53	23.37
Philadelphia, Pa.	2,071,605	30.25	61	18.45
Washington, D. C.	802,178	21.64	75	16.23
Cincinnati, Ohio	503,998	27.80	50	13.90
Kansas City, Mo.	456,622	41.80	30	12.54
Worcester, Mass.	203,486	52.00	70	36.40
Jacksonville, Fla.	204,517	50.58	50	25.29

STATE CORPORATION INCOME TAX RATES

STATE	CORPORATION NET INCOME TAX RATES	DEDUCTIBILITY OF FEDERAL INCOME TAX
Alabama	3%	Allowed
Arizona	Graduated from 1% on first $1,000 to 5% on all above $7,000	Allowed
Arkansas	Graduated from 1% on first $3,000 to 5% on all above $25,000	Not Allowed
California[1]	4%	Not Allowed
Colorado[2]	5%	Allowed
Connecticut[3]	3%	Not Allowed
District of Columbia	5%	Not Allowed
Georgia	4%	Not Allowed
Idaho[4]	Graduated from 1.5% on first $1,000 to 8% on all above $5,000	Allowed
Iowa	3%	Allowed
Kansas	2%	Allowed
Kentucky	4.5%	Allowed
Louisiana	4%	Allowed
Maryland[5]	4.5%	Not Allowed

(continued on next page)

(STATE CORPORATION INCOME TAX RATES—continued)

STATE	CORPORATION NET INCOME TAX RATES	DEDUCTIBILITY OF FEDERAL INCOME TAX
Massachusetts[6]	6.765%	Not Allowed
Minnesota[7]	6%	Allowed
Mississippi[8]	Graduated from 2% on first $5,000 to 6% on all above $25,000	Not Allowed
Missouri	2%	Allowed
Montana[9]	3%	Allowed
New Mexico	2%	Allowed
New York[10]	5.5%	Not Allowed
North Carolina	6%	Not Allowed
North Dakota	Graduated from 3% on first $3,000 to 6% on all above $15,000	Allowed
Oklahoma	4%	Allowed
Oregon[11]	8%	Not Allowed
Pennsylvania	5%	Not Allowed
Rhode Island[12]	4%	Not Allowed
South Carolina[13]	5%	Not Allowed
Tennessee[14]	3.75%	Not Allowed
Utah[15]	4%	Allowed
Vermont[16]	5%	Not Allowed
Virginia	5%	Not Allowed
Wisconsin	Graduated from 2% on first $1,000 to 7% on all above $6,000	Allowed

[1] California: Financial corporations other than banks are allowed a limited offset for personal property taxes and license fees. Minimum tax, $25.

[2] Colorado: For the calendar year 1955 and fiscal years beginning in 1955, the tax is reduced 20%.

[3] Connecticut: 3¾% for income years beginning in 1955 and 1956. Or, if tax yield is greater, 1½ (1.9 for 1955 and 1956) mills per dollar of capital stock, surplus and indebtedness. Minimum tax, $15 ($20 for 1955 and 1956).

[4] Idaho: Increased by 7½% for taxable years beginning after December 31, 1954. Surtax expires December 31, 1956.

[5] Maryland: Domestic corporations are allowed credit for so much of their franchise taxes as are in excess of $25.

[6] Massachusetts: All corporations pay additional tax on corporate excess. Domestic property holding and property dealing corporations, not less than 1/20 of 1% of gross receipts.

[7] Minnesota: A property and payroll credit is allowed against the tax equal to 10% of the average of the ratios of tangible property and payroll in the state, applicable to corporations. Minimum tax, $10.

A surtax equal to 5% of the above rate and a tax of $5 per year are imposed for years beginning after 1948 and before 1959. An additional tax of 1% for two taxable years beginning Dec. 1, 1954.

[8] Mississippi: 14% surtax from April 1, 1955, to June 30, 1956.

[9] Montana: Minimum tax, $5.

[10] New York: Corporations are subject to a 5½% tax on net income or a tax on three alternative bases, whichever produces the greatest tax.

[11] Oregon: Utilities, 4%. Mercantile, manufacturing and business corporations and utilities are allowed a personal property tax credit up to 50% of the excise tax. Minimum tax, $10.

[12] Rhode Island: 5% of net income from 1951 through 1955. Or 40¢ on each $100 of corporate excess if tax yield is greater.

[13] South Carolina: For corporations, not less than 3% of the entire net income plus salaries and other compensation to elective and appointive officers and to any stockholder owning in excess of 5% of the issued capital stock, after deducting $6,000 and any deficit for the year.

[14] Tennessee: Insurance companies are entitled to credits for gross premiums taxes paid. Fees paid by state banks for the use of the State Banking Department are credited. Corporations are also subject to the tax on dividends and interest.

[15] Utah: Corporations are subject to the 4% tax or a tax of not less than 1/20 of 1% of the fair value of tangible property in the state, whichever is greater, but in no case less than $10.

[16] Vermont: Subject to reduction if there is sufficient surplus in the general fund. Minimum tax, $25.

Source: Commerce Clearing House, Inc.

STATE BUSINESS TAXES

STATE	FRANCHISE TAX	INCOME TAX	STOCK TRANS-FER TAX	SALES TAX	USE TAX
Alabama	Yes	Yes	Yes	Yes	Yes
Arizona	No	Yes	No	Yes	No
Arkansas	Yes	Yes	No	Yes	Yes
California	Yes	Yes	No	Yes	Yes
Colorado	Yes	Yes	No	Yes	Yes
Connecticut	Yes	Yes	No	Yes	Yes
Delaware	Yes	No	No	Yes	No
D. C.	Yes	Yes	No	Yes	Yes
Florida	Yes	No	Yes	Yes	Yes
Georgia	Yes	Yes	No	Yes	Yes
Idaho	Yes	Yes	No	No	No
Illinois	Yes	No	No	Yes	No
Indiana	No	No	No	Yes	No
Iowa	Yes	Yes	No	Yes	Yes
Kansas	Yes	Yes	Yes	Yes	Yes
Kentucky	Yes	Yes	No	No	No
Louisiana	Yes	Yes	No	Yes	Yes
Maine	Yes	No	No	Yes	Yes
Maryland	Yes	Yes	Yes	Yes	Yes
Massachusetts	Yes	Yes	Yes	No	No
Michigan	Yes	No	No	Yes	Yes
Minnesota	Yes	Yes	Yes	No	No
Mississippi	Yes	Yes	Yes	Yes	Yes
Missouri	Yes	Yes	No	Yes	No
Montana	Yes	Yes	No	No	No
Nebraska	Yes	No	No	No	No
Nevada	No	No	No	No	No
New Hampshire	Yes	No	No	No	No
New Jersey	Yes	No	No	No	No
New Mexico	Yes	Yes	No	Yes	Yes
New York	Yes	Yes	Yes	No	No
North Carolina	Yes	Yes	No	Yes	Yes
North Dakota	No	Yes	No	Yes	Yes
Ohio	Yes	No	No	Yes	Yes
Oklahoma	Yes	Yes	Yes	Yes	Yes
Oregon	Yes	Yes	No	No	No
Pennsylvania	Yes	Yes	Yes	Yes	Yes
Rhode Island	Yes	Yes	No	Yes	Yes
South Carolina	Yes	Yes	Yes	Yes	Yes
South Dakota	No	No	No	Yes	Yes
Tennessee	Yes	Yes	Yes	Yes	Yes
Texas	Yes	No	Yes	No	No
Utah	Yes	Yes	No	Yes	Yes
Vermont	No	Yes	No	Yes	No
Virginia	Yes	Yes	Yes	No	No
Washington	Yes	No	Yes	Yes	Yes
West Virginia	Yes	No	No	Yes	Yes
Wisconsin	No	Yes	No	No	No
Wyoming	Yes	No	No	Yes	Yes

STATE AND LOCAL TAXES AS A PERCENT
OF INCOME PAYMENTS: 1952-1953

STATES	STATE TAXES ($ 000)	LOCAL TAXES ($ 000)	TOTAL TAXES ($ 000)	INCOME PAYMENTS IN PRIOR CALENDAR YEAR ($ MILLIONS)	PERCENT OF TAXES OVER INCOME
48 States	$11,750,149	$12,686,955	$24,437,105	$253,589	09.63
North Dakota	69,162	49,938	119,100	734	16.22
Louisiana	340,221	120,652	460,873	3,396	13.57
New Mexico	96,271	27,714	123,985	965	12.84
Florida	269,076	246,545	515,621	4,088	12.61
Minnesota	274,256	282,717	556,973	4,505	12.36
Wyoming	33,134	27,381	60,515	495	12.22
Arizona	87,974	60,223	148,197	1,287	11.51
Oklahoma	223,912	110,858	334,770	2,910	11.50
Mississippi	124,177	79,383	203,560	1,778	11.44
New Hampshire	32,948	60,801	93,749	823	11.39
Colorado	128,398	135,314	263,712	2,316	11.38
Nevada	20,336	25,737	46,073	405	11.37
California	1,236,892	1,350,551	2,587,443	23,146	11.17
Idaho	46,970	50,583	97,553	874	11.16
Iowa	189,289	259,440	448,729	4,087	10.97
Vermont	29,275	25,146	54,421	497	10.94
Wisconsin	279,454	357,173	636,627	5,837	10.90
South Carolina	175,846	77,049	252,895	2,341	10.80
Washington	209,050	183,732	481,782	4,466	10.78
Maine	64,027	63,871	127,898	1,203	10.63
New York	1,188,962	2,067,367	3,256,329	30,935	10.52
Massachusetts	340,679	539,849	880,528	8,385	10.50
Utah	57,783	53,731	111,514	1,069	10.43
North Carolina	315,083	142,112	457,195	4,383	10.43
Oregon	146,310	140,882	287,192	2,763	10.39
Montana	49,190	53,856	103,046	1,003	10.27
Georgia	234,909	169,383	404,292	3,998	10.11
Michigan	649,241	539,418	1,188,659	12,172	09.76
Kansas	153,708	171,067	324,775	3,400	09.55
Arkansas	111,374	58,405	169,779	1,785	09.51
Alabama	182,364	105,890	288,254	3,089	09.33
Nebraska	74,215	125,523	199,738	2,147	09.30
Texas	536,532	544,733	1,081,265	11,887	09.09
Tennessee	196,585	134,022	330,607	3,669	09.01
Indiana	320,409	299,625	620,034	6,917	08.96
New Jersey	226,330	606,809	833,139	9,996	08.33
Virginia	227,024	154,897	381,921	4,624	08.25
Maryland	186,402	176,154	362,556	4,449	08.14
Kentucky	149,521	119,869	269,390	3,311	08.13
West Virginia	134,418	60,920	195,338	2,404	08.12
Connecticut	156,208	183,728	339,936	4,375	07.76
Ohio	534,587	640,674	1,175,261	15,378	07.64
Pennsylvania	656,693	716,488	1,373,181	18,245	07.52
Illinois	537,175	800,730	1,337,905	17,681	07.56
Missouri	219,829	249,950	469,779	6,420	07.31
Rhode Island	60,128	38,224	98,352	1,352	07.27
Delaware	37,288	14,378	51,666	764	06.76

The impact of specialized state and local taxation must be carefully analyzed by the investigator seeking a new plant location. Manufacturers, for example, who move a large volume of freight via motor carrier will be affected, to a varying degree, by the gasoline taxes.

Rates of general application in 1955, exclusive of municipal taxes, license and inspection fees, are tabulated below:

	CENTS PER GALLON		CENTS PER GALLON
Alabama	7	Nebraska	6
Arizona	5	Nevada	6
Arkansas	6½	New Hampshire	5
California	6	New Jersey	4
Colorado	6	New Mexico	6
Connecticut	6	New York	4
Delaware	5	North Carolina	7
Dist. of Columbia	6	North Dakota	5
Florida	7	Ohio	5
Georgia	6½	Oklahoma	6-58/100
Idaho	6	Oregon	6
Illinois	5	Pennsylvania	5
Indiana	4	Rhode Island	4
Iowa	6	South Carolina	7
Kansas	5	South Dakota	5
Kentucky	7	Tennessee	7
Louisiana	7	Texas	5
Maine	7	Utah	5
Maryland	6	Vermont	5½
Massachusetts	5	Virginia	6
Michigan	6	Washington	6½
Minnesota	5	West Virginia	6
Mississippi	7	Wisconsin	4
Missouri	3	Wyoming	5
Montana	7	Source: Commerce Clearing House, Inc.	

LABOR LAWS

Virtually all industry is subject to state labor controls, legislation for which may be found in the statutes, codes and session laws of each state. Because state laws are frequently more stringent and specific, they often supersede Federal laws.

The regulation of labor unions, strikes, picketing and boycotting, collective bargaining agreements, unfair employment practices, anti-injunction laws and wage and hour laws differ radically from state to state.

In Florida, for example, union officials and organizers must secure a license from a Board composed of the Governor, Secretary of State and Superintendent of Education, under the following provisions:

No person will be granted a license

"(1) who has not been a citizen of and has not resided in the United States for a period of more than ten years next prior to making application,

(2) who has been convicted of a felony,

(3) who is not a person of good moral character. Suspension or revocation of a license for violations shall be commenced by the Attorney General upon complaint of any interested party."

Labor organizations may be sued in Florida, the closed shop is prohibited, picketing by force or violence is unlawful, there are no anti-injunction laws, no Fair Employment Practices Law, no industrial homework laws, and wage and hour laws are at a minimum level.

In New York State, a "closed shop agreement between an employer and the exclusive bargaining agency of the employees is not contrary to public policy even where a monopoly of labor in the locality is created". There is no regulation of labor unions. "No officer or member of any association or organization, and no association or organization participating or interested in a labor dispute (as these terms are herein defined) shall be held responsible or liable in any civil action at law or suit in equity, or in any criminal prosecution, for the unlawful acts of individual officers, members, or agents, except upon proof by the weight of evidence and without the aid of any presumptions of law or fact, of

(a) the doing of such acts by persons who are officers, members or agents of any such association or organization, and

(b) actual participation in, or actual authorization of, such acts, or ratification of such acts after actual knowledge thereof by such association or organization."

New York State has legislation covering minimum wages for both women and men and a mandatory Fair Employment Practice Act. The state of New Jersey, for example, has stringent restrictions on the employment of females after midnight. Certain industries are exempt, e.g., canning and glass manufacturing —others must seek executive order of the governor for exemption.

Interested manufacturers can secure complete digests of state labor legislation from the Department of Labor (or Industrial Commission) in the respective state capitals. Briefly, those states now having labor relations acts include:

Colorado	Massachusetts	New York	Rhode Island
Connecticut	Michigan	Oregon	Utah
Kansas	Minnesota	Pennsylvania	Wisconsin

The states of Colorado, Connecticut, Indiana, Iowa, Kansas, Massachusetts, New Jersey, New Mexico, New York, Oregon, Rhode Island, Washington and Wisconsin now have Fair Employment Practice Acts.

Those states having minimum wage orders affecting either all or some phases of industry include: California, District of Columbia, Illinois, Kentucky, Maine, Massachusetts, New Jersey, North Dakota, Oregon, Rhode Island, Washington, Wisconsin.

WORKMEN'S COMPENSATION INSURANCE

Workmen's Compensation Insurance rates are applied against every single dollar the manufacturer expends in payroll, and geographically there can be a sizable differential to the manufacturer in his annual Workmen's Compensation Insurance bill due to varying state laws. The maximum period for temporary total disability in California is 240 weeks whereas the worker in the state of Connecticut is entitled to a maximum of 780 weeks. Maximum percentage of wages ranges from 80% in Nevada down to 50% in Vermont, Georgia, California and Connecticut.

Rates payable on each dollar of payroll can produce sizable differentials depending upon the state under consideration. Iron foundries are subject to the following rates for each $100 of payroll expended: (Base rates without giving effect to the individual company's experience benefits.)

Rhode Island	$7.15	North Carolina	$2.02
New York	4.30	Indiana	1.62
New Jersey	3.66	Alabama	1.47
California	3.11	Virginia	1.11
Illinois	2.22	Pennsylvania	1.10

(Classification Code #425 for Pennsylvania, and #3081 for other states listed above)

MINIMUM AND MAXIMUM BENEFITS
FOR TEMPORARY TOTAL DISABILITY

STATE	MAXIMUM PERCENTAGE OF WAGES	MAXIMUM PERIOD	LIMIT OF PAYMENTS PER WEEK MINIMUM	LIMIT OF PAYMENTS PER WEEK MAXIMUM	TOTAL MAXIMUM STATED IN LAW
Alabama	65	300 weeks	$5.00	$23.00	
Alaska	65	Period of disability			
Arizona	65	433 weeks		150.00	
Arkansas	65	450 weeks	7.00	25.00	$8,000
California	61¾	240 weeks	9.75	35.00	7,200
Colorado	50	Period of disability	10.00	28.00	
Connecticut	50	780 weeks	9.00	36.00	
Delaware	60	Period of disability	8.00	30.00	
District of Columbia	66⅔	Period of disability	12.00	35.00	11,000
Florida	60	700 weeks	8.00	35.00	
Georgia	50	350 weeks	7.00	24.00	8,400
Hawaii	66⅔	Period of disability	8.00	35.00	10,500
Idaho	60	400 weeks; thereafter $8 per week	10.00	20.37	
Illinois	65	Period of disability	25.50	34.00	8,500
Indiana	55	500 weeks	12.10	27.00	7,500
Iowa	60	500 weeks	12.00	28.00	
Kansas	60	416 weeks	7.00	25.00	
Kentucky	65	520 weeks	7.00	24.00	10,000
Louisiana	65	300 weeks	3.00	30.00	
Maine	66⅔	500 weeks	12.00	24.00	9,000
Maryland	66⅔	312 weeks	12.00	32.00	4,500
Massachusetts	66⅔	Period of disability	18.00	30.00	10,000
Michigan	66⅔	500 weeks	11.00	24.00	
Minnesota	66⅔	300 weeks	15.00	32.00	
Mississippi	66⅔	450 weeks	10.00	25.00	8,600
Missouri	66⅔	400 weeks	8.00	30.00	
Montana	66⅔	300 weeks	21.50	27.50	
Nebraska	66⅔	300 weeks; thereafter 45 percent of wages for life, maximum $16, minimum $8 (or actual wage, if less).	11.00	26.00	
Nevada	80	433 weeks		24.23	
New Hampshire	66⅔	300 weeks	10.00	30.00	7,500
New Jersey	66⅔	300 weeks	10.00	30.00	
New Mexico	60	550 weeks	12.00	30.00	
New York	66⅔	Period of disability	12.00	32.00	6,500
North Carolina	60	400 weeks	8.00	30.00	6,000
North Dakota	66⅔	Period of disability	25.00	42.00	
Ohio	66⅔	312 weeks	10.00	32.20	6,000
Oklahoma	66⅔	300 weeks; may be extended to 500 weeks	15.00	25.00	
Oregon	66⅔	Period of disability	25.38	45.00	
Pennsylvania	66⅔	500 weeks	12.50	25.00	12,500
Puerto Rico	50	104 weeks	3.00	15.00	
Rhode Island	60	1,000 weeks	15.00	28.00	14,000
South Carolina	60	500 weeks	5.00	25.00	6,000
South Dakota	55	312 weeks	10.00	25.00	
Tennessee	60	300 weeks	10.00	25.00	
Texas	60	401 weeks	9.00	25.00	
Utah	60	313 weeks	29.50	34.38	9,750

(continued on next page)

(MINIMUM AND MAXIMUM BENEFITS—continued)

STATE	MAXIMUM PERCENTAGE OF WAGES	MAXIMUM PERIOD	LIMIT OF PAYMENTS PER WEEK MINI-MUM	MAXI-MUM	TOTAL MAXI-MUM STATED IN LAW
Vermont	50	260 weeks	12.00	25.00	
Virginia	60	500 weeks	6.00	20.00	7,800
Washington		Period of disability	23.08	42.69	
West Virginia	66⅔	156 weeks	15.00	25.00	
Wisconsin	70	Period of disability	8.75	37.00	
Wyoming		Period of disability	21.23	43.85	
United States:					
Civil employees	75	Period of disability	25.96	121.15	
Longshoremen	66⅔	Period of disability	12.00	35.00	11,000

STATE UNEMPLOYMENT COMPENSATION TAX RATES[a]

BY TYPE OF PLAN AND BY STATE. Rate Year Beginning in 1953

TYPE OF PLAN AND STATE[b]	EMPLOYER CONTRIBUTION RATE (PERCENT) RANGE POSSIBLE[c] MAXIMUM	MINIMUM	AVERAGE[d]	PERCENTAGE OF EXPERIENCE RATED ACCOUNTS WITH REDUCED RATES
Reserve-Ratio Plan				
Arizona[e]	2.7	.4	1.2	94.3
Arkansas[e]	2.7	.1	1.3	94.4
California	2.7	.0	1.4	63.5
Colorado[e]	2.7	.0	.4	98.2
Georgia	2.7	.25	1.2	96.5
Idaho	2.7	.9	1.75	95.8
Indiana[e]	2.7	.1	.7	93.6
Iowa[e]	2.7	.0	.6	95.7
Kansas	2.7	.35	1.0	92.9
Kentucky[e]	3.2	.0	1.7	59.0
Louisiana	2.7	.3	1.4	74.8
Maine	2.7	.9	1.6	88.3
Massachusetts	2.7	(f)	2.7[f]	(f)
Missouri[e]	3.6	.0	.6	96.4
Nebraska[e]	2.7	.1	.5	96.8
Nevada	2.7	.1	1.9	86.0
New Hampshire	2.7	.5	1.7	77.0
New Jersey[e]	2.7	.3	1.6	81.5
New Mexico	2.7	.1	1.35	93.9
North Carolina[e]	2.7	.1	1.2	94.3
North Dakota[e]	2.7	.25	1.5	90.1
Ohio[e]	2.7	.3	1.05	92.2
Oregon[e]	2.7	.3	1.2	90.7

(continued on next page)

(STATE UNEMPLOYMENT COMPENSATION TAX RATES—continued)

TYPE OF PLAN AND STATE[b]	EMPLOYER CONTRIBUTION RATE (PERCENT)			PERCENTAGE OF EXPERIENCE RATED ACCOUNTS WITH REDUCED RATES
	RANGE POSSIBLE[c]		AVERAGE[d]	
	MAXIMUM	MINIMUM		
Pennsylvania[e]	2.7	.5	1.1	84.3
South Carolina[e]	2.7	.25	1.4	90.1
South Dakota[e]	2.7	.0	.8	92.5
Tennessee	2.7	.5	1.5	89.9
West Virginia[e]	2.7	.0	1.0	85.1
Wisconsin[e]	4.0	.0	.9	95.3
District of Columbia	2.7	.1	.5	92.5
Hawaii[e]	2.7	.0	.9	86.4
Benefit-Wage-Ratio Plan				
Alabama	2.7	.5	1.0	95.0
Delaware	3.0	.2	.5	98.3
Illinois	2.7	.25	.9	86.7
Oklahoma	2.7	.2	1.0	91.6
Texas	2.7	.1	.5	98.2
Virginia	2.7	.1	.6	96.0
Benefit-Ratio Plan				
Florida	2.7	.0	.7	94.2
Maryland	2.7	.2	.8	94.2
Michigan	4.0	.1	1.6	86.3
Minnesota[e]	2.7	.1	.8	79.5
Vermont	2.7	.6	1.3	90.8
Wyoming	2.7	.1	1.1	88.6
Pay-Roll Variation Plan				
Mississippi	2.7	.9	1.2	99.7
Rhode Island	2.7	(f)	2.7[f]	(f)
Utah	2.7	.9[g]	1.1	99.6
Washington	2.7	1.5[h]	1.7	94.7
Alaska	2.7	(f)	2.7[f]	(f)
Compensable-Separations Plan				
Connecticut	2.7	.5	1.2	91.1
Combination Plans				
Pay-Roll Variation and Reserve-Ratio				
New York	2.7	.7	2.1	68.8
Pay-Roll Variation and Benefit-Ratio				
Montana	2.7	.5	1.3	80.8

[a] Standard rate is 2.7 percent in all states. The rate for any employee may be below the standard rate depending upon his experience rating; in a few states a penalty rate above 2.7 may apply.

[b] States classified by type of plan in effect during rate year beginning in 1953.

[c] The maximum and minimum rates as shown are the latest effective rates assigned employers during 1953 rate year.

[d] Preliminary; does not include effect of voluntary contributions from employers.

[e] State law provided for voluntary contributions during 1953.

[f] Employers not assigned any reduced rates during 1953 rate year.

[g] Rates determined by distribution of surplus, in specified proportions, to employers according to their experience rating.

[h] On the basis of experience and pay-roll, credit is allowed employers on their future contributions; reduced rates represent credit factor converted to net contribution rates.

Source: Tax Foundation.

CHAPTER 8

Climate: Its Effect on Industry

It is a proven fact that weather exerts great influence on human efficiency and behavior. More crimes are committed during the hot, humid period between July and August than at any other period of the year. The desire to work and capacity to produce are affected by weather. Air pressure, humidity and climatic conditions play a large role in a thousand different industrial processes. Snow, rain, glaze and sunshine all have an effect on both employer and employee, on total costs of doing business, and even on the type of structure necessary to house an industrial operation.

The New England Electric System recently published a booklet in defense of its power rates, in which the first question and answer were as follows:

> Q. Does electricity cost more in New England than in other parts of the country?

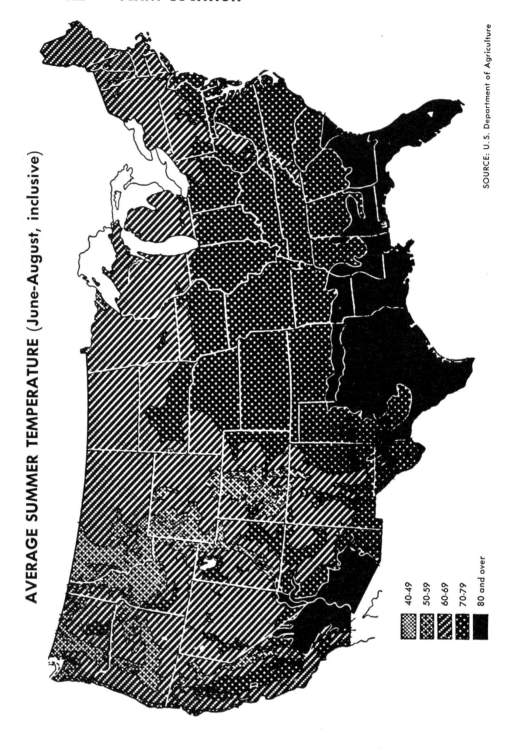

AVERAGE SUMMER TEMPERATURE (June-August, inclusive)

SOURCE: U. S. Department of Agriculture

40-49
50-59
60-69
70-79
80 and over

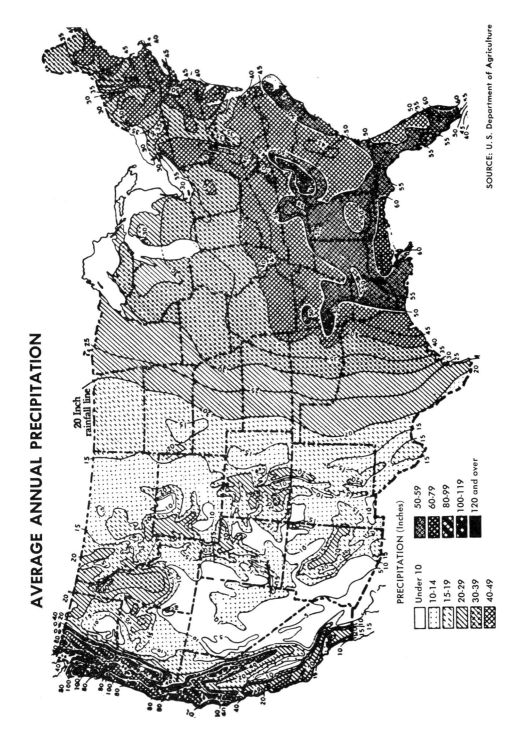

AVERAGE ANNUAL PRECIPITATION

20 Inch
rainfall line

SOURCE: U. S. Department of Agriculture

PRECIPITATION (Inches)

Under 10
10-14
15-19
20-29
30-39
40-49
50-59
60-79
80-99
100-119
120 and over

A. Yes. And for some very good reasons: :

Coal and oil cost more here because we are so far from the source of supply. Transportation amounts to about as much as the cost of the fuel itself. *It costs more to build and to maintain transmission and distribution lines because in New England we need extra strength and durability to withstand sleet, storms and high winds* and also because of our rough and rocky terrain.

One of the nation's principal airplane manufacturers, when a choice had to be made between a location in either of two fine communities, one in Pennsylvania and the other in Tennessee, finally selected the Tennessee city because of its higher percentage of days with sunshine. He realized that grounding of his planes would cost him money. The above is a type of climatic problem that does not yield readily to the installation of air-conditioning!

Each area of the United States has a characteristic climate. If certain industrial processes require minimal seasonal differences, the manufacturer would do

Victaulic Company of America, Hillside, New Jersey. Plant Location Study—FANTUS FACTORY LOCATING SERVICE.

well to examine southern California—no other section of the country offers so slight a difference between winter and summer temperatures. On the other hand, the Pacific Coast region experiences the greatest degree of fog in the United States.

If a manufacturer requires an area in which he can recruit common labor at competitively low rates, he would consider the "Cotton Belt," whose climate makes it possible to subsist at lower cost than perhaps anywhere else in the country. Heavy winter clothing is unnecessary, heating bills are insignificant, and food crops can be raised at low cost.

Manufacturers utilizing large amounts of floor space in proportion to total number of employees, where maintenance is a factor, will prefer areas where there is no frost line problem and no freeze and thaw cycle—thus eliminating continuous pointing up of brick work, removal of ice and snow, elimination of enclosed loading platforms, and the winterizing of trucks and other plant equipment.

In areas where temperatures seldom fall to freezing level, concerns requiring open storage of drums and other materials can operate with no time lost due to weather conditions.

The velocity and direction of prevailing winds may affect the ventilating problems of large plants, and the orientation of a new plant on a proposed site will vary greatly, dependent upon the characteristics of the area. This is especially true if any phase of the operation, or neighboring plants, produces noxious odors, fumes or heat. In the city of Chicago, average wind velocity in the month of June is 15 miles per hour and wind direction is Southwest. In Kansas City, average velocity is 9.1 miles per hour and wind direction is North. In Albany, New York, velocity is 6.7 miles per hour and wind direction is South. The weatherman is not at all satisfied with the above inconsistencies—in many areas, wind direction reverses or shifts during periods throughout the year. Prevailing winds in Seattle, for example, are South in June and North in July.

Manufacturers interested in ideal working conditions should seek a climate with frequent but moderate weather changes and gradual seasonal changes. Periods of continuous wet spells or constant sunshine lead to weather "monotony" and may reduce initiative and accomplishment. Approximately 40° during the winter season and 64° in the summer are considered ideal temperatures.

From a personnel standpoint, geographic extremes should be avoided. Exceptional dryness, anything below 25 per cent of relative humidity, promotes susceptibility to the common cold and other respiratory diseases. It is a well known fact that pneumonia is more prevalent in large cities than in rural areas, due perhaps to dust and other conditions.

Even future marketing policies are dictated by climatic factors. Despite

CLIMATIC CHARACTERISTICS
Selected Industrial Cities of the U. S.

CITY	ELEVA-TION	TEMPERATURE		PRECIPITATION		RELATIVE HUMIDITY	SUNSHINE HOURS
		WINTER	SUMMER	RAIN	SNOW		
Atlanta, Ga.	1,054	44.0	77.9	49.75	2.3	72	2,776
Asheville, N. C.	2,192	39.2	71.6	38.02	10.5	75	2,519
Boston, Mass.	15	29.7	69.4	40.14	43.1	72	2,561
Buffalo, N. Y.	693	25.5	67.8	36.00	74.9	77	2,346
Charleston, S. C.	9	51.3	80.4	45.22	.3	79	2,945
Chicago, Ill.	594	27.0	70.9	32.81	33.4	73	2,645
Cincinnati, Ohio	761	33.6	75.1	38.40	18.2	76	2,670
Detroit, Mich.	77	26.4	70.4	31.47	39.7	74	2,367
Galveston, Texas	6	55.6	82.6	46.55	0.2	80	2,850
Kansas City, Mo.	741	31.9	77.1	36.32	21.4	68	2,880
Los Angeles, Calif.	312	56.4	69.5	15.40	Trace	68	3,217
Minneapolis, Minn.	830	16.7	70.4	27.19	41.1	72	2,614
New York, N. Y.	10	32.4	71.9	42.99	30.9	70	2,685
Norfolk, Va.	11	42.5	76.9	42.25	9.1	76	2,735
Philadelphia, Pa.	26	34.3	74.1	40.41	22.4	70	2,627
Pittsburgh, Pa.	1,226	32.0	72.4	36.00	34.1	71	2,313
Portland, Oregon	30	40.9	65.3	41.62	12.9	73	2,155
St. Louis, Mo.	465	34.1	77.5	39.23	17.5	68	2,693
San Francisco, Calif.	52	51.4	59.0	22.08	0.2	78	2,935
Seattle, Wash.	14	41.8	62.9	33.33	11.2	75	2,049

the population increase in the past several decades west of the Mississippi River, economists claim that rainfall deficiency reduces the number of people who might otherwise be supported by a minimum of 75%.

The U. S. Weather Bureau is most helpful in supplying data on weather conditions in every section of the country. Every area has been charted as to elevation, temperature, precipitation, relative humidity, number of sunshine hours, wind speed and the number of days with rain, snow, fog, etc.

On the opposite page is a compilation from statistics of the Weather Bureau showing climatic characteristics of selected industrial cities of the United States. Elevation noted is the ground elevation at the respective Weather Bureau office. Winter temperature is the average of the daily maximum and minimum temperatures for December, January and February. The months of June, July and August are used for the summer average. Relative humidity is an average based on the 7:30 a.m. and p.m. records for all months.

Not only is the Weather Bureau prepared to furnish data on temperature, humidity and precipitation, it can also supply information on the average number of days of clear, cloudy, rainy or foggy days. In the table which follows, note that an unusually high number of cloudy days prevails on the West Coast. (Records indicate that Roseburg, Oregon has the astonishingly high average total of 47 foggy days annually.) Severe smog conditions, such as exist at Los Angeles, are of course aggravated by the number of foggy days prevalent in that area. The Weather Bureau measures a clear day when average cloudiness does not exceed "3/10 of the sky"; partly cloudy—when average cloudiness is 4/10 to 7/10; cloudy—average cloudiness is 8/10 or more.

HEATING COSTS

The type of construction necessary, the amount and kind of insulation required, and the heating costs of a proposed plant in any area can be determined quite accurately through the utilization of data on "degree-days." Engineers have discovered that the fuel required to heat an enclosed area is contingent upon the number of degrees by which the average temperature falls below 65° F.

The degree-day is officially defined as "a departure of one degree per day in the mean daily temperature from an adopted standard reference temperature, usually 65° F." For instance, if the mean outside temperature was 45, we would record 65-45 or 20 degree-days.

Today, heating engineers depend upon degree-day computation to deter-

TYPE OF WEATHER

CITY	AVERAGE WIND SPEED	NO. OF DAYS A YEAR							TEMPERATURE		
		CLEAR	PARTLY CLOUDY	CLOUDY	RAIN	SNOW	THUNDER-STORMS	FOG	90° OR HIGHER	32° OR LOWER	0° OR LOWER
Albuquerque, N. Mex.	8.0	197	114	54	50	5	43	4	49	126	1
Amarillo, Tex.	12.5	198	109	58	75	14	39	6	52	102	2
Atlanta, Ga.	9.9	129	108	128	122	2	49	20	57	43	0
Asheville, N. C.	7.8	122	131	112	134	25	55	31	4	82	—
Bismarck, N. Dak.	9.7	146	114	105	94	70	30	5	18	183	48
Boise, Idaho	9.6	124	95	146	93	14	17	17	40	120	1
Boston, Mass.	11.5	118	118	129	125	42	18	14	9	106	3
Brownsville, Tex.	10.6	112	146	107	75	—	26	14	104	3	0
Buffalo, N. Y.	14.5	74	130	161	165	98	30	12	1	128	3
Burlington, Vt.	10.2	73	111	181	148	48	29	9	4	148	19
Charleston, S. C.	10.4	130	134	101	111	*	56	14	27	9	0
Cheyenne, Wyo.	11.3	124	152	89	96	69	45	14	7	175	12
Chicago, Ill.	11.0	117	120	128	124	59	38	10	11	109	8
Cincinnati, Ohio	7.2	112	118	135	131	19	46	10	26	89	1
Cleveland, Ohio	13.1	90	121	154	154	45	35	5	4	114	3
Denver, Colo.	7.4	146	152	67	84	49	44	2	22	136	8
Des Moines, Iowa	9.7	124	118	123	104	50	46	6	24	128	16
Detroit, Mich.	11.0	97	124	144	134	38	29	11	9	124	4
El Paso, Texas	9.2	216	112	37	50	2	29	1	88	44	*
Fort Worth, Texas	10.3	158	115	92	76	4	49	6	90	29	6
Galveston, Texas	10.7	148	123	94	99	*	49	18	13	4	0
Helena, Montana	8.0	101	125	139	98	42	29	2	9	153	22
Huron, S. Dak.	10.9	136	132	97	94	—	38	8	24	169	35
Jacksonville, Fla.	8.8	125	142	98	121	0	77	11	59	6	0
Jackson, Miss.	—	—	—	—	100	—	—	—	—	—	—

CITY	AVERAGE WIND SPEED	NO. OF DAYS A YEAR							TEMPERATURE		
		CLEAR	PARTLY CLOUDY	CLOUDY	RAIN	SNOW	THUNDER-STORMS	FOG	90° OR HIGHER	32° OR LOWER	0° OR LOWER
Kansas City, Mo.	10.1	148	112	105	106	34	56	9	39	96	4
Knoxville, Tenn.	6.6	124	122	119	134	17	47	18	30	63	*
Little Rock, Ark.	7.5	141	107	117	107	7	58	9	51	40	*
Los Angeles, Calif.	6.1	179	128	58	39	*	5	24	14	*	0
Memphis, Tenn.	8.5	142	107	116	111	3	50	5	45	40	*
Miami, Fla.	9.8	101	151	113	134	0	69	2	6	*	0
Minneapolis, Minn.	11.2	104	114	147	107	71	39	8	14	147	30
Montgomery, Ala.	6.9	133	119	113	113	2	55	5	67	19	0
New Orleans, La.	7.8	119	139	107	119	—	74	15	53	4	0
New York, N. Y.	14.8	106	133	126	125	35	31	21	7	92	*
Norfolk, Va.	11.4	133	115	117	125	6	37	15	25	41	0
Oklahoma City, Okla.	11.1	163	109	93	83	6	44	8	64	70	*
Omaha, Nebr.	9.3	132	120	113	97	22	41	8	30	120	14
Pensacola, Fla.	10.4	135	125	105	112	*	71	14	16	7	0
Philadelphia, Pa.	10.4	114	121	130	124	29	27	10	13	79	*
Phoenix, Ariz.	5.8	118	90	47	39	—	—	—	152	10	0
Pittsburgh, Pa.	10.4	85	129	151	150	64	40	23	16	102	2
Portland, Maine	9.9	130	109	126	237	37	15	28	3	135	6
Portland, Ore.	6.9	93	100	172	153	14	4	9	6	27	0
Raleigh, N. C.	7.3	133	114	118	120	4	41	12	37	50	*
Reno, Nev.	6.9	195	100	70	49	39	14	3	32	154	2
Roseburg, Ore.	4.3	110	121	134	134	5	2	47	15	33	*
St. Louis, Mo.	11.0	138	118	109	111	31	48	10	36	79	2
San Francisco, Calif.	9.1	157	115	93	67	*	2	15	1	*	0
Seattle, Wash.	8.8	77	107	181	150	14	5	27	1	21	0

* Less than one.

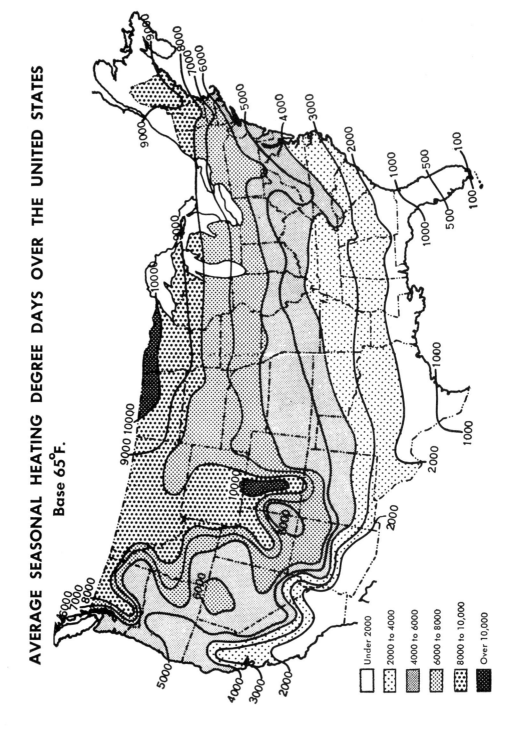

AVERAGE SEASONAL HEATING DEGREE DAYS OVER THE UNITED STATES

Base 65°F.

Under 2000
2000 to 4000
4000 to 6000
6000 to 8000
8000 to 10,000
Over 10,000

Westinghouse Electric Corporation (Meter Division), Raleigh, North Carolina. ARCHITECTS AND ENGINEERS: *Roberts & Co. Associates.* Plant Location Study—FANTUS FACTORY LOCATING SERVICE.

mine heating capacity and size of boilers, radiators and all other heating devices. In areas with mild weather, space or wall heaters are used instead of costlier central heating plants. As a result, less costly above-grade utility rooms are usually installed in such homes instead of basements.

In considering the relative cost of air-conditioning the Weather Bureau can also be helpful in furnishing the number of degree-days over 85°.

Average seasonal degree-days in selected cities (Base 65° F.):

	SEASON TOTAL		SEASON TOTAL
Minneapolis, Minn.	7966	New York, N. Y.	5280
Buffalo, N. Y.	6925	Baltimore, Md.	4487
Detroit, Mich.	6560	Richmond, Va.	3922
Chicago, Ill.	6282	Nashville, Tenn.	3613
Cleveland, Ohio	6144	Raleigh, N. C.	3275
Hartford, Conn.	6113	San Francisco, Calif.	3137
Providence, R. I.	5984	Atlanta, Ga.	2985
Boston, Mass.	5936	Dallas, Texas	2367
Newark, N. J.	5500	Mobile, Ala.	1566
Pittsburgh, Pa.	5430	Los Angeles, Calif.	1391

CHAPTER 9

Final Analysis
of Communities

Up to this point in his plant location analysis, the investigator has charted his markets, the geographic "pull" of his necessary raw materials, his labor requirements, the power, fuel and water costs of various areas and the effect of various state taxes and laws in his specific operation. He has, through a process of careful elimination, selected a general area within which he must indicate the one outstanding community for his specific manufacturing requirements.

It is in this stage of the survey that the executive usually bogs down. The Federal Reserve Banks, Federal Trade Commission, Interstate Commerce Commission, U. S. Geological Survey, U. S. Department of Interior and the U. S. Department of Commerce are in a position to provide much information. But it is on a *local level* that manufacturers often fail to amass sufficient data, particularly as to the important *intangibles* involved, and correctly interpret their significance.

Perhaps the most important single element in the conduct of a community investigation is the necessity for secrecy. A slip of the tongue, return address on a letter, or the license number of a car may cause troublesome labor turnover and allied problems long before the manufacturer is ready to shift his operation or establish a branch plant. Rumor can also result in harmful competitive repercussions.

The gathering of *objective* information is fundamental in any important step of this nature. Hence, the fewer community pressures to which the investigator is subjected, the more successful the result. The executives of one large company, just a few years ago, landed at a comfortable hotel in a medium sized city of the south, after a rainy ten day tour. The splendid chicken dinner they received through the courtesy of the Chamber of Commerce upon their arrival was a pleasant relief from the tiresome trip. It is no exaggeration to state that the gracious social amenities with which they were greeted accounted in no small measure for their decision to locate their plant there.

The above case is not an extreme example—numerous instances can be cited where social pleasantries have taken the place of bedrock economics. Surface facts are easily available. It takes hard work and genuine probing to penetrate beneath the superficial and determine the true "climate" of the community.

Promotional conversation on the part of civic representatives, no matter how well intended, cannot be substituted for fact. Many questions should be answered before a final decision is reached—What is the true nature of the people of the community? Do they own their own homes? Do they have deeply imbedded roots in the city—or is the working force transient and disinterested in the general community good? Have there been many strikes, what were the issues, what was the reaction of local law enforcing agencies? How have the tax assessors treated *present* industry? Have zoning boards been sympathetic to the unique problems of industry? Are there hidden but powerful antagonisms and resentment to industry that do not appear on the surface? Is there a traffic problem in the community that has been met with forceful action? Or will employees meet with congestion and delay in getting to and from the proposed plant?

Maurice Fulton, partner of the Fantus Factory Locating Service, in a speech before the Oklahoma Development Council at its 1951 Annual Meeting (reprinted by the University of Oklahoma), said, in part:

> Finally, and probably the most important of all general considerations, is that of community attitude. Too frequently, the efforts of a city are the lengthened shadow of one man. A

paid Chamber of Commerce executive or a utility representative may be the only individuals who ever make contact with the location investigator. Rosy promises of full and complete cooperation are made. However, an investigation of local ordinances, state legislation, municipal services, and tax treatment indicate that the community is not really anxious to have the industry locate there. At least, no real effort has ever been made to make the manufacturing or business background of the community attractive. I am not advocating a huge banquet and the 'red carpet treatment' every time an industrial prospect comes into a town. The important and objective investigator is not interested in being treated like an Oriental Nabob. I am saying, however, that the manufacturer must be satisfied that he is completely welcome, that is, at the site, in the city, in the county, and in the state. He must feel that he is wanted by the working people, the business leaders, the townspeople as a whole, the local government, and the state administration. There is little the city can do at that point. Mere protestations of cooperation are in vain. The entire history of the area will convince the industrialist—not just an expression of 'complete cooperation' to come.

The administration of the community is important. The form of government, police and fire personnel and equipment, streets and highways, sewers and, of course, the taxes and budget set up to activate community services all have a bearing on the ultimate safety and protection of a new plant.

The average city employs 1.13 fire department employees (full-time) for every 1,000 residents but the index of insurance rates on a property are dependent upon the city's fire insurance classification. A community's classification is determined by the number of points of deficiency assessed because conditions are below certain established standards. Classifications range from 1 (best) to 10 (worst) and depends upon water supply, records of fire department, alarm system, police, structural conditions, etc. In 1950, 53 communities between 10,000 and 25,000 population were in class 9 or 10. Obviously, the plant safety position in these towns was low and insurance rates were abnormally high.

Cities with a high incidence of crime, abnormal losses from theft and attack against property, or high ratio of juvenile delinquency should be avoided. Police personnel may be inadequate or civic authorities may be lethargic in combating these influences.

Under pressure of state legislation, many small and medium sized communities are facing large expenditures for sewage disposal systems. The extent of the program is important to the industrialist as he will be required to contribute to its construction cost through increased taxes, sewage assessments, etc. Some rule-of-thumb estimate of the cost can be determined by calculating a disposal plant capacity of 100 gallons per day per capita and a cost range of $90,000-$150,000 per million gallons. The cost of sewer lines varies greatly depending upon the layout of the community, terrain and soil conditions and possible use of existing lines now dumping into streams.

As a yardstick for comparing communities, the following chart* is suggested:

ADMINISTRATION

1. Political party
2. Form of government
    a. Police
        1. Personnel
        2. Equipment
        3. Do industrial properties receive patrol service?
        4. Incidence of crime
    b. Fire
        1. Personnel
        2. Equipment
        3. Annual losses
        4. Insurance class
        5. Do existing plants have sprinkler tanks?
        6. Water pressure
    c. Streets and highways
        1. How cleaned
        2. Miles paved and unpaved
        3. Contemplated building program
    d. Sewers
    e. Garbage disposal
    f. Hospital facilities
        1. Number of doctors
        2. Number of beds
    g. Judiciary

* Standards of Industrial Analysis. Copyright 1950. Fantus Factory Locating Service.

3. Taxes
   a. Rate
      1. Real estate
      2. Personal property
   b. Assessments, per cent of value
   c. Rates for
      1. Township taxes
      2. Municipal taxes
      3. County taxes
      4. Park Board taxes
      5. School taxes
      6. Other taxes
   d. Poll tax
   e. Business license fees
   f. Exemptions
   g. Contemplated expansion of city facilities affecting tax rate

BUDGET

1. Income and expenditures

2. Indebtedness

Preliminary territorial analysis has already revealed that the general area in which the community is located has a superficial satisfactory labor background. Now, a more detailed study is necessary. Total supply of labor, local skills available, wage rates and characteristics of the labor supply should be ascertained. Seasonal fluctuations, labor turnover, degree of labor stability, worker productivity, training facilities are also elements to be appraised. Chapter 4 has outlined some of the techniques involved in developing this type of objective data.

Suggested labor work sheets* for a comparison of communities within a specific area follow:

LABOR

1. Total employment

2. Chart supply of suitable labor available

3. Chart supply of unskilled labor

---

* Standards of Industrial Analysis. Copyright 1950. Fantus Factory Locating Service.

4. Elements of labor unrest
    a. Labor organizations
    b. Radical groups
    c. Unemployed councils

5. Past history of labor disturbances
    a. History of:
        1. Strikes
        2. Threatened strikes
        3. Wage disputes
        4. Walk-outs
        5. Lockouts
    b. Determine number of employees directly and indirectly affected in each instance.

6. Prevailing wage scale for all classes of employment

7. Minimum, average, and maximum hour shifts

8. Labor turnover

9. Characteristics of labor
    a. Rural
    b. Urban
    c. Agricultural-lumber-mining-industrial
    d. Percent illiteracy
    e. Percent foreign born by nationalities

10. Sex and type
    a. Percent male gainfully employed
    b. Percent female gainfully employed

11. Efficiency of labor

12. Bonus systems
    a. Describe existing piece work and bonus systems

13. Seasonal variations
    a. If they occur, inquire as to cause and effect

14. Training facilities
    a. Apprenticeship courses
    b. Trade schools
    c. Foremen's courses

15. Housing
    a. Number of units available for lease and rentals
    b. Number of units available for sale and prices

New plant of Binney & Smith Co., Winfield, Kansas. Plant Location Study—FANTUS FACTORY LOCATING SERVICE.

TRANSPORTATION FACILITIES

The manufacturer considering decentralization from urban centers must re-orient his thinking. He has become accustomed to picking up his telephone and beckoning any and all types of transportation service to his plant. In heavily industrialized areas there is seldom a problem in receiving service; rather the only problem is choosing which of the many competitive carriers to use.

In less industrialized communities transportation facilities are usually less numerous, and it is preferable to locate in a community that is served by more than one major railroad in order to obtain the element of competition which insures good service.

A helpful guide to the service offered has been shown in an accompanying list. The emphasis will be different in each industry depending upon its particular transportation requirements. Accordingly, those sections involving carriers which handle the bulk of the shipments should be expanded while others can be minimized. The existence of reciprocal **switching** agreements within a community is of utmost importance. In this manner the carrier serving the plant can handle cars whether or not he actually participates in the line-haul from origin or to the destination. In the absence of such agreements, the industry will be assessed switching charges whenever cars are routed via other carriers serving the city and these may amount to $12.00 to $30.00 per car.

For those industries seeking to utilize transit or stop-off privileges for partial loading or unloading enroute, it is imperative that responsible carrier representatives be consulted to determine whether or not such privileges will be extended in the community.

For those industries using LCL services the existence of scheduled merchandise trains is of utmost importance. In this manner full cars for important key cities will be loaded directly from the local railroad station. Time-in-transit will be competitive with the most efficient trucking services between the community and these major cities.

The existence of arrangements for store-door pickup and delivery service is sometimes overlooked but is a vital factor for those companies utilizing LCL service. Recently the railroads have begun to assess charges for such service. In most instances, the cost will be less than if the industry were forced to use common carrier truck service between the railroad station and their plant. It is assumed that the freight rate relationship of the community has been charted in advance of field inspection. If this has not been done, it is imperative that the project be completed prior to site selection.

The number of motor trucking companies offering service in the city is important. However, of greater importance is the existence of direct single-line truck service to all major markets served by the plant. In a recent survey conducted by the Fantus Factory Locating Service the following ratio of direct single-line service was determined for competitive communities.

LOCATION	RATIO OF MARKET CITIES SERVED BY DIRECT SINGLE-LINE MOTOR TRUCK SERVICE
Present Location	81%
Cincinnati, Ohio	70%
York, Pa.	51%
Providence, R. I.	25%

Of course the market to be served and the product manufactured will have a bearing on the degree of direct service available. Hence, to a New England market, the order of these cities might be completely reversed.

The existence of motor truck facilities in the community will tend to reduce time in transit, inbound and outbound movements. Accordingly, those locations should be selected which are trucking "gateways", if there is much dependence on this type of service. Trucking gateways can be determined readily from various public routing guides. The normal definition is as follows: "A point at which carriers have pickup facilities including a telephone listed in their company name."

One major caution should be observed. There may be restrictions on the service offered by the carriers in terms of the minimum weight for which they will place a vehicle into the plant. Some carriers insist upon a truckload, many others have restrictions, such as 10,000 lbs. or 5,000 lbs. Those areas served by waterways have distinct competitive advantages. If the industry is of sufficient magnitude that it can utilize barge loads of inbound commodities, or even ship outbound products in this manner, the total annual freight bill can be substantially reduced. The presence of the waterway is another competitive factor in rate making. The industry should be able to negotiate lower rates because of this situation via all competing types of transportation service.

Those companies presently located near Atlantic port and Gulf port cities have become accustomed to shipping via the intercoastal and coastwise steamships with corresponding saving compared to overland routes. Removal of the plant facilities to inland communities requires a complete revaluation of the cost of serving markets which were normally reached by use of the lower-cost water service. For example, the differential in rail rates between Ohio plants and eastern seaboard cities is frequently insufficient to offset cost from present tide-water locations to West Coast points served via the intercoastal waterways.

Manufacturers are frequently disturbed to find an absence of freight forwarder service in less industrialized areas. This is a natural consequence of the insufficient volume of freight business in and out of the communities to sustain a carloading operation. In other instances, rates from major cities in the manufacturing belt to the smaller communities may be too low to provide sufficient margin between carload and less-than-carload rates to pay for the costs in assembling and distributing miscellaneous merchandise.

The absence of freight forwarder service is one of those disadvantages of removal to areas with less industrial population. It can be partially overcome by careful review of the company's distribution policy. Pool cars can be consigned to points normally served by forwarder service and the savings may be of such magnitude that the company will wonder why it has not resorted to such practices in the past. Similarly, local non-profit pooling associations can be joined which will reduce the total costs on distributing LCL freight.

The manufacturer should carefully investigate facilities for parcel post and railway express shipments as they will undoubtedly differ from the present location.

The existence of public warehouses can be of utmost importance. There are those inevitable periods in every manufacturing operation when inventories of raw materials or finished products exceed space availability in the plant. During such periods the manufacturer seeks "elbow room" in either public space or some short-term lease arrangement. In small communities the availability of lost space and unused antiquated industrial structures is limited compared to their availability for storage purposes in urban areas. Unless the manufacturer has local warehouses offering these facilities, he may find it necessary to build such emergency space into his plant at additional cost.

TRANSPORTATION FACILITIES*

1. Railroads
    a. Trunk lines
    b. Short lines and switching lines
    c. Volume of freight traffic
        1. CL
        2. LCL
    d. Reciprocal switching agreements and switching charges
    e. Transit privileges
    f. Facilities for handling LCL traffic
        1. Frequency of service
        2. Scheduled merchandise trains
        3. Trap car service—weight minimum
        4. Store-door pick-up delivery service
    g. Freight rates
        1. Inbound raw materials
        2. Outbound products
    h. Time in transit

2. Motor trucking
    a. Over-the-road companies serving city
        1. Frequency of service
        2. Terminal facilities
    b. Local drayage companies and pool-car distributors
    c. Motor freight rates
        1. Inbound raw materials
        2. Outbound products
            (a) TL—minimum weight
            (b) LTL—weight breakdown
    d. Time in transit

* Standards of Industrial Analysis. Copyright 1950. Fantus Factory Locating Service.

3. Waterways
    a. River (or lake) transportation
        1. Description of system
        2. Frequency of service
        3. Water freight rates
            (a) Inbound raw materials
            (b) Outbound products
        4. Time in transit
        5. Incidental costs
    b. Intercoastal and coastwise transportation
        1. Description of system
        2. Frequency of service
        3. Water freight rates
            (a) Inbound raw materials
            (b) Outbound products
         4. Time in transit
        5. Incidental costs

4. Other traffic information
    a. Freight forwarder service
    b. Air service
        1. Air cargo and forwarder service
        2. Passenger service
    c. Parcel Post (including Air Parcel Post)
    d. Railway Express (including Air Express)
    e. Public warehouses
    f. Electric railways
    g. Local bus service

EDUCATIONAL, RECREATIONAL AND CIVIC DATA

Enrollment in schools, quality of newspapers, hotel facilities, cultural and recreational advantages all play a part in attracting and holding personnel in a new location, especially when the demand for certain skills far outstrips the supply. The following table* will serve as a chart for community comparison:

*Standards of Industrial Analysis. Copyright 1950. Fantus Factory Locating Service.

1. Schools (with enrollment)
    a. Primary
    b. High Schools
    c. Junior College
    d. Universities
    e. Parochial
    f. Facilities for occupational training

2. Churches

3. Fraternal organizations

4. Libraries

5. Parks

6. Playgrounds

7. Motion picture theatres

8. Facilities for recreation:
    a. Golf
    b. Swimming
    c. Tennis
    d. Fishing
    e. Hunting
    f. Boating

9. Newspapers
    a. Weekly
    b. Daily
    c. Circulation

10. Special agencies

11. Hotels

12. Hospitals

13. Public buildings

POPULATION, COST OF LIVING, CLIMATE

Population statistics and expenditure standards are excellent indices of growth and stability of the area under consideration. Data on climate is easily secured and may be important in certain processes.

The following schedule* lists the most important factors to consider:

POPULATION STATISTICS

1. Growth
2. Corporate limits
3. Suburban
4. Labor drawing area
5. Brief historical sketch

CLIMATE

1. General weather conditions, elevation, etc.
2. Temperature
    a. Annual average
    b. Seasonal average
    c. Maximum temperature
    d. Minimum temperature
3. Precipitation
    a. Average (annual) rainfall
    b. Average (annual) snowfall
4. Humidity
    a. Average relative humidity
5. Days with sunshine, rain, fog, etc.

COST OF LIVING (per capita)

1. Rent
2. Food
3. Clothing
4. Other necessities
5. Luxuries
6. Department and merchandise store expenditure
7. Residential rates
    a. Power
    b. Gas
    c. Water

---

*Standards of Industrial Analysis. Copyright 1950. Fantus Factory Locating Service.

COMPARISON CHART

BASIC FACTORS	PRESENT LOCATION	CITY A	CITY B	CITY C	CITY D	CITY E	CITY F
TOTAL TRANSPORTATION COSTS							
Inbound materials							
Outbound products							
Total	$						
LABOR							
Direct production							
Non-productive							
Total	$						
PLANT OVERHEAD							
Rent or carrying costs, excluding taxes							
Additional costs due to inefficient layout, lack of siding, etc.							
Real estate taxes							
Personal property taxes, etc.							
Fuel for heating purposes only							
Total	$						
UTILITIES							
Power							
Gas							
Water							
Total	$						
STATE FACTORS							
State taxes							
Workmen's Compensation							
Insurance							
Total	$						
MISCELLANEOUS							
Other cost factors inherent or peculiar to your present location(s)							
Total	$						
GRAND TOTAL	$						

8. Transportation
   a. Street car fares
   b. Bus fares
   c. Bridge tolls

FINAL SELECTION OF THE COMMUNITY

A proper summation of all the cost factors will provide a dollar and cents analysis of the present industrial location and theoretical costs at projected other points of operation. The accompanying "Comparison Chart" will serve as a guide in comparing the *recurring* annual totals existing in each community.

This chart does not take into account the non-recurring costs of site acquisition, building costs, etc. Neither does it consider the many intangible factors that deserve great weight and attention, i.e., community attitudes, labor productivity, background of labor stability, general surroundings for executives, etc.

Occasionally, superior "intangibles" together with outstanding community or state cooperation, in the form of bond issuance for new plant construction, tax consideration and financial aid in the building of access roads, installation of water mains, sewers and railroad siding as well as free sites, may actually motivate the selection of a location having a less favorable dollar and cents advantage. Since every case is different, it will be up to the manufacturer to evaluate correctly all interrelated factors and reach a sound conclusion.

The method is illustrated by the following actual calculations for a fabricated metal products plant, covering three cost elements as they affected production costs in three communities compared with present location:

LOCATION	COST OF MAJOR ITEMS			TOTAL	SAVINGS PER $100 OF OUTPUT
	LABOR	STEEL	FUEL		
Present	$30.92	$22.26	$11.71	$64.89	$ —
A	29.26	21.41	13.34	64.01	.88
B	28.79	21.20	12.86	62.85	2.04
C	23.60	21.20	9.60	54.40	10.49

CHAPTER 10

Selecting the Site

It is the opinion of the author that more mistakes are made because of the temptation of a fine site or attractive building than any other single phase of plant location engineering. An investigation of the specific site is recommended only *after* a community has been chosen that combines the most favorable economic features. Rarely is it necessary to reject a community because of the lack of sites—especially with the definite trend toward peripheral rather than central city operations.

Contrary to general procedure, the first and most important consideration in orienting the proposed plant in the community is the labor pool that is to be employed. Whether the new production facilities are to be near the central district of the city, or in one direction or another of the city, will depend upon a number of labor-related factors.

Female employees and unskilled male workers usually depend upon local transit systems to reach their place of employment. Where the majority of workers fall into these classifications, the site should be oriented to local bus routes. The amount of the fare, relationship of the site to fare zone boundaries, and the availability of free transfers will affect recruitment. While transit authorities are often willing to extend routes to serve a plant offering new riders, careful investigation of the system may reveal "blind spots" requiring excess transit time and extra fares between the majority of worker residences and the plant site. Female labor will be easier to obtain if the plant location offers opportunities for noon-hour shopping.

The automobile and improved rural roads have made the mill village obsolete. Experience indicates that the maximum commuting distance by automobile is 30 miles each way under average driving conditions provided wage levels offered are average for the area. Poor roads, natural geographic obstacles, or inadequate wages reduce the labor-drawing radius.

From the site selection viewpoint, orientation to the highway network is a paramount consideration where employees are expected to commute by automobile. If the majority of workers must drive through busy, congested areas to reach the plant, recruiting may be affected. If access to the site is via residential streets, public opposition can be expected. Some industrial psychologists believe that commutation each day through the better residential areas tends to lower worker morale.

Another factor commonly overlooked is the influence of neighboring industries—wage rates, radical tendencies, working hours, shift schedules, and even fringe benefit patterns of manufacturing plants in the immediate neighborhood may have as much effect on the future of the proposed plant as your own carefully worked out personnel policies.

When the most strategic location area has been determined based upon studies of local labor conditions, examination of specific plant sites may be begun.

A list of general specifications should be prepared as follows:

1. Description of building to be constructed (including sketch).
2. Size of plot.
3. Necessary railroad, highway and waterway facilities.
4. Minimum size of water mains, gas line and power line.
5. Volume of ground water to be utilized.
6. Sewage and effluent disposal requirements.
7. Safety area for offensive odors, noise, smoke, etc.
8. Provisions for sprinkler pressure (gravity tank or local water mains).

Preliminary sketches of the proposed plant (including anticipated future additions) should be made. In this manner the basic shape of the site can be determined as well as its orientation to highways and railroads. The plan must be a flexible one, adaptable to the non-utopian conditions which will be found in the field. The need for flexibility was pointed up recently when the Fantus Factory Locating Service was engaged by a nationally known glass company to find a suitable site in a community after previous attempts by the manufacturer had failed. Several excellent tracts were made available by simply *reversing* the original building plan thereby reorienting it to existing rail lines. The final plan resulted in less wasted space for rail siding construction, reduced site preparation costs and lowered landscaping allocations.

Generally a site of not less than five times the actual size of the plant is considered minimum to allow for siding, loading platforms, truck ingress and egress, parking facilities, storage area and for future expansion. If possible, open land should be available on two or more sides to allow for future site expansion.

Unfortunately, too many manufacturers tend to tighten their purse strings at this point. Examples abound of sites which were outgrown by manufacturing plants because future expansion requirements were underestimated. The price of land is normally a very small percentage of final construction costs. Why limit the future of a good location by restricting it to an inadequate site?

In most communities the local Chamber of Commerce, railroad industrial agent, power company representative, or a good industrial realtor will be familiar with sites meeting the general specifications. However, it is unnecessary to rely solely on local sources for this information. Likely site areas can be readily selected by consulting county land maps, topographic quadrangles, aerial photographs, or even street maps.

Alexander Smith, Inc., Greenville Mills operating division, Greenville, Mississippi. Plant Location Study—FANTUS FACTORY LOCATING SERVICE.

From a topographical map (showing configuration of the land surface) it is possible to determine not only the relationship of highway and railroad but also the terrain conditions in the area. One can almost select possible site areas from his desk. At least the amount of time spent in the field can be substantially reduced by eliminating from consideration those sectors which lie in swampland or rough terrain.

The U. S. Geological Survey has been making a systematic survey of surface features of the nation since 1882. Maps covering individual quadrangles have been published for nearly 80% of the country, identified by the name of a city or prominent natural feature in the area. Copies can be obtained at low cost.

Unfortunately the scale and contour interval used on the maps is not equal in all sectors. This sometimes makes it difficult to interpret adjacent quadrangles.

The maps show three classes of information:

1. Water features, such as oceans, lakes, rivers, canals and swamps. (These are printed in blue.)
2. The works of man, such as roads, dams, buildings, railroads, etc. (These are printed in black.)
3. The configuration and elevation of the land. (These are printed in brown.)

One of the most amazing manifestations of economic suicide is the seeming persistence on the part of some manufacturers to ignore nature and locate plants in known flood areas. The high seasonal volume of rain, the melting of large quantities of snow, and the backing up of water in river channels due to ice jams have caused frequent floods along major rivers. Of even more danger are the flash floods which occur without warning on tributary streams, annually taking their toll in industrial stoppages and damage to equipment.

Topographic maps will reveal important information on drainage conditions in the vicinity of sites. From a study of land gradient and drainage basins of creeks, the experienced engineer can predict the absence or presence of flood danger at specified points.

On the accompanying contour map, note area A. No evidence of water was available upon inspection of the site, but the swamp symbol on the contour map indicated need for caution. A subsequent interview with a local farmer confirmed that flood water had been "higher than tractor wheels" the previous Spring.

Conversely, site B has never been affected by high water despite its proximity to the river. Careful check revealed that much of the surrounding territory had been flooded in 1903, including the area occupied by the large plant which appears on the map southwest of site B.

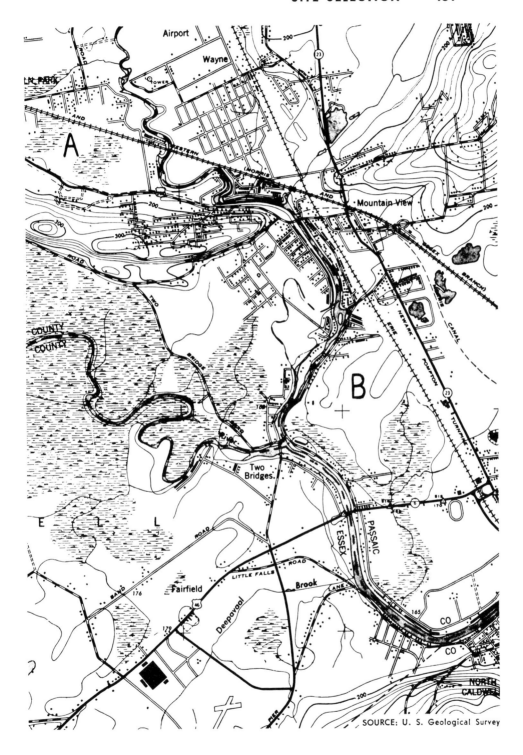

SOURCE: U. S. Geological Survey

PUBLISHED TOPOGRAPHIC MAPS

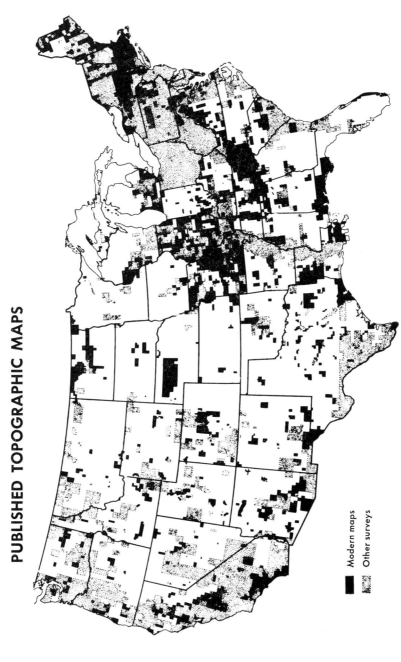

■ Modern maps

▨ Other surveys

This small map is intended to give a general picture of the areas covered by published topographic maps of the U. S. Geological Survey and other government agencies. Some additional areas have been covered by old reconnaissance surveys which are now considered inadequate. Larger size status maps of the United States covering topographic mapping, aerial photog-

raphy, aerial mosaics, vertical control, and horizontal control may be obtained on application to the U. S. Geological Survey, Washington 25, D. C. State index circulars showing the details of map coverage and the names of map sheets printed for distribution, are also available without charge.

Aerial photographs are now being made of the entire country by various governmental agencies. Some data soon will be available on areas which have not as yet been mapped topographically. From these photos it will be possible to correct those man-made features which have occurred since the original topographic surveys were prepared. The major disadvantage of an aerial photograph is that it does not allow the reading of contours for, like a one-eyed man, the camera does not possess stereoscopic vision.

Determination of the character of the ground for building and equipment foundations during *initial* inspections can save considerable expense for the occurrence of rock and soft underlying formations may necessitate a change of location in the interest of building economy. A helpful hint can be obtained from the local agricultural agent or from the state geologist's office.

Safe bearing values of foundation soils are set forth in the following chart:

MATERIAL	TONS PER SQ. FT.
Granite rock	30
Limestone, compact beds	25
Sandstone, compact beds	20
Shale formation or soft friable rock	8-10
Gravel and sand, compact	6-10
Gravel, dry and coarse, packed and confined	6
Gravel and sand, mixed with dry clay	4-6
Sand, compact, well cemented and confined	4
Earth, solid, dry and in natural beds	4
Clay, very dry and in thick beds	3
Sand, clean and dry, in natural beds and confined	2
Clay, soft	1-1½
Quicksand, alluvial soils, etc.	1

Where heavy vibrating machinery is to be utilized (such as steam hammers, shears, grinding equipment), the foundations must receive some allowance for possible compression and rearrangement of soil resulting from transmitted vibrations.

Inexpensive test pits (or shallow holes) are often sufficient to determine the thickness of strata, moisture conditions and compactness of the earth and should be dug to the estimated level of footings. If any question arises as to the load-bearing capacity of the soil, wash and core borings should be taken. This precaution is particularly emphasized in those areas of the site which will underly heavy machinery.

Before the foundation of the plant is laid, basic engineering data will have to be accumulated including:

(a) Geology of the area
(b) Resistance of rocks
(c) Possibility of slips
(d) Danger of rock disintegration
(e) Frost depth
(f) Water table level

While piling can overcome low bearing values and rock out-croppings can be blasted, bad foundation conditions may require abandonment of even the most desirable operating locations. Hence, alternate sites should always be considered as insurance against this possibility.

The recent experience of a nationally known company will be of interest. Company officials inspected an excellent site of 100 acres adjacent to highway and railroad, bordering on a stream which provided the necessary minimum flow to carry off a bothersome effluent. Negotiations on land acquisition failed, although the executives had not anticipated this difficulty. It was decided to acquire an adjacent tract, securing the necessary easements for an extensive railroad siding. When test borings were made the second site was found to be unsatisfactory. Executives, still enamoured of the location, then purchased another site in the immediate vicinity. But now the necessary rail siding was a half mile in length and had to bridge the stream at an estimated cost of $75,000. Access roads had to be constructed. Several excellent farm buildings had to be removed before construction could begin. While alternate sites were available in other sectors of the community, they were ignored in the attempt to "save face." The embarrassment over sites may have influenced a later decision not to utilize the community at all.

Since almost every sizable operation requires the use of rail facilities, the markets to be served and the quality of rail service will have great bearing on the ultimate site selected.

Ordinarily, the selected site should be on the route of a carrier *directly* connecting it with as many major markets and as many sources of raw materials as possible. In Chapter II the various major routes of the railroads were examined. If a plant offers traffic to the carriers contra the natural traffic flow pattern, it will experience poor service, terminal delays, rate and routing restrictions, extra switching charges, etc. A basic test of the location is the question: *How much of a line-haul will the carrier who serves the site get from the traffic the plant will offer?* If the carrier must immediately switch most of the outgoing cars to other lines, or cannot handle a substantial portion of the inbound tonnage via its line, then the site selection is incorrect. (Switching or belt railways who derive all revenues from switching service are an exception to this test.)

The qualitative aspect of transportation service is frequently overlooked in the selection of plant sites. Yet speed is an element in total production costs particularly affecting *working capital*. If markets can be reached quickly, expenditures for warehousing are minimized and the risks of price declines on inventory are lessened. Dependable service on inbound materials allows closer scheduling of purchased supplies and reduces capital outlay for stockpiling.

In general, service on the main line of a railroad is superior to that rendered on a branch line. The main line usually has more frequent and dependable switching service, and the carrier can meet emergency demands more easily. However, at any location consideration must be given to the number of "drills" or switchings per day, the schedules of time freight trains, yard limits, etc. Even the direction of the turnout from the private siding can affect service to the site.

Both the major railroads and the smaller connecting lines present valid arguments concerning their respective locational merits. The manufacturer considering the smaller lines, however, must investigate the ability of the connecting railroad to handle the expanded tonnage he will offer. Too, particularly in rural areas, the large railroads sometimes discriminate against the smaller roads by withholding empty box cars during harvest season car shortages.

The site investigation must include a study of the station territory to which the site is assigned. The trend toward plants in peripheral areas has intensified the possibility of site selection in station territories beyond the desired rate grouping boundary and beyond the reciprocal switching limits. The shift of a few hundred yards up or down the railroad line sometimes can prevent a rate penalty to key markets which could persist for the entire life of the plant!

Orientation of the site to the roadbed of the rail line affects plant layout. Under normal conditions it is preferable that the rail line should form the rear boundary of the site, or one side. It should be at the same elevation as the majority of the site area. The maximum gradient allowable for operation of modern railroad equipment is 2%, i.e., two feet increase or decrease in elevation per one hundred feet of rail line. The minimum radius of the siding curve is 475 feet or approximately 12°.

Even where a rail siding is not anticipated, it is wise to select a site where a side track can be constructed if desired. This is a "hedge" against the future: (1) when motor trucking rates may increase disproportionately over rail rates and (2) to increase the resale value of the plant.

If the plant anticipates extensive use of LCL or carloading services, the site must be within the pick-up and delivery range of the local station. Sites beyond the normal service radius may require the payment of penalty freight forwarder rates, and the maintenance of a company truck to handle LCL shipments from plant to station.

The desirability of highway locations has been increasing due to expanded use of private automobiles by plant workers. Some companies also consider highway locations to possess immeasurable advertising value, particularly when the plant is modern and well landscaped. A relatively obscure chemical manufacturer reports a two-fold beneficial effect by his recent location on a major highway. (1) He finds that the prestige of his company has been increased among the general public as thousands pass his attractive plant each day. (2) Recruiting has been eased because employees become identified with a plant that "everyone knows."

One major danger in the selection of plant sites is the common disregard of existing motor truck franchises. It is assumed that location on or near a highway insures service from the trucklines utilizing that highway. Such a conclusion is false and may be extremely costly.

Neglect to investigate existing authority prior to site selection may require the industry to use only those local trucking firms with present authority to serve the *specific* community in which the site is selected. Under such circumstances all inbound and outbound shipments may have to be transferred enroute with subsequent rate penalties, and the desired over-the-road carriers would continue to "ride by" within sight of the plant.

That site should be selected which can prove the maximum number of *direct* single-line truck routes to major markets if truck service is utilized entensively. Investigation should include the relative orientation of the site to carrier terminals.

Where consideration is being given to existing structures, special attention must be given to the problem of handling motor truck traffic. Most older plants have inadequate off-street truck docking space and insufficient room to allow modern semi-trailer trucks to maneuver.

If the plant utilizes an appreciable amount of water transportation, careful attention must be directed to the following considerations:

(a) Proximity to piers
(b) Lighterage limits
(c) Switching limits
(d) I. C. C. exempt zones
(e) Transit privileges

In off-highway site locations, it is imperative to determine the extent of cooperation which will be extended by state, county and local governments in the improvement of roads. If streams are crossed by existing access roads, the load limits and clearances on bridges and culverts may prove insufficient to allow modern trailer-trucks to serve the site.

Waste disposal, power, water and gas were discussed in detail in Chapter 6. Their adequacy, reliability and cost will, of course, play a large role in the final selection of the site. If large quantities of water are required for process, orientation to the supply will be a paramount consideration. The underlying aquifers will dictate the amount of ground water which may be available and the spacing of wells. If surface water is to be utilized, it will be important to calculate the pumping head of the site above the river or stream. The possibility of impounding supplies must be investigated both from a topographical and legal viewpoint.

Barring unusually heavy loads, the local power company will normally extend or improve lines to the site without cost to the industry. City water mains, sewerage lines and gas mains are less flexible and their extension may require considerable contribution on the part of the new industry.

It is important for those industries releasing extensive effluent to investigate the local sewage disposal plant to determine whether or not the type of installations is adequate to neutralize the wastes which the plant will release. If streams are to be used for disposal, it is imperative that the industry clear its proposed waste releases with state authorities, perhaps even interstate commissions. Any waste which increases the biological oxygen demand in the stream is certain to meet opposition from state wildlife and game authorities. Discoloration will anger downstream residents.

Climatic conditions may influence the location of the site selection for industries which release offensive odors or smoke impurities. The prevailing direction of the wind is a particularly important consideration in such cases. Those plants which operate noisy equipment must consider their relation to residences, particularly if the operation continues throughout the night.

In an era of uncertainty, it is advisable to minimize the danger of atomic bomb attack by choosing a site at least three miles from a vital target, especially if the community has a population of over 50,000 and harbors vital war industries. Bridges, airports, railroad marshalling yards, or military installations of any kind are to be avoided.

It is in the matter of negotiations for land purchase that many companies waste funds. If land is to be obtained at minimum cost, it is almost essential that some local resident be taken into the company's confidence and for that agent to assemble the tract as if he wished it for his own purposes. This is particularly important in rural areas where the company may be unfamiliar with land values. If it becomes rumored that an industrial plant is to be constructed on a site, the price may be inflated beyond all reason.

Initial investigation with the local land office can determine whether or not the property is under a single or multiple ownership. It is preferable to deal only with one or two individuals in assembling a tract. Experience indicates extensive difficulties in acquiring acreage where many owners are involved.

The following check list should be used in final evaluation of the site:

(a) Will local building code and zoning regulations allow the construction of the type of building proposed?

(b) Are there area restrictive covenants, easements, or other legal entanglements that will interfere with maximum use of the property?

(c) Who will remove snow, where necessary, and maintain access roads?

(d) Can definite long-term commitments be received on the valuation of a proposed plant for tax purposes?

(e) Even though it may be outside city limits, will the plant receive full police and fire protection?

HINTS ON NEW PLANT CONSTRUCTION

The enlightened manufacturer will build his plant *around the manufacturing process* in order to insure smooth functioning. Today, the type of building to be constructed is determined *after* the floor plan has been developed and not before.

The flow of work, the problems of material handling, floor loads required, possible segregation of objectionable processes and many other factors will determine the layout of the plant and whether buildings are to be isolated, single floor, or multiple story construction.

When the floor plan calls for a one-story plant, certain advantages can be expected as a matter of course:

1. Installation of foundations and heavy floor loads are more feasible.

2. Wide bays and elimination of obstructing columns are obtainable.

3. Straight flow production and assembly lines are possible.

4. Elimination of elevators saves many formerly wasted man-hours.

5. Elimination of stairwells, elevators, additional lavatories, etc. saves formerly wasted space.

6. Departments can be readily contracted or expanded, and additions to the building can be more easily planned or executed.

Multiple story plants are recommended when:

1. Gravity-flow is required for the industrial process.
2. "Nuisance" phases for the operation should be isolated, i.e., fumes, noise, etc.
3. The cost of land is prohibitive.

The type of material selected for the plant will vary with climatic conditions, load bearing characteristics of the soil, building codes, construction costs, ceiling clearance and spans required, durability and general exterior appearance, and a host of other factors.

Corrugated metal siding, for example, is inexpensive but is a poor insulating wall for the average manufacturing plant. It is nevertheless often utilized for warehouses and other buildings where heat loss in the winter or radiation in the summer is not important. Transite siding, a lightweight covering with considerably more insulating value than metallic sheets, might be an alternative.

Each of the basic building materials, brick, steel, concrete, wood, possesses their own characteristics and their use in a specific construction problem will, of course, depend greatly on the type of building required and the product manufactured therein.

Steel has great strength in comparison to its weight, can be shop-fabricated and is well adapted for use in buildings requiring heavy loads, high ceiling clearance and wide spans.

Reinforced concrete is relatively strong, resists fire and assures a long building life when good material is used. It is used to greatest advantage in single story structures and in buildings where strength and mass are desired.

Cinder and concrete blocks, as well as brick, are used as bearing walls in single story plants and are entirely acceptable for many manufacturing operations.

CHAPTER 11

Hints for Industrial Development Groups

An amazing paradox exists in the field of industrial development. Manufacturers are eager to receive data and communities are desperately anxious to present it, yet, *parallel as their interests may be,* conflicts and misunderstandings seem to continually arise. Since the attraction of new industry has become the primary objective of most Chambers of Commerce, and since millions of dollars are expended annually in advertising by all types of industrial development groups, it is the aim of this chapter to help channel these activities as productively as possible.

Securing a new industry is not an easy task. Competition among states and cities is keen. Throughout the United States there are thousands of communities that have some form of organized industrial development program. Almost every state government has an agency devoted to the promotion of industrial development. State universities engage in formalized economic development programs.

Most Class I railroads have industrial departments concerned with securing new industries along their lines. Many public utilities, particularly electric power companies, engage in long term promotional programs to generate economic activity in their respective territories.

THE DEVELOPMENT AND PROMOTION PROGRAM

Any community or area program must have a clear-cut objective if it is to be successful. This is especially true of the industrial development program where the cost and effort involved normally exceeds other types of activity sponsored by these groups.

The program must be geared to the *potential* of the community or area which undertakes it. Obviously it would be foolish for a small or medium sized population group to engage in a program of the magnitude of the Territorial Information Department of the Commonwealth Edison Company of Chicago, or the Industrial Development Board of Kentucky, or the Pennsylvania Railroad. These latter agencies employ a staff of well paid engineers and men trained in the field. Large sums made available through giant corporations or state governments are expended on research and the preparation and printing of elaborate material.

Most communities or groups of communities have neither the resources nor the potential to justify an elaborate industrial development program. However, it would be economic folly for these communities to pass up opportunities resulting from the huge industrial expansion and decentralization under way in the United States. For these communities it would be wise to follow a middle-of-the-road approach, avoiding extravagant waste through fruitless advertising, but preparing themselves to intelligently handle industrial prospects resulting from selective promotional work.

THE VOLUNTEER COMMITTEE

The first major step is the establishment of a Volunteer Committee to lead the program. Responsible leadership is essential to the success of the industrial development program. Such leadership must be of a stature to invoke complete cooperation of the entire community.

It is not usually necessary in this minimum program to incur the expense involved in hiring full-time personnel. The work can be divided among several willing and capable individuals. The most important assignment is that of the committee chairman, a role reserved for a person willing to spare no effort in his work and also able to command the attention of both the community and the industrial prospects.

One of his prime functions is to make the initial contact with industrial prospects, intelligently provide the answers to the infinite number of questions such prospects will ask, arrange for visits to the community, inspections of sites and meetings with local manufacturers and act as spokesman for the community in any negotiations which may arise.

The actual number of committee members is not nearly as important as the knowledge and ability of the members chosen. Each member should be the best informed individual in this field, who is locally available. He should be willing to offer information based upon his experience and must cheerfully investigate problems for which he may not have an immediate answer. Each member will be accountable for the accuracy and timeliness of those sections of the committee work which falls within his sphere.

Admiral Television Corporation, West Chicago, Illinois. Plant Location Study—FANTUS FACTORY LOCATING SERVICE.

The selection of the proper committeeman is all-important. Sometimes the not-so-obvious choice may be the proper one. For example, the local office manager of the State Employment Service (Employment Security Division) is an excellent source of information on labor availability. However, the better committeeman, from a promotional viewpoint, would be a personnel manager from a local plant. His presence on the committee is reassuring to the industrial prospect who may have some concern as to the welcome he will receive from other manufacturers in the area.

A well informed realtor or builder should be a member of the committee. It is essential that he be willing to place community interest before profit.

A city official or attorney, who is familiar with aspects of local tax and assessment policies, should be a committee member. He should be a student of both local and state taxes and must be prepared to estimate taxes as they apply to the given fiscal condition of the prospect.

It is important that the committee membership contain a representative of transportation agencies. This committeeman must remember that he is working for his city or area in this respect and must not attempt to minimize services rendered by competitors.

A representative of the local bank, preferably an officer, will be a helpful member of the committee. Normally, the banking groups are very active in such programs and it may be necessary to set up a sub-committee made up of representatives of all the banks to avoid offending local interests.

One committee member must be qualified to speak on utilities and fuels. While a representative of the local utility company is the most logical choice for this position, he must be willing to discuss competitive energy sources.

Public relations

As a preliminary, it is vital that all local interests be made aware of the importance of new payrolls and their ultimate effect on the growth and prosperity of the community. The industrial payroll is one of the few forms in which *new money*, as contrasted to re-circulated currency, can be provided in the base economy of the area. While not as dramatic, a new plant payroll can be as much an economic boon as the local discovery of oil! Community leaders, particularly employers, must be made to realize that diversified industry is essential to healthy growth, and that labor tends to migrate from an area where employment opportunities are static.

Once all civic and private interests are convinced through an intelligent public relations campaign that industrial expansion is vital and desirable, the community is ready to launch into a sound industrial development program.

Physical appearance

The second step of the program involves the physical appearance of the community. The first impression that a manufacturer receives is at the airport, railroad station or incoming highway. Cleanliness and courtesy at public terminals and lack of traffic congestion on important arteries will provide an immediate favorable impression. Good hotel facilities, well-paved streets, well-maintained homes, the absence of slums, modern public buildings (yes, even the Chamber of Commerce office!) will create a receptive attitude in the mind of the prospect who visits a city for the first time.

Many an executive has arbitrarily eliminated a location from further consideration when the area has a down-at-the-heels look, reflecting lack of community interest and pride. This is particularly true when the concern contemplates transplanting its executive family and entire plant to a new location. In one case, a manufacturer rejected a community in Pennsylvania because the city streets had not been cleaned of a heavy snowfall that had stopped 48 hours before. In an Ohio town, a prospect arriving by automobile at night was dismayed at the abysmal lack of street lighting, a condition often leading to automobile accidents, crime and juvenile delinquency.

It is well to remember that further investigation into purely physical aspects of the city will surely include at least an outward inspection of school plant, parks and playgrounds, hospitals, club and recreational facilities, etc. Such manifestations of community well being are not improved overnight, but it is truly astonishing what can be accomplished if the community at large is enthused over industrial development and will cooperate in a general paint and clean up program.

Self-evaluation

In Chapter 1 of this book, the manufacturer was advised to "cast out personal predilections and honestly determine what makes his company 'tick'. *Critical self-evaluation is essential.*" Simply substitute the word "community" for "company" and the suggestion still holds good. Following are a series of indices that may assist you in measuring your own assets and liabilities—you may find it necessary to liquidate some of your liabilities and improve your balance sheet before you are even in a position to discuss new industry!

1. Are you treating your present manufacturers fairly? This question has nothing whatever to do with altruism—most prospective industries will eventually talk to presently located concerns anyway—and it is suggested that civic interest make certain they are satisfied—if not, a remedial program should be instituted without delay.

2. How many companies have moved out? Why? Are there reasons that can be corrected?

3. Is your city in good financial condition? Is your per capita net debt out of line? Do you supply a full measure of community service for the tax dollar you assess?

4. Are your law enforcement and public safety agencies functioning properly? Or is there graft and laxity in public office?

5. Do you have sensible industrial restrictions against waste disposal, fumes, etc.? Or are existing regulations antiquated nuisance laws that are certain to repel industry?

6. Have your zoning ordinances and building codes been modernized? Or are they geared to a horse and buggy era?

The above list is intended solely as a thought prober, since it would be impossible to cover all of the many situations that exist throughout every region, in the short space allotted. Critical self-analysis and improvement are important, however, before the community is ready for its industrial campaign.

Community data book

All truly significant community data should be collected in loose leaf form. In this manner information which may become obsolete over a few months time can be kept up-to-date.

Reading of Chapters 4 and 5 of this book will give the community repre-

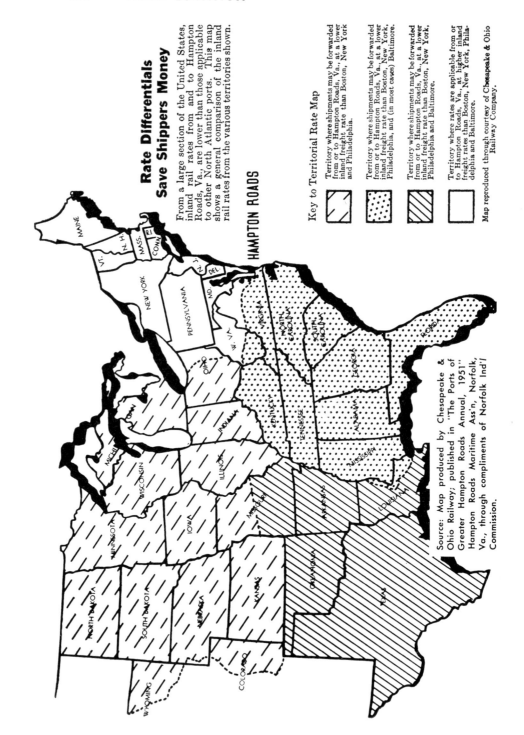

Rate Differentials Save Shippers Money

From a large section of the United States, inland rail rates from and to Hampton Roads, Va., are lower than those applicable to other North Atlantic ports. This map shows a general comparison of the inland rail rates from the various territories shown.

HAMPTON ROADS

Key to Territorial Rate Map

Territory where shipments may be forwarded from or to Hampton Roads, Va., at a lower inland freight rate than Boston, New York and Philadelphia.

Territory where shipments may be forwarded from or to Hampton Roads, Va., at a lower inland freight rate than Boston, New York, Philadelphia, and (in most cases) Baltimore.

Territory where shipments may be forwarded from or to Hampton Roads, Va., at a lower inland freight rate than Boston, New York, Philadelphia and Baltimore.

Territory where rates are applicable from or to Hampton Roads, Va., at higher inland freight rates than Boston, New York, Philadelphia and Baltimore.

Map reproduced through courtesy of Chesapeake & Ohio Railway Company.

Source: Map produced by Chesapeake & Ohio Railway; published in "The Ports of Greater Hampton Roads Annual, 1951" Hampton Roads Maritime Ass'n, Norfolk, Va., through compliments of Norfolk Ind'l Commission.

sentatives an insight into what industrial management requires in the form of labor data. The manufacturer seeks a stable productive labor nucleus of sufficient size to staff the proposed plant at satisfactory wage levels.

It is important, therefore, to develop complete background information showing characteristics of population, growth, present employment, seasonal characteristics, extent of unemployment. As an outgrowth of this data, the need for additional employers of male or female labor will be manifested. Too many towns "scatter their shots" in seeking new industry when in reality they should be concentrating only on those which will absorb their specific labor surplus.

The labor member of the industrial development committee must keep this data current, familiarizing himself with the labor rates prevailing for specific job classifications in all plants in the city, the names of local union organizers present, the total number of male and female employees, extension plans, if any, recruiting practices, fringe benefits, and all other labor matters as they apply to *all* of the city's plants. If it is not readily available, an education program may be necessary in order to bring out the data.

The community analysis must contain exhaustive information on tax rates, methods of assessment and the actual assessment of the city's various factory buildings. It should treat state taxes as well as local taxes.

The utility and fuel section must contain estimates of the cost of extending lines to various sites, the type of service which can be rendered, etc. Information on the location of water lines, sewer lines, depths, pressures, analysis and capacities of all utility systems should be gathered along with current rates and charges. The fuel section should include F. O. B. prices and freight costs to sites.

The transportation section should contain schedules of all railroads, bus lines, airlines, and major truck lines serving the community. The distance and elapsed travel time between the community and major national market centers is equally pertinent information. This is especially true with respect to delivery schedules on express and freight shipments from the city to such major markets as St. Louis, Chicago, Cincinnati, New York, Detroit, New Orleans, Dallas and Los Angeles. Those manufacturers utilizing less-than-carload lots will want to know of local availability and transit time of "package car" and "trap car" services. If more than one railroad serves the community, prospective shippers will want to know if the railroads have reciprocal switching agreements, or what switching charges may be in effect. A helpful addition to the traffic file will be the first-class rail exception rates and Docket 28300 rates to major consuming points.

The basic data book should contain information on sites, the financing of plant construction, the availability of loans for working capital and other pertinent financial information.

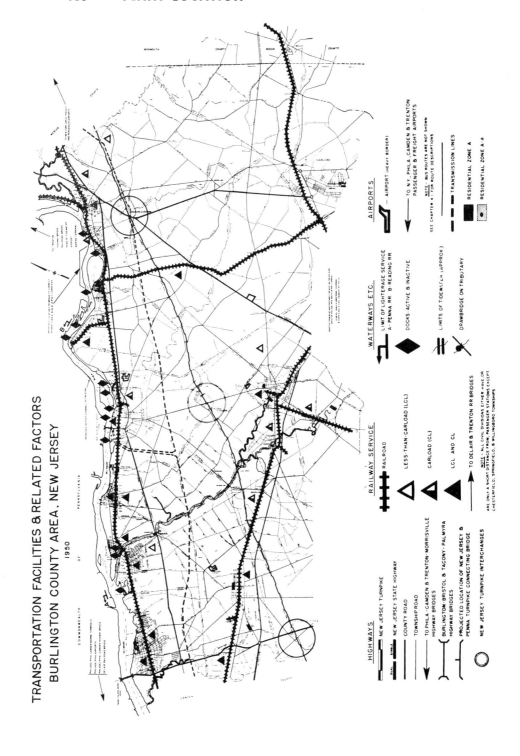

TRANSPORTATION FACILITIES & RELATED FACTORS
BURLINGTON COUNTY AREA, NEW JERSEY
1950

It may be a formidable job to analyze all sites in an area, but it is certainly advisable to have a working knowledge of at least the major *types* of sites in various key sizes. Several prominent highway locations, acreage with rail siding, a site with surface water supply and disposal facilities if available, and even sites in several peripheral areas or satellite communities should be charted. Site inspection should be made as simple as possible for the prospect since waste motion leads to impatience on the part of the manufacturer.

Local civic agencies should be in a position to provide at least the major part of the following background data on all sites:

1. Topography, land bearing characteristics, utilities, rail siding, etc.
2. Employee accessibility and transportation.
3. The labor force in the immediate neighborhood.
4. Tax rates, average assessment, type of community service (fire protection, water pressure, etc.)
5. Flood hazards or other *adverse* conditions.
6. Zoning.
7. Cost per acre.

A coalition of local builders, working as a group or committee, should sketch a plan of a proposed one-story plant, utilizing local materials to maintain minimum cost. Two purposes are fulfilled by this test or experimental project:

(A) Since plant location surveys usually take far longer than anticipated, speed is often a crucial factor in final community selection. The presence of a group of contractors or even a single contractor who has actively worked on the problem may be sufficient to influence the decision.

(B) When discussing the cost of a sprinkler system, roofing material, type of insulation required for the area, or foundation conditions, the "contracting group" with their pooled experience can be invaluable in providing specific answers to prospects' inquiries.

Site and construction data are important. In fact, many communities have considered it advisable to raise funds by public subscription and erect medium-sized, one-story straight line industrial plants, *prior* to securing a prospect. This is an extraordinary solution, however, and is not to be recommended, except in unusual circumstances.

In addition to information on sites, the community data book should contain current information on available industrial buildings or floor space, housing, construction, programs, etc. Accurate data on rentals and sale prices of selected homes should be available so that the prospect may single out a representative group to ascertain the cost of housing.

The data book should cover as many phases of the community life as possible. Other suggested topics are living costs, location of production materials, climate, educational and cultural facilities, recreational advantages, etc.

The following list sets forth sources of helpful information for the data book:

TOPIC	SOURCE
Location of Production Materials	Agricultural agent
	Chamber of Commerce Secretary
	Industrialists
Labor	Local office State Labor Department
	Employment Security Division
	Chamber of Commerce Secretary
	—or—
	Make field survey
Sites	Real estate agents
	Railroad agents
	Planning Commission member
Industrial Fuels	Coal dealer
	Oil company agents
	Gas utility agent
Transportation Facilities	Railroad agents
	Motor carrier agents
	Port Authority
	Postmaster
Market	Chamber of Commerce Secretary
	Industrialists
	Bankers
Distribution Facilities	Banker
	Transportation agents
Power	Power utility company agent—
	or—
	Manager of municipal plant
Water	Water utility company agent—or—
	Manager of municipal plant

Living Conditions	Planning Commission
	Building inspector
	Realtors
	High school class
Laws and Regulations	Planning Commission
	City Attorney
	City Engineer
Tax Structure	Assessor
	Treasurer
Climate	Agricultural agent, State Industrial Development Commission
	U. S. Weather Bureau
Miscellaneous	Local newspaper editor
	Librarian
	Representatives of groups concerned

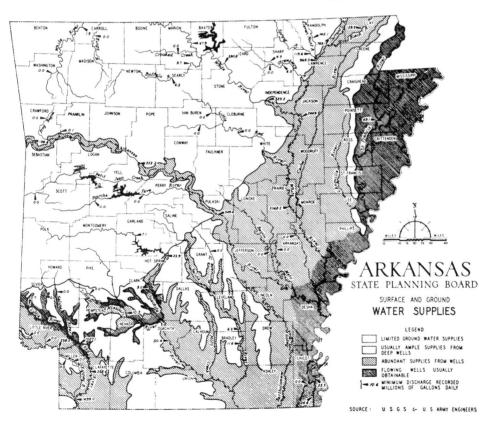

ARKANSAS
STATE PLANNING BOARD

SURFACE AND GROUND
WATER SUPPLIES

LEGEND

☐ LIMITED GROUND WATER SUPPLIES
☐ USUALLY AMPLE SUPPLIES FROM DEEP WELLS
▨ ABUNDANT SUPPLIES FROM WELLS
▨ FLOWING WELLS USUALLY OBTAINABLE
⊢ 10 6 MINIMUM DISCHARGE RECORDED MILLIONS OF GALLONS DAILY

SOURCE: U. S. G. S & U. S ARMY ENGINEERS

Comparison with other communities

By this time *the hours expended in compiling and condensing data are truly staggering;* yet the committee is not quite ready. Remember that the industrialist usually considers the community or area along with many others. Thus, while few industrial development groups take the trouble to do it, a comparison of perhaps 15 or 20 towns within a several hundred mile radius is desirable and is always of great value to the industrial prospect. Power costs, net debt per capita, tax rates, labor pools, wage rates for identical job occupations, labor stability, labor history, percentage of home ownership, are a few of the factors which should be compared.

One community in central Pennsylvania secured four sizable new industries in the space of two years by having such a study compiled for them by an industrial engineering firm.

The logical result of the volunteer committee will be the formation of an Industrial Foundation.

THE INDUSTRIAL FOUNDATION

In order to have a clear picture of the possibilities inherent in an Industrial Foundation, it is perhaps well to take a brief look at what is happening throughout the country.

It is estimated that there are currently

72 active Foundations
9 dissolved Foundations
17 cities considering the establishment of a Foundation
32 cities using some other plan to promote industrial growth

These figures, it should be noted, are not complete, but suffice to give a broad picture.

In every instance, Foundations were created with the express mission of increasing industrial payrolls in the community. There are basically three ways to accomplish this end and these can be used individually or in combination, with the emphasis being placed on that aspect of the program which promises the greatest and most prompt return.

Bristol Meyers, Sun Tube Division, Washington, New Jersey. Plant Location Study—FANTUS FACTORY LOCATING SERVICE.

1. Aiding new industry to establish facilities in the community.
2. Assisting established industries to expand their activities and, consequently, payrolls.
3. Getting entirely new local "venture" enterprises on their feet.

Of these three, the first is the best known and most widely practiced activity of Foundations, some 59 being reported as engaging in it.

The second is a less publicized activity of some 47 Foundations and it is natural that this should be the case, since established businesses usually draw on other forms of assistance to expand their activities, notably banks and insurance companies.

The third activity is reportedly undertaken by 39 Foundations. Usually, this involves making a loan and providing technical assistance to some enterprising individual with a good idea but lacking the financial and business qualifications that would make him acceptable to an investor, a bank or an insurance company. It should be noted that this last phase of Foundation work is one which should be clearly understood and definitely authorized in advance by those individuals who have a financial stake in the Foundation.

Promoting a new venture always involves a risk. If the venture fails, the Foundation will be subject to sharp criticism and may lose the support of well-to-do backers. Fear of criticism, however, should not preclude consideration of proposals which might, in course of time, open up an entirely new field of economic activity for the community. There are many examples of quite substantial businesses, operating on a national scale, that germinated from a community-sponsored "shoestring".

How do Foundations attract new industries? The most common "bait" is some kind of financial inducement. This takes several forms, among which the following are the most prevalent:

1. The provision of suitable sites at low cost or at no cost at all.
2. Provision of utility extensions and/or access roads and rail sidings to a selected site at no cost to the industry.
3. Provision of a building at low rental, with or without option to purchase.
4. Provision of a manufacturer's needed equipment on a rental basis. (This form of assistance is generally frowned upon as being economically far too risky. A manufacturer unwilling to buy his own equipment is almost certainly not worth having, though this is not invariably the case.
5. Purchase of stock in the company that proposes to establish itself in the community. Here again, considerable caution is necessary if the Foundation is not to end with worthless stock certificates on its hands . . . and, of course, no payroll.
6. Direct loans to prospective industries.

All the above "inducements" have one thing in common. They serve to provide the prospective industry with capital, either free or on extremely favorable terms. Many companies do not like to tie up their capital in "bricks-and-mortar." This is true of large companies as well as small ones; of old-established firms as well as fledgling industries. It is both proper and legitimate that an Industrial Foundation meet industry half-way in this matter.

The acid test as to whether a given industry is a good or bad risk for a Foundation is for the Foundation to attempt to sell a first mortgage on the property on the open market, with the prospective industry's lease as "security." If the lessee is good, the mortgage will sell readily enough; if he is not, it won't. In the latter case, the Foundation would be well advised to pass up the industry or, at least, refrain from making any financial concessions.

What is the economic justification for the financial assistance a Foundation offers to a prospective industry? Careful and conservative economic studies have shown conclusively that ten manufacturing jobs maintain about eight service jobs in the average industrial city. These studies also show that manufacturing payroll money usually creates business in the city in a volume of from $2\frac{1}{2}$ to $3\frac{1}{4}$ times the actual payroll. Since this is, by its very nature, incremental business in the community, it is a safe assumption that the percentage of net profit on it will be substantially higher than the percentage which derived from the level of activity existing before the new industry started up.

How can a Foundation protect its investments? There are many ways and most of them, in essence, are simply a matter of common business caution and common business sense. For that reason it is not deemed necessary to discuss the matter at length here.

How are Foundations financed? There seems to be no hard-and-fast rule nor, for that matter, any definite pattern. Capitalization of existing Foundations bears no relationship to the size of the community in which they happen to be located. The best guide here would seem to be a judicious balance between the community's needs, that is to say, what the Foundation will actually have to do to accomplish its stated ends, and the amount of money that one can reasonably expect to raise in that community.

How is the money raised? There are two accepted methods of raising funds for a Foundation?

1. A general campaign which seeks to solicit the entire citizenry of the community.
2. A limited campaign addressed only to the business community.

A general campaign is harder to manage, costlier to run and more unpredictable in its results. Offsetting these disadvantages is the fact that the whole community will have a sense of participation and will thus be more willing to back the objectives of the Foundation. A program with a broad community base is more impressive and inviting to a prospect than one which has the backing of a small group of interested parties. In the event that re-zoning or some municipal expenditures are involved in accommodating a prospect, wide public support may prove to be very helpful.

While the prime objective of such a program would be the industrial development of the community, there are many other phases of civic improvement in which the Foundation can participate. For example, it can be empowered to make loans for revenue bearing public improvements.

Funds may also be available on loan from local banks, individuals or organizations, or under the terms of special statutes which exist in many states which permit the levying of taxes for industrial development purposes.

Organizing the foundation

At an initial meeting of the community business and civic leaders, a chairman and temporary secretary can be chosen. The meeting is designed to acquaint those present with the objectives of the Foundation and to arrive at a decision concerning the type of foundation to be formed, that is, whether profit or non-profit.

This Foundation may be staffed with personnel who are also members of the Chamber of Commerce; it is essential, however, that it have a distinct identity and a high degree of autonomy. Cooperation with the Chamber of Commerce is of course natural, but it should be clearly understood that this Industrial Foundation ought not to be subservient to the Chamber of Commerce. The reason for this clear-cut divorcement is that the interests of members of the Chamber of Commerce and the interests of the Industrial Foundation are at times sufficiently divergent to cause friction. This becomes particularly awkward when an industrial member of the Chamber of Commerce objects to the establishment of another industry in the community, on the grounds that this new industry will compete with established industries for the available supply of labor. This objection can be overcome if, as noted above, local industrialists are participants in and supporters of the program.

What has been referred to as "the Industrial Foundation" can, of course, be called by a wide variety of names. However, the term "Industrial Foundation" has become widely known in industrial circles and most industrialists will understand what the functions of such organizations are supposed to be.

Three committee chairmen should be appointed, each with three or four committeemen. The committees should be:

1. *Legal Committee.* This group will draft articles of incorporation and by-laws, arrange for a charter, and advise on all legal matters.

2. *Finance Committee.* This committee will determine the amount and par value of the stock, the amount for which to incorporate, the extent of general public participation, and methods of stock sale.

It should be made clear from the very outset that investment in foundation bonds is not, in and of itself, a bonanza to the investor. Investors will receive their return through other channels, notably through increased economic activities which will redound to the advantage of their other business enterprises in the community.

The term "non-profit" does not mean no income. The Foundation should, indeed, have income to cover its operating expenses and this income can best be derived from a modest profit on real estate purchased for industrial resale from its leases to industry, and from donations from the Chamber of Commerce and city government. These latter donations should not be too hard to secure since the operation of the Foundation is for the betterment of the community, and the Foundation could legitimately be considered as a worthwhile expense to both the Chamber of Commerce and the taxpayers of the community.

3. *Publicity Committee.* Working closely with the Finance Committee, this group assists in making the aims and objectives of the Foundation known to potential subscribers as well as to the general public.

The articles of incorporation should be broad enough to allow for all functions which can conceivably aid in the economic and industrial development program. Among the stated purposes should be the following: (1) to encourage the industrial and commercial growth of the community and general area, (2) to encourage and assist existing industries, (3) to buy, sell, mortgage or lease real estate, construct buildings and conduct an industrial real estate business.

Purposes of the industrial foundation

The Industrial Foundation can perform a variety of functions. Among these, of course, is the collection and maintaining of accurate data relating to the community. It should also be its purpose to keep careful track of industrial development throughout industry, to establish a file of prospects, to circularize these prospects, to determine the sites desirable for industry in and around the community and, if possible, either to acquire them outright or obtain options on them. This activity is most important, for it precludes the possibility of real estate speculation and puts the Foundation in the position of being able to offer suitable property to prospects at a reasonable, rather than an inflated, price.

In many communities throughout the country, industrial foundations are prepared to build factory-type buildings for a prospective industry, and lease them to industry at attractive rentals. It is desirable that a Foundation have the authority and the financial backing necessary to undertake this type of activity since many companies, even large national corporations, are strongly attracted by the possibility of acquiring a good modern plant without the necessity of heavy investment on their part. A word of caution is necessary here: No Industrial Foundation should under any circumstances finance a special purpose building that can only be used for a limited type of industrial activity (e.g. cold storage warehouse, foundry, etc.). The vicissitudes of economic life are such that a seemingly prosperous company can go under with extraordinary rapidity, leaving the Industrial Foundation with an empty building. It is, of course, quite obvious that the wider the range of tenants who can be attracted to the premises, the greater the chance of finding a successor to the enterprise that has failed. Many a small manufacturer, for example, would be quite content with a concrete block and wooden truss building. Another manufacturer, having a higher investment in equipment, would prefer to have it housed in a somewhat more substantial and fireproof shell. It is, hence, to the advantage of the Foundation to build a substantial building, provided the rental at which it must be offered is not so great as to discourage promising new enterprises.

In addition to the selection and acquisition of suitable industrial acreage, it will also devolve upon the Foundation to secure the proper zoning of such property by petitioning for the re-zoning of areas not already zoned for industry.

The Industrial Foundation will also have to take upon itself the task of keeping a vigilant eye on all utilities that serve the area. Rate increases for utilties are invariably the object of discussion at public hearings, and a representative of the Industrial Foundation should be able and prepared to attend hearings to submit the views and sustain the interests of the Foundation.

The Foundation will also be called upon occasionally to negotiate with railroads and trucking lines for advantageous commodity rates for prospective or established industries. In the same area, it would be the function of the Foundation to persuade public carriers to provide the community with the best possible passenger service.

The Foundation should also maintain close contact with the state agencies concerned in such matters as road construction and maintenance, irrigation, drainage, flood control, mosquito abatement and the like, even though these activities may duplicate those of the Chamber of Commerce.

The Foundation should also make certain that the labor force of the community is working at highest possible skills. It may establish a training school, if one does not already exist, to furnish present plants with skills in short supply. This school can then serve as a nucleus for training labor for new industry.

SPECIAL INDUCEMENTS

Communities endowed with physical, geographical or climatic advantages which serve to attract industry and commerce to them need rely upon few inducement devices. Accessibility of markets, availability of raw materials, abundance of labor supply, and the presence of other special factors essential

climate

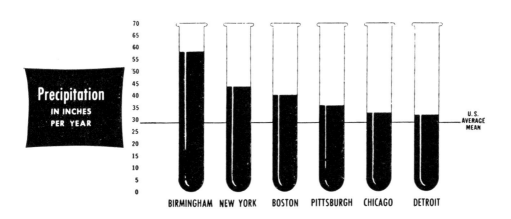

Temperature
A - AVERAGE MAXIMUM
B - AVERAGE MEAN
C - AVERAGE MINIMUM

90
80
70
60
50
40
30
20
10
0

U.S. AVERAGE MEAN

BIRMINGHAM   PITTSBURGH   NEW YORK   BOSTON   CHICAGO   DETROIT

Precipitation
IN INCHES
PER YEAR

70
65
60
55
50
45
40
35
30
25
20
15
10
5
0

U.S. AVERAGE MEAN

BIRMINGHAM   NEW YORK   BOSTON   PITTSBURGH   CHICAGO   DETROIT

SOURCE: The Pittsburgh Industrial Development Council

for development of specific industries are sufficiently important in themselves to attract industries. The managements of progressive, growing concerns are continually alert to the problem of locating their plants at points where the best balance between all elements of production, distribution and cost may be attained. When they are aware of such a location, they require neither a special invitation nor any bonus from the community to establish a plant at that point. Most of our older and larger industrial centers owe their existence to this fact.

In some instances however, communities lacking the proper combination of natural advantages present in other localities have found it necessary to offer artificial inducements. The belief that all special inducements are uneconomic and should not be offered at any time is not entirely well founded. Certain types of inducement differ in no respect from the means employed by formal financing channels. Others are purely temporary, aimed at easing the shocks of relocation which frequently occur in cases of industrial migration.

A complete analysis of special inducements is beyond the scope of this book. Of the many variations of bonus and concession, only a few are desirable for most cities, and fewer yet are feasible. Thus cash grants, bonuses, moving expenses, etc. are not advocated. The mortality rate among plants located through such devices has always been high. Equally undesirable is the investment in capital stock of the new enterprise unless such investment represents only a small share of the total worth.

Special tax treatment may be a sound practice in inducing a new industry to locate in the community provided the circumstances are correct. It should not be extended unless it can be done without serious disproportion between the benefit and the cost to the community. No local taxing districts should be required to absorb the loss of revenue in exempting a property whose use does not confer a reasonable local benefit.

In considering the extension of special tax treatment, it should be borne in mind that exemptions to particular property owners are demoralizing to those who continue to pay taxes. Competition is rarely welcome and less so when it is subsidized competition. Attempts to restrict exemption to those industries which will not compete with those who are already present may vitiate the entire program since the established industries are generally those best suited to a given location. In spite of this, seventeen states grant some form of exemption and innumerable communities offer special low assessments for a number of years.

Whether tax exemption will be possible in some states is questionable. If permissible under the Statutes, the community would be wise to consider such inducements only under the following circumstances:

1. It should be limited in duration, not to exceed five years.
2. Local citizens should vote upon it, in order to secure the full assent of the people.
3. It should be extended only to strong or promising industries.
4. It should be brought to the attention of local manufacturers who should be sold on the wisdom of the inducement. Antagonism must be avoided.

One form of special tax treatment should be offered unqualifiedly to the new industry, viz., a low assessment for the first few years followed by truly reasonable assessments in the future. This, incidentally, is a consideration which the community should perpetually extend to its *existing* industrial family.

The most satisfying and economic way in which a typical city can make itself interesting to an industrial prospect who is inducement conscious is through the functioning of the Industrial Foundation. Construction of a modern factory building to the *general* requirements of an industry, available at *reasonable rentals,* plus a moderate tax base on machinery and equipment, is the limit to which most cities should go.

If an industry is willing to construct its own plant, the city should be willing to donate the site and extend roads and utilities, if asked to do so. This is not an uncommon practice. The South abounds with examples of this practice. It is also true in the Middle West. For example, Lincoln, Nebraska presented the Elgin National Watch Company with a site worth $700,000 upon which the Company is expanding its present plant. The same thing was done by Lincoln for the Goodyear Tire and Rubber Co. Fort Smith, Arkansas built a $500,000 plant for the Dixie Paper Cup Co. Although the Fort Smith Foundation had only $150,000, some $350,000 was borrowed from banks.

Many other examples of such assistance exist, ranging all the way from 100% community financing of the plant to joint community-industry-financial institution programs.

PUBLICITY

Publicity can serve an industrial development program in many ways. Among these are: (1) Show evidence of having a definite program of development, (2) Encourage and back up local development, (3) Possibly obtain direct inquiries from industrial prospects and, (4) Make the location better known.

There is in the United States almost no community so small that it does not feel called upon to print and distribute a brochure. Community brochures range all the way from inexpensive one-page mimeographed flyers to elaborately bound, multi-colored books. Whether they are printed, photo-offset, done in 4 colors, bound in plastic, or simply mimeographed, is relatively unimportant. Two essential points must be considered in presenting data:

> (a) Provide factual information to the prospect.
> (b) Advertise *specific* factors.

Probably the one factor which is most significant is that of complete honesty on the part of the community. The establishment of a plant based on misrepresentation of facts can result in economy disaster in certain cases. Be completely factual in your approach to this important problem.

Advertise specific factors. Shy away from such hackneyed phrases as "Intelligent labor," "Excellent transportation," "A good place to work, live and play." Remember that all communities have characteristics in common—all have people, most have railroads and power, most show population growth, all have a local market of one size or another. The question is—how is your community distinctive? What are its unique advantages? Why can a manufacturer gain by relocating there? These are the elements to emphasize—in specific terms and not in generalities.

Periodical and newspaper advertising is also resorted to in industrial promotion programs but usually only by the larger, well-financed development agencies. And some areas have even employed television as a sales device. The use of direct mail for distribution of promotional materials is, of course, common.

Most cities would be wise to leave newspaper and periodical advertising to agencies better equipped and better financed to engage in a sustained program. Few results in terms of dollars or jobs can even be directly attributed to such advertising. It is effective only as a part of a comprehensive promotional program which includes other elements such as personal contacts, direct mail, community education, close study of industrial trends, and a thorough follow-up of industrial prospects. A recent analysis by the University of Santa Clara of 200 such advertisements revealed that 182 were placed by state agencies, railroads and utilties. Only 12 were placed by cities and local chambers of commerce, and the remaining 6 were spread among banks, newspapers, etc.

It is also suggested that the detailed community data book which was set up in loose leaf form be mimeographed. It should be distributed only to bona fide prospects in response to an inquiry, and made up in the light of that prospect's requirements. Thus, if the availability of water is a major locational factor for this particular prospect, complete data on the water supply, cost and necessary treatment, etc. should be included. Pages relating to other community features that are less significant may be omitted.

By so compiling the informational brochure submitted to a prospect, the community avoids bulky presentations which the prospect will not take the time to read through. In addition, this procedure eliminates the cost of printing and distributing a large volume of paper that serves no purpose. A typical loose leaf data book condenses materials subject to rapid obsolescence into as few pages as possible. These pages should be mimeographed or printed in small quantities and brought up to date at stipulated intervals. Other data which does not out-date rapidly can, of course, be printed in substantial quantities (e.g., location, history, climatology and the like).

It is suggested that sample sketches be made of all suitable industrial sites. These sketches should show the outline of the site, adjacent roads, railroads, power lines, water lines, gas lines, sewer mains, and if there are any unusual topographical features, these, too, should be shown (e.g., a drainage ditch or gulley). In the event of an inquiry for a five-acre site, for example, send only those plats of sites approximating that acreage or larger tracts which can be subdivided.

SOURCES OF ASSISTANCE AND LEADS

The Industrial Foundation can and should call upon a number of sources for assistance in collecting data of economic importance to the location. Among these sources are the State Development Commission, if any, the State University, the several executive departments of the government of the State, the State Employment Commission, the U. S. Department of Commerce, the Corps of Engineers, the Geodetic Survey, the Federal Communications Commission, the industrial departments of the railroads and utilities that serve the area, and other similar bodies.

It is usually very hard to determine in advance what industries are contemplating relocations. Such moves are not often published until they are virtually an accomplished fact. It should be the business, therefore, of the Foundation to scrutinize as many trade publications as it can conveniently secure; the *Wall Street Journal* and the financial sections of prominent New York and Chicago newspapers. If an eastern manufacturing concern has issued $5,000,000 worth of stock for the purpose of expansion, it may be that a letter of inquiry addressed to the company will strike a responsive chord. Likewise, mergers and consolidations are worthy of close scrutiny since the merger is frequently entered into to strengthen the financial structure of both parties and, occasionally, implies a prospect of growth. This is by no means an exhaustive list of sources of leads but should suffice to convey in a general way how the search for these should be organized. It is taken for granted that the public spirited business men in the area who hear of impending moves will report these to the Foundation.

In determining whether a possible "lead" seems likely of conversion into a "prospect," the Foundation can apply the following criteria:

1. Is the product manufactured now used or likely to be used or consumed in the region in large enough quantities to warrant interest in its local production?

2. If the product is used or can be used in the region, is it physically capable of production in the community? That is, are there any unusual requirements which cannot be met locally?

3. If the product is physically capable of production locally, can it be produced more economically or *as* economically here as at any other location?

Occasionally it will be found the consumption or need for a product far exceeds its production in a given area. If transportation costs or time-in-transit are a factor in such a product, the presentation of such data may help you secure a new industry—very often the manufacturer himself is unaware of the true situation.

In a recent study conducted by the Fantus Factory Locating Service, it was found that 13,560 tons of a building materials product were manufactured in one of the central states, but 96,000 tons were consumed! Investigation revealed that the one small company now located there was not progressive and made no attempt to meet the demand of the markets, obviously a perfect situation for the establishment of a plant with progressive management.

Development of data on the natural resources of the area may lead to the establishment of new plants for their exploitation. Bear in mind that the more loss of weight incurred in the processing of the raw materials, the more important its geographic pull.

Strangely enough, *present* industry is usually a good source for new industry, even though existing plants may be limited in number. Thorough analysis is of course necessary on a local basis, but the following suggestions may serve as a stimulus to specific action.

Assume that yours is a community in the southeast that is the location of a pulp mill. Some of your logical prospects would include plants in these categories:

Paper and paperboard

Fiber tubes and drums

Paper bags

Envelopes

Wallpaper

Paper converters

Paper boxes

A large local saw or veneer mill might logically lead to development of industrial prospects in the following categories:

Radio and television cabinets

Office and store fixtures

Furniture

Toys and miscellaneous

Prefabricated buildings

Supplementary industries can often be attracted to an area where local services are inadequate. For example, a cooperage plant should easily be secured where there is a combination of a saw mill (primary raw materials) and the customers for the product which would include plants in any of the following categories:

Blended or rectified liquors

Abrasives

Paint products

Nails

Lubricant oils and greases

Glycerine and soaps

Chemical products

Cider, vinegar

Roofing coatings and felts

Wines

Asbestos

As a further example, an electroplating plant could be attracted into an area if power costs are unusually low and if any of the following types of industry could provide a satisfactory sales volume:

Costume jewelry

Fabricated metal products

Mechanical pencils and pens

Photography equipment

Lighting fixtures

Surgical instruments

Industrial machinery and equipment

Occasionally special studies of existing industry will attract like industry (recommended only for fairly large metropolitan areas). The South Texas National Bank of Houston compiled a study in 1950, titled "Chemicals In The Texas Gulf Coast," in which were listed all the "producers of chemicals in the Houston area and the organic and inorganic materials manufactured . . . to indicate the area's potentialities to producers and processors alike."

Special industry studies by the Territorial Information Department, a group of prominent utilities in Northern Illinois, such as "The Radio Industry" and "The Steel Industry," have attracted plants producing allied products.

CHAPTER 12

Puerto Rico:
A New Factor
in Plant Location

The great majority of American manufacturers who expand or relocate plants do so within the continental limits of the United States. PLANT LOCATION, therefore, is concerned primarily with the factors involved in selecting a mainland site.

Location abroad involves a completely different set of problems. Discussion and analysis of foreign exchange controls, tariffs, trade restrictions and the like would require a disproportionate amount of space in this study since comparatively few companies are in a position to benefit from the establishment of foreign manufacturing subsidiaries. Most of the U. S. territories also have little attraction. Alaska and Hawaii both have high wage levels resulting from the demands of non-manufacturing industries on limited populations. Other U. S. possessions are very small and remote.

The one exception is Puerto Rico, which has a population larger than 23 of the 48 states and where a considerable number of mainland firms have already established plants, many of which have been successful.

Ten years' exemption from income and other local taxes, automatic exemption from Federal taxation, labor training facilities and ease of obtaining loans have intrigued industrialists.

Puerto Rico is about 3½ hours by air southeast from Miami with an area of 3,435 square miles and a population of 2¼ million. Its people are largely of Spanish descent and Spanish is the principal spoken language. They have been American citizens since 1917, however, and today Puerto Rico, the only Commonwealth in the American Union, has a status similar to the 48 States with two important exceptions: no voting representation in Congress and no Federal taxation.

Until recently, Puerto Rico has not shared in the industrial expansion that has taken place in the United States since 1900. From the turn of the century, industry has grown more rapidly than population in the North Central, Far Western and Southeastern regions of the country.

In Puerto Rico, meanwhile, there has been an exceptionally rapid population growth. Population density is now 646 per square mile compared with 51 for the continental United States. Only Rhode Island, which consists mainly of industrial cities, has a comparable figure. An industrial state like Ohio has 194, New York has 233 and Alaska has only 0.2 persons per square mile.

As these figures suggest, unskilled labor is plentiful in almost any part of the island. Moreover, in spite of heavy migration to the mainland and substantial industrial growth during the past few years, about 15% of the labor force remains unemployed. Many others earn such low wages in agriculture, trade and service that they are available for any industrial job openings.

This readily available labor supply in Puerto Rico, at a time when the labor market has been tight in most sections of the mainland, is an important factor in the sharp recent increase in the selection of Puerto Rico as a location for new plants. In the 3-year period ending in June 1951, 102 new factories were opened. During the next 3 years, 237 were established.

But, as a number of firms have learned belatedly, plentiful labor at low wages, together with substantial government assistance, does not insure profits. *Tax exemption is meaningless for the plant that cannot earn a profit.* Successful operation in Puerto Rico depends on the same locational and management factors that apply on the mainland.

TRANSPORTATION

Distance, and therefore, transportation, is the most obvious drawback to location in Puerto Rico and is most often the critical element in determining its feasibility as a manufacturing location.

Sugar milling and refining, rum manufacture, cigar making and coffee roasting are *materials-based* industries that have long existed in Puerto Rico. The reduction in bulk involved in the extraction of raw sugar from cane is so great, in fact, that the sugar mills, which require substantial industrial plants, are spotted right in the cane fields.

Plants producing cement, structural clay products, glass containers and processed foods, have been established more recently. These industries are characteristically among the first to be established in a developing area which is starting to supply its own basic needs, and they have a two-way transportation advantage.

Development in some of these industries, however, has not stopped at the Puerto Rican market. Cement and bottles are shipped to Venezuela, Cuba, Colombia, and in the case of cement, to Florida. For these bulk commodities, the factor of distance has been upset by the economy of ocean freight over land transportation. Some processed foods, such as citrus juice, pineapple, and other local specialties, now find their largest market on the mainland and a large, modern cigar factory exports practically all its output.

A few *market-based* industries which import their raw materials have also long existed in Puerto Rico. Some, such as bakeries, beverage bottlers, printers, and machine shops, still sell primarily or exclusively in the local market. Others, such as furniture and fertilizer companies are now expanding into the mainland and nearby Caribbean markets. Apparel, which was started early as an export industry in Puerto Rico because of the very low wages then prevailing, is now finding an expanding local market.

Moreover, industrial expansion itself makes new materials locally available and creates new local demands. One firm sets up to draw wire and another is established to make wire products. A plant is established to make pens and a metal stamping firm adds the pen caps to its line. The development of a substantial plastic molding industry leads to the establishment of a tool and die shop to manufacture the molds. New plants doing metal stamping, wire insulating, and tin can manufacture are the result of new industrial demands. Plastic and metal working industries are becoming large enough to open up economic possibilities for the collection and processing of scrap.

Industrial opportunities such as these, deriving their transportation advantage from a new local source of demand or supply, tend to appear and then to disappear quite rapidly because in most cases only a single plant is required to fill the vacuum. To seize this type of transportation advantage in Puerto Rico, a firm almost has to know not only what its competitors are doing, but what they are thinking.

It is believed that the combination of recent expansion and new technology has now begun to open up in Puerto Rico some more basic and larger-scale opportunities for the development of major industrial complexes. Two oil refineries now under construction can be the base of petrochemicals, synthetic fibres, and further expansion and integration of the existing textile and apparel industries. Geological investigation has turned up limited iron ore resources which, with the increasing amount of scrap available, opens up the future possibility of an integrated steel and metal working industry. New technology and rising pulp wood costs may soon mean that bagasse from the sugar mills will be manufactured into paper and cardboard, instead of being burned as fuel and as waste. This may give Puerto Rico a major transportation advantage in book publishing and a lower-cost material for its construction and millwork industries.

In a sense, Puerto Rico appears to be a distant, ocean-bound laboratory in which there is being reproduced, quite rapidly, a small replica of the industrial giant which has grown up on the mainland over a period of many years. Actually, however, Puerto Rico is developing into an integrated, though necessarily somewhat isolated, part of the U. S. economy.

This economic integration has been facilitated by common citizenship, a common currency, an interlocking legal and judicial structure, common jurisdiction of Federal Government agencies and many other links. There is also some mutual trade made possible by the few commodities which move from Puerto Rico into the mainland market with a natural transportation advantage because of proximity to raw materials or the comparative economy of ocean freight. These conditions, most of them of successful long standing, merely permit industrialization. Establishment of new plants requires that, on balance, favorable cost factors outweigh the unfavorable.

Most of the new plants in Puerto Rico have been located there in spite of a disadvantage, sometimes slight but often quite large, in transportation costs. In practically all such cases in which operations have proved to be successful, lower labor cost has been the principal offset to the transportation disadvantage.

Some sort of generalized yardstick might be helpful in rapidly assessing the relative advantages and disadvantages of a move to Puerto Rico.

One possible rule is: Measure labor, tax and government assistance savings against the added costs of transportation. But even transportation may turn out to be a blessing in disguise if your product is the right shape or weight and your markets are in the right places. For instance, reaching such growing centers as New Orleans and Galveston, Texas, by water carrier has proved extremely inexpensive. In fact, one Boston candy manufacturer recently learned to his surprise that while it took $2.11 to ship 100 pounds of lollipops to Los Angeles by rail, it cost only $1.16 by water from Puerto Rico all the way through the Panama Canal.

TAX INCENTIVES

Tax exemption is in many ways the keystone of Puerto Rico's continuing program to attract new industry.

Tax exemption has special significance in Puerto Rico because it accompanies the blanket exemption from all Federal taxes which applies to all residents of Puerto Rico, including corporations that are subsidiaries of mainland firms. Most new firms are also eligible for the following exemptions from Commonwealth and municipal taxes:

1. Corporate income tax—*ten years from the start of operations.*
2. Municipal license fees—*ten years from the start of operations.*
3. Personal income tax on dividends paid out of the first seven years earnings *to residents of Puerto Rico.*
4. Real and personal property taxes—five to ten years, depending on the size of investment.

Eligible firms include those manufacturing a product that was not in commercial production in Puerto Rico on January 2, 1947 and those making any of a long list of products enumerated in the Industrial Incentives Act of 1954. Firms that close a mainland plant to relocate in Puerto Rico are ineligible.

Exemption is in the form of a contract between the firm and the Commonwealth Government. It is subject to revocation if the firm fails to live up to its obligations as to minimum employment and continuance of operations after a specified date. These obligations are based on the manufacturer's own estimates.

After the exemption periods have expired, the firm becomes subject to regular Puerto Rican taxes, but the exemption from Federal taxation continues. Since the Puerto Rican income tax on corporations ranges between 59% and 70% of the Federal rates, there is a substantial permanent tax advantage.

In the final analysis tax exemption can make a tremendous difference—sometimes between business success and failure. Two simple examples bring this point home:

	TAXES IN U.S.	TAXES IN P.R.
Case 1. Individual Enterprise $100,000.00 Net Income	$67,320	$0
Case 2. Corporation $100,000.00 Net Income	$46,500	$0

LABOR

The labor force in Puerto Rico is large, young—and greatly under-utilized. It is possible to recruit plant labor with ease in nearly all localities and severe unemployment holds wage rates down to levels far below those in comparable occupations on the mainland.

Here are some of the salient facts (mid-1954):

Total population	2,239,000
Number 14 years of age and over	1,272,000
Total labor force	*626,000*
Employed	536,000
Unemployed	*90,000*
Employed in manufacturing	*95,000*
Home needleworkers	29,000
Employed in factories	*66,000*
Sugar mills	6,000
Other foods and beverages	7,000
Tobacco manufacturing	11,000
Textiles and apparel	23,000
Other manufacturing	19,000

Some further facts:

About 40% of the labor force is between 20 and 35 years of age—almost half of the island population is now under 14 years of age.

Unemployment varies seasonally from a low of about 70,000 during the

sugar season to almost 120,000 in the "dead" season. Seasonal swings in employment give promise of flattening out somewhat in the long run with gradual
mechanization in the sugar industry.

Underemployment (persons not working full-time or close thereto) is estimated at double the outright unemployment. Underemployment in agriculture
is so great that an estimated 40,000 male agricultural workers could be drawn
into manufacturing if jobs were available.

About half of all factory workers are women. But if females constituted the
same proportion of the labor force that they do on the mainland (one-third),
about 50,000 additional female workers would be available for manufacturing.
The principal reason these women are not now in the labor force is lack of jobs.

The results of this kind of labor surplus are reflected in average hourly wage
rates in manufacturing ranging from one-third to one-half those of the mainland.
Here are the comparative averages for production workers in June 1954:

	AVERAGE HOURLY EARNINGS	
INDUSTRY GROUP	PUERTO RICO	U.S. MAINLAND
ALL INDUSTRIES	*52.7¢*	*$1.81*
Food and kindred products	70.2	1.68
Tobacco manufacturers	35.2	1.35
Textile mill products	50.3	1.36
Apparel and related products	39.7	1.33
Chemicals, petroleum and rubber	71.6	1.92
Leather and leather products	44.7	1.39
Stone, clay and glass products	65.6	1.75
Metal products	64.1	1.89
Instruments and miscellaneous	52.9	1.83

Manufacturing wage rates have been rising, of course. In 1951, they aver-
aged around 45 cents an hour. Their gradual rise is a result of the interacting
effects of (1) upgrading of jobs and (2) minimum wage legislation.

The sharp decline in home needlework and the rapid expansion of the far
more efficient factory apparel industry, which pays 5 times as high weekly earnings, is an outstanding example of *job upgrading*. Puerto Rico can not and does
not want to compete with such very low-wage areas as the Philippines and
Japan for starvation business. A manufacturer considering a substantial investment in Puerto Rico will be well-advised to project carefully his probable ability
to pay a gradually rising level of wages.

But this wage rise is clearly limited by one all-important consideration—*it
costs less for a worker to live successfully and even comfortably in Puerto Rico*

than in most areas of continental United States. In other words, an employer can assure a higher standard of living at a relatively lower payroll cost. There are a number of important reasons for this. Among them:

1. *Favorable Climate*—In this warm and almost rainless country, overcoats, rain apparel and so forth are of course unnecessary. Clothing, therefore, takes a smaller percentage of the total family budget, while insulation and other cold weather housing aids are unnecessary. Equally important, since temperature remains unusually stable throughout the year, there are no summer or winter slumps in worker output, and high production can be maintained year-round.

2. *Lower Food Costs*—The traditional healthy Puerto Rican diet, largely vegetables and rice, costs considerably less than the typical mainland meat, potatoes and ice cream combination. In addition, most Puerto Rican families, particularly in the country, maintain their own gardens, which furnish a large part of their nutritional requirements.

3. *Government Assistance*—Housing and health are also less expensive for a large proportion of factory workers. Today, low cost public housing is the rule in metropolitan centers like San Juan, while out-of-city housing is even less expensive. A liberal and growing government-sponsored hospitalization program has also been designed and is now within reach of many thousands of industrial workers.

There are two sets of *minimum wage regulations* in Puerto Rico. Industries selling in interstate and foreign commerce are subject to the Federal Fair Labor Standards Act. Purely local industries are regulated by the Puerto Rico Minimum Wage Board. Most new manufacturing firms are under Federal jurisdiction.

The Federal Act exempts Puerto Rico from the minimums now in force on the mainland. Instead, special minimum wage boards are convened periodically to recommend to the Administrator of the Federal Wage and Hour Division minimum wage rates for each separate industry. The rate is required by law to approach as near to the continental U. S. minimum as possible without causing layoffs or restricting hiring. The Administrator reviews the rate recommended, entertains any protests, and then, usually after a considerable lapse of time, establishes the new minimum rate for the industry.

Even if the Fair Labor Standards Act is amended to provide a higher flat minimum on the mainland, Puerto Rican operations will be protected from sudden shock by this special machinery. Following are some of the typical Federal minimums in force (November 1954):

	CENTS PER HOUR
Costume jewelry	36
Fertilizers	75
Cigars and cigarettes	36
Structural clay products	40
Beverages (non-alcoholic)	42½
Other food products	35
Handicrafts	26
Hosiery	50
Leather goods:	
General rate	40
Baseballs and softballs	32
Furniture	38
Men's and boys' clothing	35
Leather gloves:	
Hand sewing	25
Machine operations	52
Other operations	29
Infants' wear:	
Hand sewing	17½
Other operations	30
Brassieres, etc.	55
Paperboard	40
Paper bags	45
Paper boxes	55
Shoe manufacturing	40
Crocheted slippers	32
Sugar manufacturing	75
Vegetable, fruit and nut processing and packing	30

Low wage rates mean nothing, of course, if labor productivity is correspondingly low. But managers of newly established plants report that Puerto Rican workers soon approach and often surpass production rates for comparable mainland operations.

The manager of a plastic plant revealed to this investigator that productivity in Puerto Rico compares with that of the company's plant in Ohio after a thirty-day training period. The personnel manager of an internationally known electric products firm stated "Our productivity today is excellent—comparable to the mainland in every way."

Frawley Manufacturing Corporation, makers of "Paper-Mate" pens, began in October 1952 as purely an assembly operation with 80 workers. All parts were flown to California. Yet, despite transportation and initial expansion costs, the first certified balance sheet for three months in December 1952 showed a net profit of $326,000. In the last two years, Frawley has constructed two buildings and is now completing a third. They produce as well as assemble an average of more than 80,000 pens a day and have increased their pay roll from 80 to over 400 Puerto Rican workers.

Productivity in companies requiring highly developed skills is often not as high, however. For example, an automatic screw machine plant reports that workers are only 80% as efficient as in similar mainland operations.

The big difficulty is in the higher costs of starting up operations. Any vocational training the new employees have had must almost always be supplemented by a period of money-losing, on-the-job training. Higher-skilled and technical personnel must usually be brought from the States, at least for this early period, which means higher incentive pay.

The Commonwealth Government (see below) frequently helps with some of these extra expenses and local managerial talent is being developed. A November 1954 survey showed that 34% of the new plants have managers born in Puerto Rico. Finding a qualified local man is still not easy, but is worth time and effort because of his understanding of the language, the workers and local conditions.

Overtime must generally be paid *in operations engaged in interstate commerce* at time and a half for hours in excess of 8 in a day or 40 in a week, *and in operations engaged exclusively in intrastate operations,* at double time if in excess of *8 hours per day* and 48 hours per week. *All work* on the seventh consecutive day of work *per week must be paid at double the rate.* With certain exceptions, *notably in the manufacture of textile products,* women may not be employed between 10 p.m. and 6 a.m. Dismissal without *just* cause must be accompanied by a month's pay; but workers may be kept in a probationary status *for a limited time* at the beginning of employment during which this requirement does not apply. Workmen's compensation *insurance* is mandatory for any establishment employing more than two persons.

There is no mandatory sick or vacation leave, but this *fringe benefit* is customary to a certain extent. All told, fringe benefits in different industries are estimated to range between 2% and 5% of direct payroll.

Unions are not a factor in most industries. Only 12% of the new plants are organized and strikes in manufacturing have been infrequent. The strongly organized waterfront workers, however, have engaged in long walkouts causing significant losses to manufacturers through interruption of raw-materials flow and shipments of finished products. The latest of these strikes was serious enough to prompt emergency seizure action by the Commonwealth Government and the institution of legislative action for permanent control of the situation.

In late 1954, in a conference with Governor Luis Munoz Marin, the author was told that a committee had been formed which would be responsible for the future smooth running of the dock area.

OVERHEAD COSTS

While the balance between transportation and labor costs is frequently decisive in one direction or the other, it is tipped in many specific cases by differences in overhead items.

Puerto Rico has a very complete network of plainly marked, paved highways and roads, a modern school system with special emphasis on vocational education, low-rent public housing projects and excellent public health services, supported in part by Federal funds.

Electric power, water, sewerage and telegraph utilities as well as port and airport facilities are operated on an island-wide basis by public corporations and their expansion is planned and carried out in anticipation of rapidly rising industrial demands.

Electric power in Puerto Rico is currently 25% hydyroelectric and 75% steam generated. Output has risen from 65-79,000,000 KWH in 3 years and the entire island is connected by a well developed high tension grid. The system provides dependable single phase and three phase 60 cycle alternating current at standard voltages. Rates are comparable to those in mainland areas which depend primarily on recently installed steam generating power plants, such as New England and the Middle Atlantic States. In 1952-53 average cost per KWH for industrial use was 1.76 cents, with some large industrial users paying as little as 1 cent.

Communications on the island are provided by the Puerto Rico Telephone Company, a subsidiary of I. T. & T., by the telephone and telegraph services of the Communications Authority, and by regular U. S. mail service. Communications with the mainland or overseas is by radiotelephone, cable, or radiotelegraph. The island is also served by regular and air mail and parcel post.

All major urban centers have adequate supplies of pure safe water. There is a wide variation in the degree of hardness of the island's water, depending on location. Underground water resources are ample in many areas and are well charted. Large industrial users will find it more economical to sink their own wells. Sewer connections are generally available, and assistance is provided in the disposal of large volumes of industrial waste.

Most manufacturers in Puerto Rico use oil for industrial process heating. Completion of two refineries now under construction will provide a local source for petroleum products including, from one refinery, commercial LPG.

The new $15,000,000 San Juan Airport is now completed and initial contracts have been let for a $20,000,000 port development on the south side of San Juan Bay. A central wholesale market, bulk handling facilities, a meat packing plant, a grain mill, and other water based and supporting industries are included in the plans. Public transportation in San Juan is modern, and is also distinguished for having still retained the 5-cent fare. Low-cost transportation by bus and public passenger car is available throughout the island.

CLIMATE AND SITE SELECTION

The climate of Puerto Rico is generally mild, with mean temperatures fluctuating between 73 degrees in the winter and 78.6 degrees in the summer. Striking local differences in weather arise from variations in rainfall and altitude. The central mountains have 80-100 inches of rainfall per year and the mean temperature from 68 to 74. Mean temperature around most of the coast is 76 to 78, but rainfall ranges from 80 inches along the northeast coast to about 40 inches along the south coast. This makes for a variety of locations with different but comparatively stable combinations of temperature, rainfall, and humidity.

Air-conditioning is seldom regarded as necessary, except when required in connection with a specific process, and there are no winter-time heating and maintenance problems or costs.

U. S. Geological Survey maps cover all of Puerto Rico and the periodic census data on population, labor force, and markets in each municipality are supplemented by special surveys to aid in site selection.

LAND AND BUILDING COSTS

Land costs are relatively high in Puerto Rico because of the great density of population. A recent cost survey may be summarized as follows:

	COST PER ACRE
Undeveloped Land	
Small communities	$1,000 to $2,000
Larger cities	$4,000 to $5,000
San Juan metropolitan area	$4,000 to $17,000
Improved Land	
Small communities	up to $5,000
Larger cities	about $10,000
San Juan metropolitan area	$17,000 to $30,000

The Government has reserved large tracts suitable for industrial purposes which it subdivides and sells, or uses as sites for the construction of factory buildings for rent or sale.

Where the nature of the industrial operation permits the use of a locally-prefabricated steel frame and asbestos cement structure, construction costs are about $3.50 per square foot. Concrete industrial buildings cost from $5.50 to $6.00 per square foot and steel frame structures cost from $4.50 to $5.00 per square foot.

Rentals of new privately-owned industrial space, reflecting these land and building costs, vary from $0.60 to $1.00 per square foot. The Industrial Development Company maintains in various communities a supply of standard buildings, either 11,500 to 23,000 square feet in size, for rent with purchase option at a rate between $0.40 and $0.75 a foot depending on proximity to the San Juan metropolitan area.

COMMUNITY ATTITUDES AND POLICIES

The commonwealth government

People who are not familiar with Puerto Rico's history and politics, but who are acquainted with the Latin American scene, are likely to be apprehensive about the island's political stability. Actually the earliest settled area now within the Union has never had a revolution.

The party now in power (the Popular Democratic Party) has won every election, with increasing majorities, since it first gained control of the legislature in 1940. It first won on a platform of more jobs and higher incomes, and its position is solidly in favor of continued association with the United States, as is also that of the Statehood (Republican) Party. The minority Independence Party (not to be confused with the outlawed Nationalist Party, a tiny lunatic fringe) puts its trust in the ballot box as the means to gain its objective.

All parties are agreed on the need for industrialization to meet the island's serious economic problem. Relations between the legislative and executive branches of the government are unusually harmonious—the executive budget is seldom cut in any major particular by the Legislature. There is deep respect, even among his political opponents, for Governor Munoz; the government officials appear to be thoroughly honest and competent.

The economic development program

Industrial development is a part of Puerto Rico's comprehensive development program, which also embraces the promotion of rum sales and the tourist business, agriculture, utilities, and transportation. All have met with some success but industrialization is by far the most dynamic and is believed to have the greatest potential. During the last three years it has been adding about $20,000,000 a year to Commonwealth net income.

The promotion aspect of the industrial development program is carried on vigorously but on the basis of solid facts. Current statistics are maintained and available on such matters as:

1. Labor availability
2. Wage rates
3. Productivity
4. Absenteeism and turnover
5. Transportation facilities and cost
6. Material suppliers, sub-contractors, etc.
7. Living conditions for personnel from the mainland.

Information and promotion are backed up by a specific set of incentives and types of assistance. Each one is granted in accordance with the provisions of the enabling legislation and under established administrative procedures. They include:

1. Recruitment, testing, and training of workers.
2. Government Development Bank loans, up to 50% of the

uninstalled value of machinery and equipment, usually for 5 years at 5%.

3. Loans by the Puerto Rico Industrial Development Company (PRIDCO) in cases not suitable for bank financing.

4. Special incentives to firms servicing local industry, or processing local raw materials, or locating in smaller towns, or employing 500 or more workers. Grants to individual firms limited to $25,000 and to be used only for the following purposes:

   (a) One year's rent free.

   (b) Half the cost of shipping machinery and equipment from the mainland.

   (c) The salaries of instructors brought from the mainland to train workers.

5. New industrial buildings at 40¢ to 75¢ per square foot per year, but if specially built to the manufacturer's specifications, *they must be purchased with a down payment in excess of 10%, the balance to be amortized on a long-term basis with interest at 5%.*

THE RECORDS OF THE NEWLY-ESTABLISHED FIRMS

Financial data are available as of the end of the 1953 tax year covering 210 of the firms established up to that date with some form of government assistance. All but 17 are tax exempt and the bulk of them were then three years old or less. The 210 firms earned total profits amounting to $15,577,000 on a total paid-in capital and surplus of $49,669,000—*an average rate of return of 31%.*

The significant fact buried in this average, however, is that 67 of these *firms lost money.* About half of them were in their first year of operations, with the usual heavy start-up costs and so the record is still inconclusive. Firms with losses had a lower average capitalization ($119,000) than the firms that made profits ($291,000). This limits still further the possibility of appraising the record from a purely locational standpoint.

For perhaps as many as 30 firms, however, the losses may be attributable to inadequate analysis of locational factors and a faulty decision to locate in Puerto Rico.

The following table suggests that there may be some systematic variation by industry in the comparative advantages and disadvantages of locating in Puerto Rico.

PERFORMANCE BETTER THAN U.S. AVERAGE		PERFORMANCE WORSE THAN U.S. AVERAGE	
RATIO OF PROFITABLE TO UNPROFITABLE FIRMS		RATIO OF PROFITABLE TO UNPROFITABLE FIRMS	
Leather goods	3.3 to 1	Textiles	1.0 to 1
Electronics	3.2 to 1	Stone, clay, glass	1.0 to 1
Plastics & misc.	2.6 to 1	Food & Tobacco	1.4 to 1
Apparel	2.5 to 1	Metal Products	2.8 to 1

Broad industrial groupings such as this, however, conceal many differences in raw materials, products, processes and markets which must be separately analyzed. Only the individual firm is in a position to know and properly appraise all the factors involved in making a sound locational decision.

In December 1953, a study was conducted by the Economic Development Administration of 23 "EDA-aided Plants" closing or changing ownership.

Here are the most relevant statistics:

Closed because of management problems 6

Successful firms, either sold as going concerns or closed
    for reasons other than lack of success 5

Closed due to reduction in defense spending 4

Actually represent contractions of enterprises which
    continue to operate successfully 3

Other and unknown reasons 4

Evidently, *sound decisions were made* by the managements of the 147 firms that located in Puerto Rico and operated at a profit. Their return of $17,212,000 on an equity investment of $48,452,000 represents 35% "after taxes." An expanding firm should certainly not overlook the possible advantages it may gain from locating in Puerto Rico.

CHAPTER **13**

Safety
from Enemy Attack

Will your plant survive the first wave of bombing attacks launched by an unscrupulous enemy? Or will your facilities be neutralized, smashed and burned beyond recall? The answer lies with you and you alone.

Every top executive must reach a decision now—*no one else will make it for him*. Simply stated, the problem for most executives is this: shall our productive facilities remain in congested, heavily concentrated industrial areas—or shall we decentralize at once?

It should be noted, at the outset, that "decentralization" is meant in the strictest sense. No matter how many times government agencies change their definition, *"dispersal"* will not work. The U. S. Department of Commerce has issued a handbook purporting to assist the manufacturer in selection of safe locations for "new defense-supporting plants." They have suggested location on the peripheral radia of concentrated industrial areas and have indicated the

AN UNREALISTIC GOVERNMENT FORMULA
FOR PLANT DISPERSAL

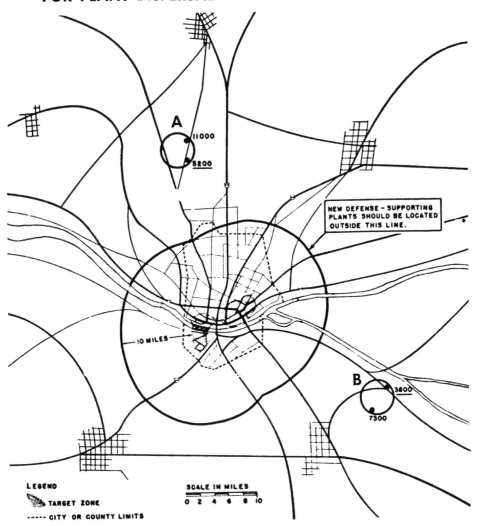

The outline of the potential A-bomb target zone is placed on an over-all map of the entire metropolitan area.

A map of a hypothetical metropolitan area with one target zone plotted in this manner is shown above. A line has been drawn around the target zone in such a manner that any point along it is 10 miles from the nearest point on the target-zone boundary. New industrial plants should be located in the area beyond this line.

At sites A and B the underlined figures are proposed new plant total employment. (The other figures are the total employment of existing plants within the 4-mile circles.) The proposed plant at site A would not meet dispersion requirements because a new target area would be created. Site B would be satisfactory because the proposed employment would total less than 16,000.

center of such metropolitan areas as "target zones." A series of concentric circles based on industrial and population density is the suggested guide.

From the standpoint of production continuity, it would be foolhardy to follow this impractical advice. The most recent H bomb possessed a blast power of 14 megatons equal to the explosive force of 700 Hiroshima type bombs. There is reason to believe that a 40 to 50 megaton bomb is entirely feasible.

Complete obliteration of a 100 square mile area is possible with such a bomb, and partial destruction over an area of more than 1,000 square miles.

How safe, then, is a plant on the outskirts of a large city even if it is twenty miles from the blast center? Assuming that the plant itself weathered the H bomb attack, would the factory be able to continue production?

Probably not. While lives of executives and personnel may be saved if the attack occurred during working hours, production would cease just as surely as if the building were at the heart of the blast. Every "dispersed" plant is simply a satellite depending for its existence on the central city for its power, gas, transportation and personnel. When these life lines are gone, the peripheral plant is paralyzed. Every main highway leading out of principal cities is labeled "In the event of enemy attack, this highway will be closed to all traffic except military or civilian defense vehicles."

The only answer to the problem of possible H bomb attack is "decentralization," that is, the relocation of plants in communities of not more than 25,000 population, or preferably less, at least 40 miles away from a concentrated industrial area. Drastic? Certainly! But such a step will mean survival!

SELECTING A "SAFE" COMMUNITY

Those factors to be considered in determining the general area of the country in which to locate proposed new facilities are outlined in detail in various chapters of PLANT LOCATION. This analysis covers all problems connected with markets, raw materials, transportation, labor costs, power, water, gas and fuel costs, taxes, etc.

Once the general area is selected that will conform to all economic indices, the problem of plant safety must then be resolved. It is suggested that, within this area, the following types of communities be screened out:

1. Cities within 40 miles of an industrial center.
2. All cities of over 25,000 population.

3. Areas where more than 5,000 persons are employed in heavy industry.

4. Communities near large power plants, water systems, oil fields, dams, bridges or railroad marshalling yards.

5. Cities with ordnance, airplane or other important military production or installations.

6. Cities served by only one railroad and where alternate sources of power, gas and water are unavailable.

These stringent requirements may tend to eliminate any but rather small communities. A plant of average size, however, will be able to utilize smaller towns when it is realized that labor can be drawn not only from the community itself but from the surrounding countryside. Unless hampered by mountains, large bodies of water or other physical barriers, workers may easily commute 25 miles in each direction. It has been found that 70-75% of the work force in rural plants will use automobiles (including car pools) as a means of conveyance.

SABOTAGE

The problems of internal security against espionage, sabotage and other subversive efforts are minimized by virtue of location in a rural or semi-urban area.

In a community of say 10,000 population, the reputation and character of all workers in a plant can be established without a question of doubt. Employee recruitment becomes a much simpler matter than in huge metropolitan centers.

Even external sabotage, such as the damaging of buildings, power systems, equipment, communications, exposed water supplies, etc. is less likely. Strangers can be recognized almost immediately in the small town where natives—unlike their city cousins—are well acquainted.

ECONOMICS OF A NON-URBAN LOCATION

To an industrialist who has spent a lifetime manufacturing his products in a metropolitan center, the small community may be looked upon with some misgivings. Since many towns located in agricultural areas possess no tradition of manufacturing experience, and because no apparent skills are in evidence,

CRITICAL TARGET AREAS FOR CIVIL DEFENSE PURPOSES

LOCATION AND POPULATION

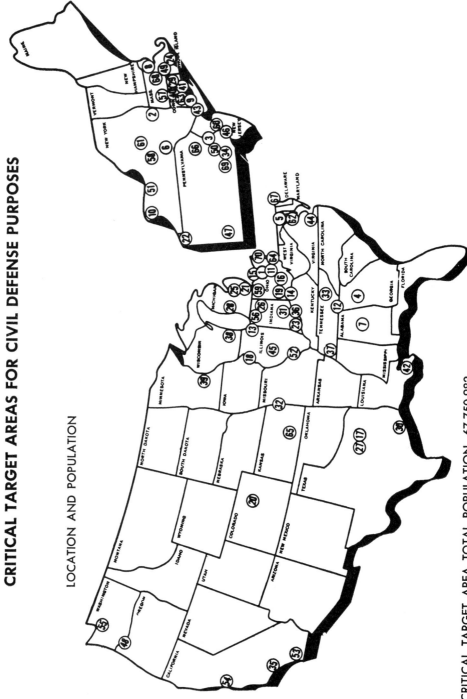

CRITICAL TARGET AREA TOTAL POPULATION—67,750,982

CRITICAL TARGET AREA & STATE	POPULATION	% TOTAL		CRITICAL TARGET AREA & STATE	POPULATION	% TOTAL
1. Akron (Ohio)	410,032	.6052	37.	Memphis (Tenn.)	482,393	.7120
2. Albany-Schenectady-Troy (N. Y.)	514,490	.7594	38.	Milwaukee (Wisc.)	871,047	1.2857
3. Allentown-Bethlehem-Easton (N. J.-Pa.)	437,824	.6462	39.	Minneapolis-St. Paul (Minn.)	1,116,509	1.6480
4. Atlanta (Ga.)	671,797	.9916	40.	New Britain-Bristol (Conn.)	146,983	.2169
5. Baltimore (Md.)	1,337,373	1.9739	41.	New Haven (Conn.)	264,622	.3906
6. Binghamton (N. Y.)	184,698	.2726	42.	New Orleans (La.)	685,405	1.0117
7. Birmingham (Ala.)	558,928	.8250	43.	New York-N. E. New Jersey (N. Y.-N. J.)	12,911,994	19.0580
8. Boston (Mass.)	2,369,986	3.4981	44.	Norfolk-Portsmouth-Newport News (Va.)	589,427	.8700
9. Bridgeport (Conn.)	258,137	.3810	45.	Peoria (Ill.)	250,512	.3698
10. Buffalo (N. Y.)	1,089,230	1.6077	46.	Philadelphia (Pa.-N. J.)	3,671,048	5.4184
11. Canton (Ohio)	283,194	.4180	47.	Pittsburgh (Pa.)	2,213,236	3.2667
12. Chattanooga (Tenn.-Ga.)	246,453	.3638	48.	Portland (Ore.-Wash.)	704,829	1.0403
13. Chicago (Ill.-Ind.)	5,495,364	8.1111	49.	Providence (R. I.-Mass.)	737,203	1.0881
14. Cincinnati (Ohio-Ky.)	904,402	1.3349	50.	Reading (Pa.)	255,740	.3775
15. Cleveland (Ohio)	1,465,511	2.1631	51.	Rochester (N. Y.)	487,632	.7197
16. Columbus (Ohio)	503,410	.7430	52.	St. Louis (Mo.-Ill.)	1,681,281	2.4816
17. Dallas (Texas)	614,799	.9074	53.	San Diego (Calif.)	556,808	.8218
18. Davenport-Rock Island-Moline (Ill.-Ia.)	234,256	.3458	54.	San Francisco-Oakland (Calif.)	2,240,767	3.3074
19. Dayton (Ohio)	457,333	.6750	55.	Seattle (Wash.)	732,992	1.0819
20. Denver (Col.)	563,832	.8322	56.	South Bend (Ind.)	205,058	.3027
21. Detroit (Mich.)	3,016,197	4.4519	57.	Springfield-Holyoke (Conn.-Mass.)	407,255	.6011
22. Erie (Pa.)	219,388	.3238	58.	Syracuse (N. Y.)	341,719	.5044
23. Evansville (Ind.)	160,422	.2368	59.	Toledo (Ohio)	395,551	.5838
24. Fall River-New Bedford (Mass.-R. I.)	274,767	.4055	60.	Trenton (N. J.)	229,781	.3392
25. Flint (Mich.)	270,963	.3999	61.	Utica-Rome (N. Y.)	284,262	.4196
26. Fort Wayne (Ind.)	183,722	.2712	62.	Washington (D. C.-Md.-Va.)	1,464,089	2.1610
27. Fort Worth (Tex.)	361,253	.5332	63.	Waterbury (Conn.)	154,656	.2283
28. Grand Rapids (Mich.)	288,292	.4255	64.	Wheeling-Steubenville (Ohio-W. Va.)	354,092	.5226
29. Hartford (Conn.)	358,081	.5285	65.	Wichita (Kans.)	222,290	.3281
30. Houston (Tex.)	806,701	1.1907	66.	Wilkes-Barre-Hazleton (Pa.)	392,241	.5789
31. Indianapolis (Ind.)	551,777	.8144	67.	Wilmington (Del.-N. J.)	268,587	.3961
32. Kansas City (Kans.-Mo.)	814,357	1.2020	68.	Worcester (Mass.)	276,336	.4079
33. Knoxville (Tenn.)	337,105	.4976	69.	York (Pa.)	202,737	.2992
34. Lancaster (Pa.)	234,717	.3464	70.	Youngstown (Ohio-Pa.)	528,498	.7801
35. Los Angeles (Calif.)	4,367,911	6.4470				
36. Louisville (Ky.-Ind.)	576,900	.8515				

many executives are fearful of the cost of "educating" the community to industrial work.

Today, fortunately, the manufacturer no longer has to guess about adaptability of untrained rural labor. Young men have been leaving agricultural work for factory jobs for decades and have proven that lack of experience is no deterrent to ultimate high efficiency.

Between 1910 and 1950, the number of persons living on farms decreased by nine million, or over 25%. Yet during this same period, the total rural population *increased* by twelve million. This paradox is easily explained. While the farm element in rural population declines, the non-farm element almost doubled in the same period.

It has been found that this vast new source of industrial labor has been easily trained to top-skill status. One rural plant reports that 11% of its workers were laborers prior to hiring. Of this group, 68% are now semi-skilled production workers.

In contrast to city experience, there is almost an inverse correlation between age and skill in rural factories. In reports from several plants, over 50% of the rural employees in semi-skilled and skilled job classifications were under the age of 36, and the largest ratio of semi-skilled workers were between 19 and 25 years of age. Younger workers apparently have the advantages of better education, more initiative and the ability to acquire new skills.

WAGE RATES LOWER IN RURAL AREAS

A definite correlation exists between rural areas and low wage patterns. The charts on pages 210 and 211 illustrate this close relationship. Note, for example, that median income in the State of Indiana is matched by a low urban population. Similarly, income in southeastern states conforms with low urban population.

Thus, not only is labor available for most operations in rural areas but it is apparent that wage rates in such regions are low as well.

NEGATIVE ECONOMIC FACTORS

As operations get under way, management may be pleasantly surprised to find that rural labor responds very quickly to training, reflecting high native ability and basic familiarity with hand tools and mechanical devices.

However, management may also face some disappointments. Some workers may never adjust to indoor work and the industrial tempo. Aptitude tests may have to be amplified and augmented with emotional behavior and temperament tests to avoid excessive turnover.

Absenteeism in rural plants is frequently high at certain times of the year. Realistically, some plant managers close their plants on the first day of fishing and hunting seasons.

The social problems in rural factory operations are not to be treated lightly. In large city plants, social cleavages between management, foremen and workers are distinct. After factory hours, the paths of each group seldom cross. Not so in the small town—limited recreational, educational, cultural and religious facilities must be shared by all strata.

EVALUATION OF LABOR SURPLUS AREAS

Communities throughout the country have been classified according to "relative adequacy of local labor supply" by the U. S. Dept. of Labor, Bureau of Employment Security as follows:

Group I—Areas of labor shortage.
Areas in which labor shortages exist or are expected to occur in the near future, which will impede "essential activities."

Group II—Areas of balanced labor supply.
Areas in which current and prospective labor demand and supply are approximately in balance.

Group III—Areas of moderate labor surplus.
Areas in which current and prospective labor supply *moderately* exceed labor requirements.

Group IV—Areas of substantial labor surplus.
Areas in which current and prospective labor supply *substantially* exceed labor requirements.

Group IV-A—Areas of substantial labor surplus.

Group IV-B—Areas of very substantial labor surplus.

Government financial encouragement is no guarantee of plant security in labor surplus areas. There are "safe" communities and also highly vulnerable cities in the list prepared by the Bureau of Employment Security.

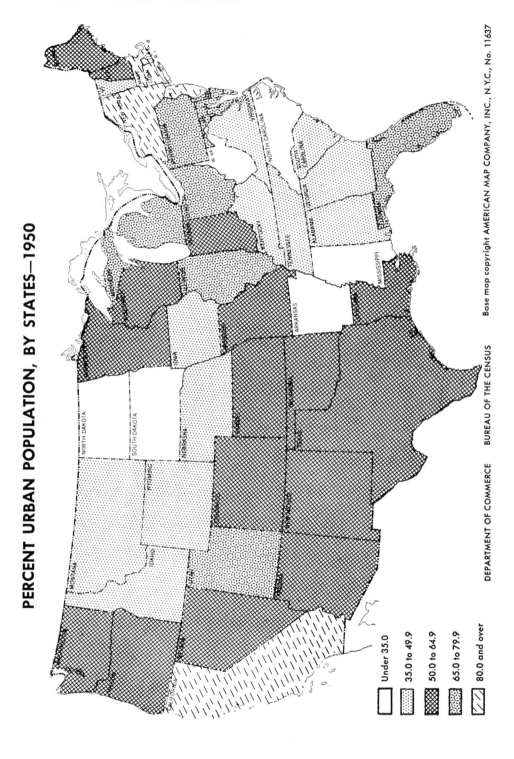

PERCENT URBAN POPULATION, BY STATES—1950

Under 35.0

35.0 to 49.9

50.0 to 64.9

65.0 to 79.9

80.0 and over

DEPARTMENT OF COMMERCE   BUREAU OF THE CENSUS

Base map copyright AMERICAN MAP COMPANY, INC., N.Y.C., No. 11637

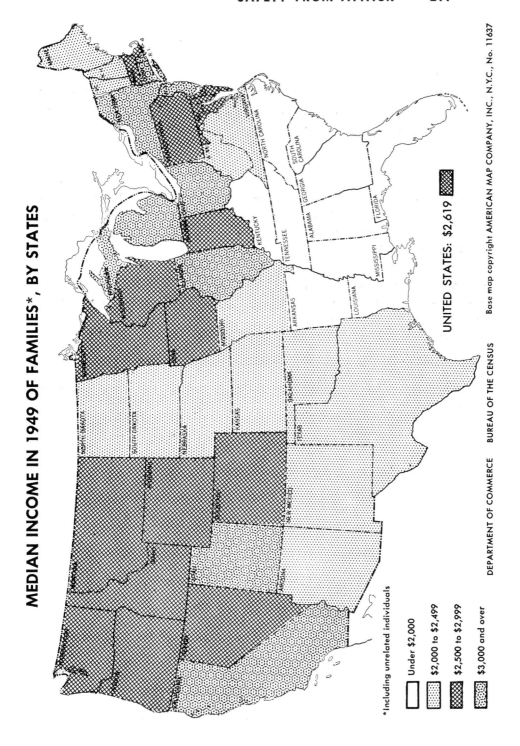

MEDIAN INCOME IN 1949 OF FAMILIES*, BY STATES

*Including unrelated individuals

Under $2,000

$2,000 to $2,499

$2,500 to $2,999

$3,000 and over

UNITED STATES: $2,619

DEPARTMENT OF COMMERCE   BUREAU OF THE CENSUS

Base map copyright AMERICAN MAP COMPANY, INC., N.Y.C., No. 11637

For example, Louisville, Kentucky is ranked as an area of moderate labor surplus but, with *one-third of the State's production workers concentrated there,* it could hardly be characterized as a "safe" area. If Kentucky is feasible as a location, less vulnerable labor-surplus towns of under 25,000 population could include Madisonville, Corbin, Hazard, etc. Other criteria, as outlined previously, would have to be applied to determine the comparative safety ranking of each community.

The mere granting of a certificate of necessity is no assurance of area safety. A manufacturer can still obtain a "certificate" today to amortize a plant in the Houston, Texas area, for example, as have such companies as Shell Chemical, Diamond Alkali, Sinclair Refining, Consolidated Chemicals, Rohm & Haas, Rheem Manufacturing Company, General American Transportation, Olin-Mathieson, and dozens of others.

Yet, Houston is highly vulnerable to enemy attack. Within a few miles of the river front is concentrated *86% of the nation's total petro-chemical plants—* the San Jacinto Ordnance Depot, the Sheffield Steel Company, huge petroleum storage tanks for the armed services, the Hughes Gun Plant, the Mayo Shell Company, and hundreds more.

When selecting an area, remember that the only guide to safety is your own good common sense.

The following checklist is reprinted from Studies in Business Policy, No. 55, entitled "Protecting Personnel in Wartime" by the National Industrial Conference Board, Inc.

For Both Plant and Community

Plan early and in detail—it is too late to do much when bombs are falling.

Prepare for maximum damage and casualties.

Become as self-sufficient as possible.

Cooperate closely with other CD groups.

Hold training and test exercises frequently.

Fire is still the greatest danger—there can never be too much water or too many sources.

Have a well-trained messenger group.

Accurate records must be kept—they help locate casualties, aid rescue operations, prevent wasted time and effort.

Don't pinch pennies. An adequate shelter program is essential.

Anti-aircraft batteries and searchlights should be moved

away from key plant and installations. They attract enemy aircraft.

Outside help must be guided and instructed by local authorities and plant ARP controller.

Disperse ARP groups so that all forces will not be knocked out by one attack.

Protect local and factory mobile fire-fighting equipment, or get it out of target area.

Prepare for all eventualities—not just atomic warfare, but also for high explosive, incendiary, gas, and bacteriological weapons.

Keep streets and factory traffic lanes open.

Build a nucleus peacetime organization, able to expand overnight in time of emergency.

Train sufficient reserves in all ARP duties for replacement and increased needs.

Have an alternate ARP headquarters in case the main control center is knocked out.

For the Plant

Industry must accept leadership in civil defense in its community if an effective program is to be developed.

Plan ahead to protect morale of the workers. Plan to help bombed-out employees and families with home repairs, emergency feeding, and financial assistance.

General Time Corporation, Athens, Georgia. Plant Location Study— FANTUS FACTORY LOCATING SERVICE.

The plant air-defense chief must have the confidence and respect of the workers.

An employee-management committee should coordinate and help plan all plant CD measures.

Establish good communications, with detailed instructions to all personnel.

Exchange of experiences between plants helps develop a more realistic plant-defense organization.

Give first priority to protection of workers.

Locate shelters as near the place of work as possible.

Hold drills with local fire services to familiarize them with the plant and its special problems.

An underground first-aid station and plant hospital is good insurance. Substations should be located throughout factory.

Do not assign personnel to shelters by departments—a direct hit might wipe out your key engineers, tool workers, etc.

Remember that "wars are not won in air-raid shelters" —organize so that a minimum of production time is lost without sacrificing adequate protection of lives and property.

Organize to repair damage as quickly as possible and get back to production.

Organize ARP within the normal functions of the fire, police, safety, and other departments.

Normal lines of authority should be followed in organizing plant defense—foremen as wardens, etc.

Stockpile critical repair materials, first-aid and medical supplies, and emergency food rations.

Every effort should be made to minimize damage to equipment and key facilities.

For the Community

CD headquarters must be outside the target area. If possible it should overlook the area.

Information centers and accident inquiry points are needed to inform people of conditions.

Thorough training, frequent tests, and accurate information are the best ways to prevent panic.

Evacuation plans and post-raid help for bombed-out victims must be prepared in advance—where to take, feed and house evacuees.

Following a major raid, aircraft are useful for estimating extent of damage and for directing post-raid operations.

Mobile noncombat CD troops should be trained and available in each region.

A centralized regional organization is essential if outside help is to arrive in time.

Local CD leaders or deputies must see for themselves what has happened. Otherwise they cannot make correct decisions.

Heavy rescue equipment must be available for quick dispatch to badly damaged areas.

All communities do not need the same protection. CD measures should be carried out according to importance and vulnerability of the area, so as not to waste critical material and manpower.

TAX AIDS FOR PLANT DISPERSION AND PROTECTION

The national policy for industrial dispersion was announced by the President in August 1951 for the purpose of assuring greater relative security of the nation's industrial plant and production from atom-bomb attack through proper spacing of additions to productive capacity. It provides that new defense-supporting production facilities be located 10 or more miles from highly industrialized or densely populated sections or from major military installations.

The Federal Government has made proper location of a new defense plant a condition to receiving defense-production assistance. Such aid takes the forms of certificates of necessity (the accelerated tax amortization privilege and defense loans).

Where production transfers and other methods are not satisfactory solutions, the Office of Defense Mobilization will authorize rapid tax amortization as an incentive to locate vital defense production at dispersed sites.

Applications for certificates of necessity should not be filed with ODM until

Sylvania Electric Co., York, Pennsylvania. Plant Location Study—FANTUS FACTORY LOCATING SERVICE.

after applicants have discussed their problems with the Federal agency that normally deals with problems of their industry. The appropriate Federal agency will advise whether applications should or should not be filed. The Commerce Department is the agency responsible for furnishing guidance to most manufacturing industries. Other agencies having responsibilities in this area are the Departments of Defense, Agriculture, Interior and the Defense Transport Administration.

This program is the third part of an over-all ODM policy to reduce the vulnerability of the Nation's industrial capacity to attack. Other programs call for the dispersal of new facilities and the protection of existing facilities.

ODM officials hold that the best protection for a plant against enemy bombs is for it to be located outside vulnerable areas. To encourage dispersal of new production facilities in the defense mobilization program, ODM, with certain exceptions, has been refusing tax amortization benefits to proposed facilities costing one million dollars or more, scheduled for location in congested urban areas or near major military installations. Thus far, about 80% of the plants which received the fast tax write-off privilege in this category have conformed to the ODM dispersal criteria. During 1953, for example, 215 applicants in the million dollar or over class received tax amortization on dispersed facilities which were valued at $1.7 billion.

The protective construction program permits 100% accelerated tax amortization over a five year period on money spent by management on defense plants for that purpose. This type of construction is considered as one method of reducing the extent of major damage from enemy attack which could be inflicted on important defense plants located in critical target areas. Protective construction is not a substitute for dispersion; it is urged in those cases where defense plants are already located in target areas or where dispersion of new plants is impracticable.

To qualify for the five year write off of funds spent for protective construction, the construction work must be in one of the 193 target areas designated by the Federal Defense Administration.

Poloron Products, Moosic, Pennsylvania. Plant Location Study—FANTUS FACTORY LOCATING SERVICE.

SOURCES OF OFFICIAL STATISTICS, U. S. GOVERNMENT

TREASURY DEPARTMENT
Bureau of Internal Revenue
DEPARTMENT OF DEFENSE
Dept. of the Army, Corps of Engineers
POST OFFICE DEPARTMENT
DEPARTMENT OF THE INTERIOR
Solid Fuels Administration
Defense Electric Power Administration
Defense Minerals Administration
Petroleum Administration for Defense
The Geological Survey
Bureau of Mines
Bureau of Reclamation
DEPARTMENT OF AGRICULTURE
Production and Marketing Administration
Rural Electrification Administration
Soil Conservation Service
Bureau of Agricultural Economics
DEPARTMENT OF COMMERCE
Civil Aeronautics Administration
Maritime Administration
National Production Authority
Bureau of the Census
Coast and Geodetic Survey
Inland Waterways Corporation
Bureau of Public Roads
Weather Bureau
DEPARTMENT OF LABOR
Bureau of Employment Security
Bureau of Labor Statistics
Veterans' Employment Service
OTHER
Interstate Commerce Commission
Office of Defense Mobilization

Atomic Energy Commission
Federal Power Commission
National Security Resources Board
Tennessee Valley Authority
Federal Security Agency, Public Health Service, National
    Office of Vital Statistics
U. S. Office of Education

BIBLIOGRAPHY

Alderhefer, E. B. and H. E. Michl, *Economics of American Industry* (New York: McGraw-Hill, 2nd edition, 1950)

American Society of Planning Officials, "Bibliography on Community Surveys for Industrial Development" (Chicago: American Society of Planning Officials, 1949)

Burkhead, Jesse and Donald C. Steele, "The Effect of State Taxation on the Migration of Industry" *Journal of Business* 23:167-172 (July, 1950)

Carroll, J. Douglas Jr., "Some Aspects of the Home-Work Relationships of Industrial Workers" *Land Economics* 25:414-422 (November, 1949)

Chamber of Commerce of the United States, *The Community Industrial Survey* (Washington, D. C.: Chamber of Commerce of the United States, 1940)

Dickson, Paul W., "Decentralization in Industry" (New York: National Industrial Conference Board, 1948)

Dunham, Clarence W., *Planning Industrial Structures* (New York: McGraw-Hill, 1948)

Florence, P. Sargant, *The Long-Range Planning of the Location of New Productive Capacity* (Washington, D. C.: National Resources Planning Board, 1940)

Fredrich, Carl J., *Alfred Weber's Theory of Location of Industries* (Chicago: University of Chicago Press, 1929)

Fulton, Maurice, "What Industry Looks For In a New Location" *Oklahoma Business Bulletin* 18:1-3 (February, 1952)

Hoover, Edgar M., Jr., *The Location of Economic Activity* (New York: McGraw-Hill, 1948)

Johnson, Keith W., "The Growth of Manufacturing in the Southwest" *Monthly Business Review* 35:41-51 (March 1, 1950)

Joint Industrial Zoning Committee (of Association of State Planning and Development Agencies, American Railway Development Association, American Institute of Planners, Society of Industrial Realtors, American Society of Civil Engineers), "Principles of Industrial Zoning" (October, 1950)

Locklin, D. Philip, *Economics of Transportation* (Chicago: Richard D. Irwin, n. d.)

McDonald, Douglas Moore, *A Select Bibliography on the Location of Industry*, Social Research Bulletin Series (Montreal, Quebec, Canada: McGill University, 1937)

McGraw-Hill Publishing Co., Inc., *McGraw-Hill Census of Manufacturing Plants* (New York: McGraw-Hill, 1945, 1947, 1949 on two-year intervals)

McLaughlin, Glenn E. and Stefan Robock, *Why Industry Moves South* (Washington, D. C.: National Planning Association, 1949)

National Industrial Conference Board, "Growth Patterns in Industry" (New York: National Industrial Conference Board, 1952)

Nielsen, A. M., *Economic and Industrial Geography* (New York: Pitman Publishing Corp., 1950)

Smith, T. Lynn, *Population Analysis* (New York: McGraw-Hill, 1948)

Starnes, G. T., W. M. Wilkins and P. P. Wisman, "The Labor Force of Two Rural Industrial Plants" (Charlottesville, Virginia: University of Virginia, 1951)

U. S. Congress, *Decentralization of Heavy Industry*—Hearings Before a Sub-committee, 79th Congress, 1st and 2nd sessions, October 9, 1943—March 2, 1946, on Senate Resolution 15 (Washington, D. C.: U. S. Government Printing Office, 1946)

U. S. Department of Commerce, Office of Industry and Commerce, *Industrial Development and Plant Location* (Basic Information Sources), prepared by Victor Roterus and Sterling R. March (Washington, D. C.: U. S. Department of Commerce, 1950)

U. S. National Security Resources Board, *National Security Factors in Industrial Location* (Washington, D. C.: U. S. Government Printing Office, 1948)

Wood, Richardson, "For the Community That Wants More Factory Payrolls" *American City* 63:87-88 (January, 1948)

Yoder, Dale, *Manpower Economics and Labor Problems* (New York: McGraw-Hill, 3rd edition, 1950)

—— and Donald G. Paterson, *Local Labor Market Research* (Minneapolis, Minnesota: University of Minnesota, Industrial Relations Center, 1948)

INDEX